Creation in Six Days

Creation in Six Days

A Defense of the Traditional Reading of Genesis One

James B. Jordan

Canon Press
MOSCOW, IDAHO

James B. Jordan, *Creation in Six Days: A Defense of the Traditional Reading of Genesis One*

Published by Canon Press, P.O. Box 8729, Moscow, ID 83843
www.canonpress.org
800-488-2034

04 03 02 01 00 99 9 8 7 6 5 4 3 2 1

Cover design by Paige Atwood Design, Moscow, ID

Printed in the United States of America.

ISBN: 1-885767-62-5

Contents

Introduction

This book is designed primarily as an answer to the Framework Interpretation of Genesis 1, argued from the traditional normal day (168-hour week) reading of the passage. By "Framework Interpretation" I mean any approach to the text of Genesis 1 that pits its literary features against its plain historical and narrative sense. Thus, I include as "Framework Interpreters" some who do not wear that label themselves.

In attacking this subject, I must juggle three balls and try to keep them in some kind of balance. The first is a detailed critique of the Framework Interpretation, both in its general presentation (by Bruce Waltke) and in its more "sophisticated" presentation (by Meredith Kline and his followers). This is done in chapters two and three and in appendixes A–D. This critique is rendered a bit difficult in that there is no published large-scale defense of the Framework Interpretation; the approach has yet to be presented in what I would regard as a fully worked out fashion, as a detailed theological commentary on Genesis 1.

My second task is to answer fire with fire by setting forth what I think is a proper way to read Genesis 1. John Sailhamer does present a full discussion of Genesis 1 in his book, though not from a Framework Interpretation standpoint, and in chapter seven I have used his new Limited Geography Interpretation as a foil to make an initial presentation of my own views. With this critical overview of Genesis 1, I am able to present a "positive" reading of it in chapter eight and supplement it in appendix B.

My third task, and the most difficult one, is to try to uncover the presuppositions that underlie the Framework Interpretation in order to try and explain its present-day attractiveness. My thesis is that the explanation lies in a too-ready acceptance of many of the questionable assumptions of modern science on the part of most Christians today, coupled with the pervasiveness of a gnostic, or nonhistorical, attitude toward the Christian religion. I have used two short essays by John Collins, whose position is similar to but not quite the same as the Framework Interpretation, as a springboard for a discussion of modern science in chapters five and six. I have sought to expose the gnostic root of modern thinking in chapter four to explain why a nonhistorical or pictorial approach to Genesis 1 finds such ready acceptance in Christian circles today.

I wish to thank Mr. Douglas Jones of Canon Press for his editorial criticisms of the original typescripts of this book and for his help in getting the material ready for publication. Thanks also to the many people who read parts of this book and provided encouragement and/or stimulating criticism. By no means do all of the following agree with what I have written, but they are due special mention here: Dr. Peter Wallace, Dr. Vern S. Poythress, Dr. Peter J. Leithart, Dr. John C. Whitcomb, Rev. Mark Horne, Rev. Jeffrey J. Meyers, and Dr. Gary North.

Chapter 1

In Professor Edwards's Class

William, a student at Evangelical University, had looked forward all summer to "Introduction to Christian Literature," a course taught by Professor Edwards. Enrollment for Prof. Edwards's courses always closed almost immediately because so many students wanted to take them. William was thankful he had been able to get in.

Prof. Edwards was not only highly regarded by his loyal students, but also a major figure in the evangelical world. He had authored several significant works, frequently delivered papers at scholarly societies, and was even taken seriously by liberal scholars and theologians. Moreover, William had heard Prof. Edwards speak in chapel several times and had always found him moving, inspiring, and helpful. William was excited as he took his seat for the first class.

Prof. Edwards began class with prayer and then gave out the curriculum for the course. "In this course, we'll be learning to read carefully, not superficially," he said. "And to begin with, I'm going to read to you from one of your assigned texts, and we'll discuss it today." So Prof. Edwards began reading:

> His whole life, John Pigg had lived at 17 Almond Street, a large, white house.

"This is how the story begins," said Prof. Edwards. "Do you notice anything strange about it?" No one raised his (or her) hand, so Prof. Edwards reread the sentence and asked his question again. Finally, he smiled and said, "Well, how can a house be both large *and* white?"

William was puzzled, but Prof. Edwards went on: "You see, when a book begins with a startling conundrum, a virtual contradiction, like this, the author is telling us something. He is telling us that perhaps we should not take what he is saying at face value. We should consider what 'large' and 'white' mean, perhaps, but not think that John Pigg really lived in such a house."

William could see from the expressions of the students around him that they were impressed. They had seen the light! Yes, this was a deeper sentence than they had at first thought, and the pointer to that depth was the contradiction in the sentence itself. But William was still puzzled.

So he timidly raised his hand and asked, "Prof. Edwards, sir, could you explain this further? It doesn't look like a contradiction to me. Why can't a house be both large and white? What is the problem?"

Prof. Edwards smiled. "Good question,"—and he looked at his seating chart for students—"William, is it? Yes. Well, would anyone like to address William's question?"

The student next to William raised his hand and, being recognized, said, "Sure. I mean, don't you see it, William? The house is *big* and is also painted *white!* I mean, how can it be both?"

William nodded. He did not want to get into any kind of argument on the first day of class. In fact, he did not want to argue with any Professor. The duty of a student was to learn from the Professor, not think himself his equal. But inwardly, William was still upset. What was he missing? Why did everyone else see it while he didn't?

William could not get the matter out of his mind all day long. Sure, the fact that the house was large and white might make it a symbol for God's world, signifying that it was both spacious and pure. Sure, the name John Pigg could hint that a swinish man does not belong in such a nice house. Maybe the large, white house is the Church, and John Pigg is the Christian: "John" as a saved person, and yet still a pig, still possessed of the flesh. William could see that the opening sentence might hint at depth in the narrative, though only the ensuing narrative of the story would confirm whether his conjecture was correct or incorrect. But William could not see how "large" and "white" were contradictory. The depth would still be there if such adjectives were complementary and not contradictory.

The more William thought about it in the days to come, the more disappointed he became in Prof. Edwards. To be sure, there would be a lot to learn from the Professor, but William was increasingly sure that his pitting "white" against "large" was ridiculous. And he was amazed that so many of his fellow students had fallen in line with Prof. Edwards's argument. He could only assume that their respect and affection for the Professor had blinded them to what he was actually saying on this particular matter.

In the course of the present book, we shall encounter several Professor Edwards, men who are fine scholars, godly Christians, who have made significant contributions to believing Christian scholarship. Like William, though, we shall find ourselves amazed at some of the arguments they propound concerning the opening chapter of the Bible. For like Prof. Edwards, these men see contradictions where none exist. They manufacture problems in the creation narrative that are rather obviously not present therein and that nobody ever noticed before. Like William, we shall come away disappointed.

For instance, we shall find men saying that there is a contradiction of sorts between Genesis 1:11–12 and Genesis 2:5. They will tell us that, on the one hand, all the plants were made on the third day of creation week, and on the other, they will say the plants were not made until man was created. This, they will say, is an indication that we are not to take creation week "literally" as history.

But I ask you, courteous reader, to study these two passages and see if there be any contradiction, or any problem of any sort:

> And God said, "Let the earth shoot forth shoots, grain seeding seed, trees fruitbearing fruit, according to its kind so that its seed is in it, upon the earth." And it was established. And the earth produced shoots, grain seeding seed according to its kind, and trees bearing fruit in which is its seed. And God saw that it was good. (Gen. 1:11–12)

> And none of the shrubs of the field was yet in the earth, and none of the grains of the field had yet sprouted, for Yahweh God had not sent rain upon the earth, and there was no man to serve the ground. (Gen. 2:5)

Now, do you see a problem, a conundrum, yea a contradiction, between these two statements? William does not. William notices right away that on the third day, only two kinds of plants are said to shoot forth from the earth: grains and fruit trees. Nothing is said about any other plants. To be sure, perhaps all the other plants are included, but when we come to Genesis 2:5, that initial impression is corrected. There are some plants, "shrubs of the field," that had not been made at the time Adam was created. Thus, William reasons, these were not made on the third day. Moreover, according to 2:5, the grain plants, though they existed, had not yet sprouted any grain, while according to 2:16, the fruit trees did already have fruit on them.

William meditates on what the passages say. When man was first created, the only plants in existence were two kinds of food plants: grains and fruit trees, probably including what in English we call nuts as well. But there were no grains yet to eat, only fruits and probably nuts. Thus, Adam's first food consisted of fruit and nuts, not yet grain, potatoes, broccoli, or any other food plant. And not grapes. Only fruits, nuts, and olives.

William meditates further. Olive oil is used to consecrate a man to priesthood and kingship. Thus, it is fitting that olives come first. Olive oil is not made by cooking but only by pressing the olive. Thus, it involves no tools. It requires absolutely no development of human society to make olive oil. It requires absolutely no development of human society to eat fruits and drink water.

Grains come second, William notices. Bread is made from grain, but it involves much more work as well as mastery of fire. Thus, bread comes later on.

Finally, he notices that grapes are not included in any of the third-day plants. They must be among the plants made later on, after the fall of man, when the earth brought forth thorns and thistles (and apparently grapes as well). William considers how it takes a rather advanced technology to produce wine from grapes; it is appropriate for grapes to come last. Eating bread and drinking wine presupposes the development of human beings beyond the initial infant stage.

William notices that in the second feast of the Israelite year, Pentecost, two loaves of leavened bread were raised up before Yahweh (Lev. 23:17). At the third feast, at the end of the year, wine was celebrated (Deut. 14:26). Moreover, William notices that priests ("palace servants")[1] came before kings in the biblical narrative; Israel had priests for nearly five hundred years before she had a king. He notices that priests ate the bread of the sanctuary (Lev. 24:9) but were forbidden to drink wine at the sanctuary (Lev. 10:9), while kings in the Bible are pictured drinking wine quite often (Gen. 40:5; Neh. 1:11; Esther 1:7; 3:15; 5:6; 7:1; etc.). He notices that in celebrating the Lord's Supper, the bread comes before the wine. Thus, William finds that the later narrative of the Bible confirms his suspicions about the created order of oil, bread, and wine.

[1] The Hebrew word *kohen* means "palace servant." See Peter J. Leithart, "The Priesthood of the Plebs: The Baptismal Transformation of the Antique Order" (Ph.D. diss., University of Cambridge, 1998), pp. 41–73; also Leithart, "What Is a Priest?", *Biblical Horizons* 33 (January 1992).

But William's reflections do not arise from some supposed contradiction between Genesis 1:11–12 and 2:5. Quite the opposite. It is only because he has read the passages seriously, noting the clear differences between the two, that he is able to understand them in greater depth.

In this study we shall also see men arguing that there is a contradiction of sorts between the first and fourth days of creation week. Light was made on the first day, they note, while the lightbearers were not made until the fourth day. "How can there be light without lightbearers?" they ask. "Clearly, the sun and moon were really made on the first day, not on the fourth. This shows us," they continue, "that the seven days of Genesis 1 are not to be regarded as an historical sequence of events."

William, once again, is mystified. When he goes back to his dormitory room, he flips on the lightswitch, and the light comes on. Obviously, you don't have to have the sun and moon to have light. If Genesis 1 says that God "let there be" light on the first day and did not "make" the sun and moon until the fourth, where is the problem?

William notices that the Spirit was hovering in the region between heaven and earth on day 1. He notices that the Spirit is associated with God's glory in the Bible, and that God's glory is full of light. Thus, he reasons, it was the Spirit who provided created light the first three days of the creation week. Then the Spirit gave over His light, in part, to the objects placed in the firmament, which itself was not made until the second day. Thus, William reasons, the luminaries in the firmament are only temporary. They were not there in the beginning, and they will not be there at the end. He remembers that this is just what Revelation 21:23 and 22:5 say.

In fact, William notices that in Revelation 21:11, the New Jerusalem is said to have "starlight" and is positioned between the New Heavens and the New Earth. It occurs to him that the original light of the Spirit was transferred to the firmament luminaries for the course of human history. At the end that light will be transferred again to glorified humanity, now positioned between heaven and earth.

We notice that once again, William is able to formulate these reflections precisely because he reads Genesis 1 in the traditional manner; he has *not* fallen for the notion that there are "contradictions of sorts" in the passage. Moreover, William checks out what others have said in the past, and he discovers that his "simple" reading of Genesis 1 fits with what the Church has always said.

Reading Genesis One

We could stay with William longer, but we won't. The book you hold in your hands is entirely devoted to the kinds of "problems" that William has encountered, problems that exist in the minds of certain twentieth century evangelical readers of Genesis 1 that are pretty hard to find in the text itself. At this point, then, we need to leave William behind and ask why such modern evangelical readers see such "problems" in the text of Genesis 1. Are they stupid? Are they so caught up in modern evolutionary ideas about the age of the universe that they are incapable of reading the biblical account accurately? Are they brilliant, godly men who are being influenced by unhelpful presuppositions? Or, are they right and William (and I) wrong?

It is a fact that before the modern era, nobody in the history of the church for over three thousand years ever questioned the chronology of the Bible, and only a tiny handful ever questioned that the six days of Genesis 1 were ordinary 24-hour-type days. The few who did question the six days of Genesis 1 did so for philosophical and not scientific reasons.[2] Even so, no one suggested God took a

[2] Specifically the powerful influence of Platonism on certain thinkers: Clement of Alexandria, Origen, and Augustine (to a degree), and later just before the Reformation, John Colet. On Colet's rampant Platonism, see C. S. Lewis, *Poetry and Prose in the Sixteenth Century*. The Oxford History of Literature 4 (Oxford, 1954), pp. 158ff. On the

vast amount of time. Augustine thought the six days were instantaneous. All accepted the biblical chronology and calculated the age of the earth from it. It has only been since the rise of modern science, including archaeology, that anyone has questioned the biblical chronology and traditional interpretation of Genesis 1. It is modern science, thus, that places a challenge before interpreters.

If someone said, "I noticed contradictions in Genesis 1 long before I'd ever heard of modern science," who would believe him? It is not a slur on anyone's character to say that modern science has provoked him to rethink Genesis 1. There is nothing wrong with going back and rereading the Bible after hearing a new thing to see if perhaps the Church has misread it. Perhaps she has. Only an examination of the text will tell.

Only one group of people has a problem with the biblical statements, and that group we may call "modern conservative Christians." The liberal or unbelieving expositor of Genesis has no problem with the text. It is obvious to him that Genesis 1 presents creation and world-building in 144 hours and that Genesis 5 and 11 provide a chronology of the world from creation to Abraham. The modernist and the unbeliever do not accept the Genesis account as historically true; for them it is a myth. But they perceive no problems or ambiguities in the text, nothing that indicates "gaps" in the chronology or some odd kind of "days" in Genesis 1.

Similarly, those whom we may call "traditional conservative believers" also take the text in a simple and obvious way. For them it is quite clear that God made the world

early fathers, see Robert I. Bradshaw, *Creationism and the Early Church*, chapter three (not yet published; available online at the time of this writing at www.robibrad.demon.co.uk/Contents.htm.) For a history of the matter that is unsympathetic to the traditional 144-hour view, see Stanley L. Jaki, *Genesis 1 Through the Ages* (London: Thomas More Press, 1992) and my review of this book in the online magazine *Premise* (www.capo.org).

around 4000 B.C. and in the span of six ordinary days. This group includes many conservative Lutherans, conservative Calvinists, fundamentalists, and Orthodox Jews.

Thus, we have three groups that have always seen the text as clearly and obviously teaching a recent six-day creation that is chronologically datable from the Bible: (1) the historic Church and historic Judaism; (2) present-day "traditional conservatives"; and (3) unbelievers. We are left with a small group of evangelicals and other types of conservative Christians who are committed to believing the Bible while also being very impressed with the constructs of modern science. For this small group there is a problem with Genesis 1 and with biblical chronology.[3] Unlike the other three groups we have mentioned, this group of people is motivated to search out and find evidence in the text that can relieve them of the burden of having to believe in a young earth and universe.

One way to "get around" the "embarrassment" posed by Genesis 1 is to say that the early chapters of Genesis are simply not historical at all. These texts, in other words, exist for *ideas only* and not for *history*. The person who reads Genesis 1 this way is free to say that Genesis 1 is a completely coherent narrative and that there is no "apparent contradiction" between Genesis 1's plants and Genesis 2's plants. None of it really happened historically anyway, with this view.

According to this reading, Genesis 1 presents God as creating the world and building it up over the course of a normal week of 24-hour days. Then God planted a garden, which grew almost instantaneously, and put a fully-grown, newly created man into it. God pulled a woman out of the side of the sleeping man, they ate forbidden fruit, and then they were cast out of the Garden. They and their immediate descendants lived lifespans lasting almost a thousand

[3] It should be noted that there are a few six-day creationists who are open to the possibility of gaps in the chronologies of Genesis 5 and 11.

years. Then there was a great flood that covered the entire world, and God started again with Noah and his family. This, according to such readers, is exactly and obviously what the text of Genesis says. But it never really happened. If you built a time machine and went back to watch, you would not see any of these events—because they are not events. They are just stories, "pregnant myths," designed to teach us about God and man and the world according to this view.

For reasons to be explained more fully in chapter four of the present book, orthodox Christians cannot accept this way of reading the early chapters of Genesis. In a word, such a reading is gnostic. Gnosticism entails a number of different things, but one thing it means is the rejection of history in favor of mere ideas. Liberal "Christianity," whose general approach to Genesis 1 we have just described, is gnostic. For the gnostic, it does not matter whether Jesus really rose from the grave or not. What matters is the *idea* of resurrection, or the *idea* of a virgin birth, or the *idea* of the mighty acts of God, or even the *idea* of history (as opposed to the *facts* of history). Once we understand the idea embedded in a supposedly historical narrative, we can dispense with the historical events. Christianity, however, stands opposed to all gnosticism. If there were not an original Adam and an original Fall into sin, then there could not be a final Adam (Jesus) and a redemption from sin. As mentioned, I shall address this matter more fully in chapter four.

Orthodox Christians are committed to history, to God's acts in history in creating the world and humanity, testing humanity, judging humanity, redeeming humanity, and transfiguring humanity and the world. Thus, orthodox Christians do not have the option of saying that the early chapters of Genesis are not historical.

Since Genesis 1 rather obviously does present God's creation and world-building as lasting for one normal week, orthodox Christians must either accept this and live with it or else find some indication in the text itself that Genesis 1 is not to be taken as lasting one normal week in length. There are two possible ways to get around the "normal week" interpretation.

The first is to find indications in the rest of the Bible that the week in Genesis 1 is a symbol, or rather that it is *only* a symbol. If there were a passage in the inerrant Bible that said something like, "As God portrayed Himself working in six days and resting on the seventh, so you should work six days and rest on the seventh," then a case might be made for this approach. No such passage exists in the Bible, however, nor does anything like it. Yet perhaps there are other, more general indications in the Bible that would lead us to take Genesis 1 in a nonhistorical fashion. The present book will explore such proposed possibilities.[4]

The second option is to find indications in Genesis 1 itself that the passage is not to be taken as the history of one normal week. Here is where the "apparent contradictions" come into play. Most of the first part of the present book is occupied with examining these supposed "difficulties" to see if they are really all that difficult. We have already, with William, glanced at two such proposed "apparent contradictions." We shall examine these in more depth as we go along.

The present book is a defense of the Church's traditional "normal day" reading of Genesis 1. I cannot know what the future may bring, but I am convinced that to date no one has brought forth any sound argument for reading Genesis 1 in any other way. Like William, I am disappointed in the intelligent, scholarly, godly men who have adopted other views. I can understand that young students, rightly admiring their teachers, often adopt such views and promulgate them, but it is my hope that the present series of

[4] Actually, there is only one such argument, which is that just as there is an upper-story heaven over the earth, there are also upper-story days over earthly days. This is the argument of the Klineans and will be discussed at length in due course.

essays will cause them to rethink matters and, without rejecting all that their teachers have taught them, reject them at this particular point and return to the way the Church has always read the opening chapters of the Bible.

Thesis, Purpose, and Overview

The thesis of the present series of studies is that Genesis 1 intends to provide an historical narrative of the events by which God's Spirit, over the course of six normal days, brought His initial creation to a point where it was "very good" and ready to be turned over to His Spirit-infused surrogate, humanity. The purpose of these studies is to interact with those who have advocated other views and defend the historic Christian understanding of the text of Genesis 1.

My procedure will be to analyze several important and influential essays by writers taking other views. These essays together present all the arguments against the historical understanding of Genesis 1, which are of course also found elsewhere in various evangelical writings.

I have limited myself to evangelicals. My reason for this limitation is twofold. First, I am myself in the evangelical fold. Second, as mentioned above, it is only evangelicals (and a few conservatives in other branches of the Church) who have a problem with Genesis 1. It is only among the evangelicals that we find a concerted attempt to find a way to harmonize Genesis 1 with the evanescent opinions of modern science.[5]

I have not dealt at length with two other evangelical attempts to recast the historical understanding of Genesis 1: the Gap Interpretation and the Day-Age Interpretation. This is mainly because I don't take them seriously and be-

[5] For instance, in Henri Blocher, *In the Beginning: The Opening Chapters of Genesis* (Downers Grove, IL: InterVarsity Press, 1984), and N. H. Ridderbos, *Is There a Conflict Between Genesis 1 and Natural Science* (Grand Rapids, MI: Eerdmans, 1957).

cause they have been adequately dealt with elsewhere and have few exponents any longer.

The Gap Interpretation, also called the Ruin-Reconstruction Interpretation, is based on a misreading of the phrase "without form and void" in Genesis 1:2.[6] Supposedly this phrase means that the world was in a condition of total chaos, an interpretation read back into the creation account from later passages that deal with sin and judgment. Thus, there is a time-gap between Genesis 1:1 and Genesis 1:2. Supposedly there was a pre-Adamite race, probably the angels, who governed the world and then wrecked it through sin, after which God rebuilt it in six days. There is absolutely no biblical evidence for this notion, and it flies in the face of the testimony of Genesis 1, which says that the sun and moon were not created until the fourth day of creation week. Gap Interpreters have tried to get around this by suggesting the notion that the earth had been shrouded in clouds for millennia before this fourth day, a position that assumes that Genesis 1 is written from the perspective of someone on the earth, something the text neither says nor hints. In chapter two of the present study, we shall find that Bruce Waltke, though an advocate of a pictorial understanding of Genesis 1, still holds to this discredited interpretation to some extent.[7]

[6] See John C. Whitcomb, *The Early Earth* (rev. ed.; Grand Rapids, MI: Baker, 1986), chap. 5; and Weston W. Fields, *Unformed and Unfilled: A Critique of the Gap Theory* (Phillipsburg, NJ: Presbyterian and Reformed, 1976).

[7] Less compelling, since it has few advocates, is the notion that God did not create the world in six days but revealed it to Moses or someone over the course of six days. The definitive presentation of this view is found in P. J. Wiseman, *Clues to Creation in Genesis* (London: Marshall, Morgan, & Scott, 1977). Wiseman states that God is addressing someone in Genesis 1, though we don't know who it is. Rather clearly, however, the "Let there be" statements of Genesis 1 don't have to be addressed *to* anyone; God was simply speaking to Himself, just as we, His images, often conduct internal dialogues. Other statements by God are addressed specifically to birds, fishes, and man. The rest of the Bible provides no evidence for Wiseman's conjectures.

The Day-Age Interpretation is far-fetched on the face of it. Supposedly we are to believe that plants grew on the earth for an entire eon before the sun was created and for two eons before there were insects to pollinate them. Day-Age Interpreters do themselves no service when they attempt to rescue their position by saying that plants only "came into focus" in the third eon and that the sun "came into focus" in the fourth, etc. What does such a view accomplish? The proposed scheme bears no resemblance to the understanding of cosmic development presently in vogue in the declining years of Western Civilization. The interpretation itself is based on a radical misunderstanding of the word "day" in Genesis 1, a term defined in the text itself as a period of light that alternates with a period of darkness, periods measured by the apparent movement of the sun after its establishment on the fourth day. The entire 24-hour cycle, proceeding from night to day, is called "day," since "day" is the climactic part of the cycle. Although occasionally the Bible uses "day" to refer to a larger span of time, the "day" in Genesis 1 is the "24-hour day," and it has evenings and mornings. Clearly such a "day" is not an age or eon. It is hard to understand how such an approach to the narrative ever gained credibility among thinking people, unless one bears in mind the overwhelming infuence of modern scientific constructions on the development of the cosmos.[8]

If these two attempts to rescue the historicity of

[8] About the time Western theologians have given up on such silly attempts, we find a prominent Eastern Orthodox publication advocating it. A crude attempt to mingle Genesis 1 with evolution, replete with grotesque misinterpretations of the text and misreadings of the early Church writers, can be seen in Alexandre Kalomiros, "The Divine Will: Some Thoughts Concerning Scriptural and Patristic Understanding of the Creation of Man and the World, Delivered at Mount Holly Springs Orthodox Conference in 1981," in *The Christian Activist: A Journal of Orthodox Opinion*, vol. 2, Fall–Winter 1997, pp. 8ff. This widely distributed periodical is edited by Frank Schaeffer, the wayward son of Francis A. Schaeffer.

Genesis 1 while extending time into the far reaches of the past have failed, there remain evangelicals who are not ready to discard the historicity of Genesis 1 altogether. One such is John Sailhamer, who argues that Genesis 1 is an historical account of the formation of the land of Canaan (which he says is Eden), not of the creation of the entire universe. I have determined to treat Sailhamer at length because (1) his view is quite likely to become popular, (2) Sailhamer actually moves through the text of Genesis 1, and thereby (3) he provides an opportunity for us to work through the text carefully as we answer his interpretation.

The present writer did not always hold this "strict" view. I was reared in a conservative Christian household and in a generally conservative Lutheran congregation. Like most American boys growing up in the 1950s, I had a general interest in science, and like a few of them, I developed a life-long love of science fiction literature. My ruminations in high school and college led me quite naturally to the conclusion that "God used evolution" to bring the world to its present state. To be sure, I had heard and read Genesis 1, but I had never really thought about it, or faced the fact that its account of origins does not square with the hypotheses of modern science.

By my senior year of college, I had become an active evangelical and had begun to read the works of Francis Schaeffer, brand new at the time, as well as those from whom he drew much of his thinking, such as E. L. Hebden Taylor, Herman Dooyeweerd, Rousas J. Rushdoony, and Cornelius Van Til. Eventually I came in contact with the writings of John C. Whitcomb. I was struck by the fact that someone could take Genesis 1 "literally" and wed it to the data of the world while holding to a young earth. I thought that this was interesting and curious, but no more.

As time went along, however, I found my nose pushed into the text of Genesis 1. I could not rest until I had resolved the problems that now faced me. Eventually, after much struggle, I became convinced that Whitcomb was right and became an avid follower of the "scientific creationism" advocated by Henry Morris and his associates.

Over the years since I have come to see some problems in the "scientific creationist" approach. The notion of a water vapor canopy over the earth before the Flood finds no clear-cut support in Scripture, for instance. Also, I believe that too often the creationists look to specific texts of the Bible for "scientific" information that is not really there.[9] Thus, I have remained engaged with the issue.

As a Calvinist, I found that many in my intellectual arena subscribe to a nonhistorical, pictorial view of Genesis 1. At first glance, such an approach to the passage can appear as a valid alternative to the traditional historical interpretation, but I repeatedly found that it did not stand up to close inspection. Moreover it was founded on unrecognized gnostic presuppositions, which I discuss in chapter four. Thus, over the years, I have become more and more confirmed in the traditional understanding that Genesis 1 is an historical narrative, covering the course of one normal week of time. It is my purpose here to defend that understanding.

Because of their gnostic roots and presuppositions, the nonhistorical interpretations of Genesis 1 are not minor errors. They are dangerous aberrations from Christian orthodoxy, for they are grounded in non-Christian approaches to reality and to the text of the Bible. That many of those advocating these errors are not self-conscious of the pagan roots of their thinking does not change matters as far as the truth is concerned. I hope that in this book I have been courteous toward my Christian brothers who have fallen into these errors, while at the same time standing firm in

[9] Let me hasten to add that I affirm the fundamental approach of the scientific creationists, which is to start with the statements of the Bible and then build our understand of cosmology and cosmogony on that basis.

advocating the orthodox way of understanding God, time, world, and text.

The pictorial interpreters of Genesis 1 proceed by attempting to show contradictions in the text that indicate that the text is not to be taken as an historical narrative. They complement this with discussions of the challenges posed by modern science and with discussions of the theology and literary structure of Genesis 1. My procedure, thus, is three-fold, as I mentioned in the Introduction. First, I argue that these contradictions and difficulties exist only in the minds of the advocates of the pictorial interpretation; they are not found in the text at all (chapters two, three, and five). Second, I argue that the notions of modern science are often fundamentally idolatrous, and thus they should not be allowed to direct the thinking of serious Christians (chapter six). Along with this, in chapter four, I seek to expose what I think is the pernicious tendency in post-Reformation evangelicalism to downplay the physicality and historicality of God's creation in favor of a religion of ideas.

Finally, I discuss in chapter eight the theological and literary character of Genesis 1, showing how much the pictorial interpreters have missed, showing that someone who takes the passage as historical narrative, like William, is in a better position to understand its theological and literary dimensions. Chapter eight presents in a summary the way I think Genesis 1 should be read. Most of the points in that chapter are found along the way in the chapters critical of my adversaries, but they are collected and expanded in the last chapter. Chapter eight is not what I regard as a full exposition of Genesis 1 and its meaning; that will have to wait for another occasion. I do hope it is obvious that it is not necessary to agree with my proposed interpretations in order to agree with my proposed criticisms of other views.[10]

[10] At this point, I must call attention to the fine study of Genesis 1 authored by fellow Calvinist Douglas Kelly, which appeared just as the

A couple of notes on terminology: I have often used "Genesis 1" to refer to the entire seven days of creation, which is actually found in Genesis 1:1–2:3. The chapter break between Genesis 1 and 2 is one of many really absurd chapter breaks in the Bible. The division of the Bible into chapters and verses occurred in the Middle Ages and in the Reformation era, and it badly needs to be redone.

I have also used the phrase "creation week," even though the actual act of creation happened all at once on the first day. One might write of the "world-forming week." Yet, in view of the fact that God "created" dinosaurs on the fifth day and "created" man on the sixth day, speaking of the entire week as "creation week" seems valid. The reader should always bear in mind, however, that apart from these two creative acts, the other acts of God in Genesis 1 always involve reshaping what had already been created in the beginning.

present book was being completed. Dr. Kelly does a very good job of summarizing the arguments for the historic Christian understanding of Genesis 1. His primary focus is on the interaction of Genesis 1 with modern science, while my primary focus is on the biblical theology of Genesis 1. Accordingly, his study of the text is not as detailed as mine, nor does he provide as full a commentary on the passage as does the present book. As a result, there is little overlap between his study and mine, and I heartily recommend that his book be read in tandem with the present volume. Douglas F. Kelly, *Creation and Change: Genesis 1:1—2:4 in the Light of Changing Scientific Paradigms* (Ross–Shire, UK: Mentor–Christian Focus Publications, 1997).

Chapter 2

The Framework Interpretation of Bruce K. Waltke

Bruce K. Waltke, "The Literary Genre of Genesis, Chapter One," *Crux* 27:4 (1991):2–10.

To begin with, let me write some words in praise of Bruce Waltke. Waltke is a brilliant language scholar, and he has done much work of tremendous benefit to the Christian world. His articles in *The International Standard Bible Encyclopedia*[1] and the *Theological Wordbook of the Old Testament*[2] (of which he is one of the three main editors) are rightly regarded with the highest esteem, and his co-authored *Introduction to Biblical Hebrew Syntax*[3] is the seminal text on this important topic. Moreover, Waltke is a man willing to abandon his earlier dispensationalism for covenant theology, moving from Dallas Theological Seminary to Westminster Theological Seminary and later going on to Regent College. Also, early in his career, Waltke published arguments that the fetus is not a human being from conception, and thus stated that abortion is not necessarily always wrong, but frankly reversed his opinion after further study, doing so in the most public forum he could find, the national meeting of the Evangelical Theological

[1] (Grand Rapids, MI: Eerdmans, 1979–88).
[2] (Chicago, IL: Moody Press, 1980).
[3] With M. O'Connor (Winona Lake, IN: Eisenbrauns, 1988).

Society in 1975. (I should add that back in the 1960s and 1970s, evangelicals were divided on the abortion issue, largely because the matter had not been much studied.)

All of which is to say that Dr. Waltke is a man for whom I have much esteem as a scholar and as a Christian man. But he's wrong about Genesis 1.

Waltke begins his essay with a Preface. He introduces his subject by saying that Genesis 1 (i.e., 1:1–2:3) needs desperately to be heard in the social sciences classroom, but instead it is being heard in the hard sciences classroom. Instead of seeing the implications for theology and society in Genesis 1, Christians are usually stuck debating the cosmological meaning of the passage. Waltke pits the two against each other as if we cannot have both.

Now, of course there is no need to pit the two against each other. Genesis 1 has implications for many, if not all, fields of endeavor. Moreover, it really is not correct to say that evangelicals have not applied Genesis 1 to the "social sciences." Any reading of creationist literature will find plenty about social Darwinism and about the other social and cultural implications of evolution, along with statements about the relevance of Genesis 1 in these areas.

Perhaps we should go light on Waltke at this point, however. It is not always easy to find a good introductory lead-in to an essay, and maybe all Waltke is trying to do is raise the issue in a general way.

Waltke does, however, go on to write that the question of whether Genesis 1 belongs with the hard sciences or the social sciences depends on its genre as literature. He states that the purpose of his essay is to help us identify the genre of Genesis 1 and that in so doing we shall find that it was never the intention of Genesis 1 to tell us how God actually brought the universe into being.

The Genre Question

Genre studies seem all the rage in many evangelical scholarly circles today. We are told that there are many different genres of literature in the Bible: narrative, poetry, etc. We are supposed to identify a given passage in terms of its genre and then read it accordingly.[4]

Now at first glance there is nothing apparently wrong with this procedure. If we reflect a moment, however, we can see that there is a large problem—the Bible is authored by God Himself. Just as God is beyond the limitations of human life, so God's Word is beyond the limitations of human cultural writing styles. The believer has to begin by affirming that the Bible transcends all genre considerations. Our human writings, like our human lives, are limited, partial, specialized, particular expressions of God's life, which is unlimited.

Along these lines, Vern S. Poythress has written,

> In general, the multidimensional character of the language system—or we might ultimately say, the multidimensional character of God's wisdom and his decrees—creates a multidimensional character to the nature of genre. Every particular discourse and every particular communicative purpose from a particular person belongs to any number of genres in cross-cutting fashion. Genre is not a label for the essence of a particular discourse, nor is it the definitive key to interpretation. Rather, it is a pointer to multidimensional analogies that large units like paragraphs and monologues sustain in the language system. Classifying a discourse as belonging to a particular genre can help. It highlights the similarities with other discourses belonging to the same genre, and can at times become a significant clue to authorial purposes and reading strategies. For example, to say that Matthew 13:24–30 is a parable alerts us to the fact that Matthew and his readers come with certain expectations about fictionality, the existence of a second layer of meaning, persuasive

[4] An introduction to genre classification methods, from a conservative viewpoint, is found in Tremper Longman, *Literary Approaches to Biblical Interpretation.* Foundations of Contemporary Interpretation Vol. 3 (Grand Rapids, MI: Zondervan, 1987) pp. 76ff.

> purpose, and so on. But similarities in one dimension between a particular discourse and others never exhaust the relationships that are significant for understanding the discourse. Matthew 13:24–30 also belongs to the genre of allegory.[5]

Poythress writes further:

> But in proper interpretation we meet God, who surpasses us in both beauty, order, and truth. His truth is beautiful and his beauty displays truth. His order is beautiful and his beauty displays the faithfulness and harmony of his order. Hence, order, beauty, truth each become a perspective on the others; no truncated approach provides solutions to the interpretive challenge. No human system exhausts God's beauty or his truth, or captures once-for-all the creativity belonging to both. God surpasses us in his systematic wisdom (the language system), his word of control (the particular discourse), and his person (his communicative purpose).[6]

If we look around the ancient world, we may find various kinds of literature: satires, love poems, sagas, myths, law codes, and the like. Each of these is pretty specialized and particular. When we look back at the Bible, the temptation is to try and find such genres in the Bible as well; and this is exactly what unbelieving scholars do, since they believe the Bible is a piece of merely human religious literature. When we actually look at the Bible, however, we don't find any "pure" examples of any of these genres. The "law code" of Exodus 21–23 is only superficially like the law codes of the ancient world; it includes many things that don't belong in a law code and is really more of a ser-

[5] Vern S. Poythress, *The Supremacy of God in Interpretation,* draft version 3 (Chestnut Hill, PA: Westminster Theological Seminary Bookstore, mid-1990s) p. 252f.

[6] Ibid., p. 253.

mon from Yahweh.[7] Similarly, the Song of Songs is far more than a love poem, alluding as it does to the architecture of the Temple and to the geography of the promised land.[8] Some parts of the Bible, like the Psalms, are pretty clearly poetic, and some parts come closer to modern narrative prose, but the writings of the prophets tend to fall in between.

Moreover, biblical narrative prose often contains assonances and alliterations, not to mention intricate literary structures like chiasms.[9] Notice for instance the breathy, windy sound of Genesis 2:7b in Hebrew: "of dust from the ground and He breathed into his nostrils the breath of life and the man became a living soul"—*aphar min hadamah wayipahh b'apaiw nishmath hhayim wa'y'hi ha'adam l'nefesh hhayah.*[10] You can hear the wind and the dust.

All of which is to say that the Bible transcends questions of genre. When God speaks (e.g., Leviticus, Isaiah), it is ultimately beyond genre; and when God inspires human writers (e.g., Genesis) the result is also beyond genre.

Having said that, we can give back with the left hand

[7] For instance, the "law code" of Exodus 21–23 includes this very unlegal directive: "If you ever take your neighbor's cloak as a pledge, you are to return it to him before the sun sets, for that is his only covering—it is the cloak for his skin. What else will he sleep in? And it will come about that when he cries to Me, I will hear, for I am gracious" (22:25–26).

[8] Note the repeated geographical imagery in the Song, and also that lilies and pomegranates, which had no place in the Sinaitic Tabernacle, are prominently featured in Solomon's Temple and in the Song of Songs. For a discussion of the latter imagery, see my monograph, *Thoughts on Jachin and Boaz.* Biblical Horizons Occasional Paper 1 (August, 1988; available from Biblical Horizons, Box 1096, Niceville, FL 32588).

[9] A chiasm is a literary form having an ABA structure. See appendix B for a full discussion.

[10] My transliteration of the Hebrew does not conform to the usual scholarly conventions but is designed so that the untrained reader can say it aloud.

what we have taken with the right. There are "shadows" of genres in the Bible, but only shadows. Some parts are "more like" sagas, love songs, poems, narratives, etc., but only "more like." To assume that we can "peg" a particular section of the Bible into a particular genre and then interpret it in the "light" of that genre is an unbiblical procedure, and it will surely blind us to much of what is in the text.

Thus, "genre analysis" is a tricky matter. We can make the mistake of importing into the biblical literature "genres" that are not really there, thereby distorting how we read the text. For instance, if the story of Jacob is read primarily as a "trickster tale," it is seriously misread. Or we can decide that a particular passage is a certain "genre," one genuinely found in the Bible, but make the mistake of saying that because this passage is such-and-such a genre, it therefore is nothing else. Sound biblical scholars bear all these things in mind, but even the best can fall into making too much out of genre considerations.

Waltke on the Purpose of Genesis One

In the second section of his paper, Waltke addresses the purpose of Genesis 1. He begins by telling us that the original audience of Genesis 1 was Israel in the wilderness at Sinai. The author was Moses. Moses, under divine inspiration, provided the creation story to undergird the covenant being made at Sinai.

Now, there is no biblical evidence for this notion. Yes, it is very commonly believed that Moses wrote Genesis, though the Bible never says that. But even if he did, we have no reason to think that the "purpose" of Genesis was to be a preamble to the Sinaitic covenant. For one thing, such a reading of Genesis elevates the Sinaitic covenant above the Adamic, Noahic, and Patriarchal covenants, which are lowered to the status of mere preliminaries. Certainly each covenant is preliminary to the one that follows it, but that does not mean that the record of those covenants was written at the time of the later covenant.

We might just as well assert, as some have, that the entire first seven books of the Bible were written by Samuel as an historical prologue to the Kingdom covenant. After all, Genesis 36 seems to have been finished at a time far after Moses. Aalders writes,

> in Gn. xxxvi.31 at the commencement of a list of Edomite kings we read: 'and these are the kings that reigned in the land of Edom, before there reigned any king over the children of Israel'. This can have been written only at a time when Israel actually had a king. It is not a theoretical anticipation of the possibility of a future kingship like Dt. xvii.14 ff., but has its starting-point in the reality of an Israelitish kingdom. So these words cannot have been written before the reign of King Saul.[11]

There is not a whit of biblical evidence that Moses wrote Genesis. The Bible never states or even implies that he did.[12] In fact, there is good reason to believe that he did not, though he probably added some touches to it. First of all, it can be stated as a rule that biblical writings were produced immediately after the events they described were

[11] G. C. Aalders, *A Short Introduction to the Pentateuch* (London: Tyndale, 1949) pp. 106f. Aalders is not an advocate of the idea that Samuel wrote the Pentateuch as a whole. I cite him merely to summarize some evidence that those holding such a view can point to. For Aalders, Genesis 36:31 is an insertion into Genesis by a later writer, and he is almost certainly correct. The idea that early books of the Bible may have been slightly edited later on, under divine inspiration, does not take away from the inerrancy and canonicity of the Bible. Genesis was inerrant in its first form and canonical for the people at that time. It is still inerrant, and in its last form, it is canonical for us.

[12] Nowhere is Genesis quoted and said to have been authored by Moses. Luke 24:27, "And beginning from Moses and from all the prophets, [Jesus] explained to them the things concerning Himself in the Scriptures," implies no more than that Moses put the first five books into a semi-final shape (see footnote 11 above), not that he was the original author of Genesis. John 7:22, "On this account Moses has given you circumcision—not because it is from Moses, but from the fathers—and on the sabbath you circumcise a man," refers to Leviticus 12:3.

completed. If Moses wrote Genesis, it was 144 or so years after the last event in Genesis. (Joseph died in 2369 A.M., and Israel came to Sinai in 2513 A.M.)[13]

Second, if Moses wrote Genesis, that means that the Hebrews in captivity did not have any Bible from God to read and meditate upon. All they had, perhaps, was "oral tradition." There is no reason to believe in such an oral tradition, however.[14] Rather, God's words to Moses in Exodus 3–4 and 6 seem to indicate that the people knew about the God of Abraham, Isaac, and Jacob, and that implies writings. (Some people have the idea that the Israelites were an uneducated people in Egypt. Hardly. They were the architects and artisans of Egypt, and obviously many of them were able to read and write.)

Third, evangelical scholars like Wiseman and Harrison have argued that Genesis is made up of sources marked out by the statement "these are the generations of *x*." These booklets, they suggest, existed in a series and were unified to form the book of Genesis.[15] Whatever the ins and outs of this theory, it makes a lot more sense than the notion that Moses composed Genesis from scratch at Sinai. It makes a great deal of sense in terms of progressive revelation. It means that Adam knew how God created the world; that Noah knew about creation and Adam; that Abraham knew about creation, Adam, and Noah; etc. Thus Moses might have written Genesis, but not from scratch—though I think Joseph wrote it.

Now, I imagine Waltke would agree with some of what I have stated above, but he still wants to maintain that Moses composed Genesis 1 with the Sinaitic covenant in mind. What that means is that neither Noah nor Abraham had

[13] AM stands for *Anno Mundi*, the number of years from the creation, counted as they are presented in the biblical chronology.

[14] See chapter eight, footnote 1; p. 172.

[15] P. J. Wiseman, *Clues to Creation in Genesis* (London: Marshall, Morgan, and Scott, [1936] 1977); Roland K. Harrison, *Introduction to the Old Testament* (Grand Rapids, MI: Eerdmans, 1969) pp. 547ff.

the information in Genesis 1, and thus they could not order their lives in terms of it. Is this a reasonable view to advocate and maintain?

Make no mistake about it: Waltke and those like him (and there are many) are arguing that Genesis 1 did not exist before Moses wrote it (under inspiration, of course). Genesis 1, they maintain, was not part of the thought-world of the patriarchs.

I submit that the most likely composer of Genesis was Joseph or one of his contemporaries. Joseph could have compounded the book of Genesis out of the earlier inspired books, all but the last verse (just as Moses did not write the last chapter of Deuteronomy). I suggest that this book of Genesis was the Bible of the Hebrews in captivity. It was the light to their feet and provided them the hope of a deliverance to come.

Since there is no direct evidence either way, my view is at least as good as Waltke's. In fact, my view is better because it conforms to the way God always works in history, giving His people a book at every stage of covenantal history.

Waltke continues by quoting from scholars who assert (he writes that they "argue," which they don't) that Moses wrote Genesis 1 to argue against the nature gods of the pagan religions. Supposedly Genesis 1 has an apologetic thrust, which is directed against other gods and forces, asserting that there is only one God and that He is the Creator of all things, etc. Now certainly Genesis 1 can be used that way, but what evidence is there in the text of Genesis 1 that this is any part of its original purpose? The answer is: none.[16] There is nothing in Genesis 1 that implies that it has an apologetic purpose. This notion is read into the text, not read out of it.

[16] See also appendix D.

Genesis 1:1

Waltke's next section deals with the contents of Genesis 1. He begins with Genesis 1:1, and he tells us that this verse is a summary of the rest of the chapter, not simply the first event in the chapter. Because of the importance of his argument, we shall cite him in full:

> First, "heaven and earth" is a hendiadys (a single expression of two apparently separate parts) denoting "the cosmos," the complete, orderly, harmonious universe. For example, the hendiadys "kith and kin" indicates all of one's relatives. More specifically, the hendiadys is a merism, a statement of opposites to indicate totality, like the compounds, "day and night," "summer and winter."
>
> Now the elements of a compound must be studied as a unit, not in isolation. The hendiadys, "heaven and earth," cannot be understood by treating "heaven" and "earth" as separate elements any more than "butterfly" can be decoded by investigating "butter" and "fly" in isolation. (p. 3)

Well, in isolation from everything else in the Bible, and in isolation from the rest of Genesis 1, this might make sense. It is true that heaven and earth are two sides of one cosmic coin, and so the phrase might just mean "cosmos." How do we know, however, when to take a phrase like this as a hendiadys and when to take it as two distinguished things? We can only know from context, not from the words themselves.

So what does the rest of the Bible teach us? It clearly teaches that there is a separate realm called heaven where the angels held court with God and received their marching orders, and to which the saints go after Jesus' ascension. In other words, the Bible teaches us that heaven and earth are two realms, with different functions in history and in the total cosmos. There is thus no reason whatsoever for denying that Genesis 1:1 specifically refers to these two realms.

Moreover, even in Genesis 1 we find that God called

the firmament "heaven," and this firmament-heaven is the place where the sun, moon, and stars are located. Is this the same as the "heaven" of Genesis 1:1? No, because there is water above this firmament-heaven. Where is that water located? Well, later in the Bible we see a sea of ice around the heavenly throne of God (Ezek. 1:22; Rev. 4:6). Thus, the narrative text of Genesis 1 clearly assumes that there is a created throne-heaven as well as an "earth" that, in the largest sense, is the lower cosmos including the stars.

In conclusion, there is no hendiadys in Genesis 1:1. Waltke may say that there is, but saying it does not make it so. The traditional reading of the verse is consonant with the rest of the Bible and with the rest of Genesis 1. Of course, since heaven and earth are all that God created, "heaven and earth" refers to everything, but at the same time, each noun has a specific referent. By turning "heaven and earth" into a hendiadys, we run the risk of obscuring one of the important aspects of Genesis 1, which is that the earth is developing in time toward a goal, unlike heaven, which was created finished and perfect to start with.

Waltke's second argument is that the verb "create" refers to the finished cosmos, not to a state before its completion. Waltke argues that the cosmos was not finished until the end of the seven days, so that Genesis 1:1 must be a summary introductory statement. By no means is this a sound argument, however. What Genesis 1:1 says is that God created the heavens and the earthly cosmos. This was definitely a one-time event, and a finished one.[17] The rest of Genesis 1 shows us God's Spirit working with the earthly cosmos to bring it forward from glory to glory, starting out the historical process that His Spirit-endowed image, humanity, is to complete. We notice that at each stage of His work, God saw that it was good, so that the universe was "completed" at each stage. The completed universe that God made at the beginning was formless, empty, and

[17] For further discussion, see chapter seven.

dark, but it was still good and still a completed act.

Moreover, the Spirit who entered dust to make man is the same Spirit who was working with the creation in Genesis 1. Thus, we might just as well say that the work of creation will not be finished until the Last Day. But neither Waltke nor anyone else would want to import that larger conception into the meaning of Genesis 1:1.

Genesis 1:2

Turning to verse 2, Waltke states that at the time the cosmos was created, the earth was *tohu wabohu*, "unformed and unfilled." Then he asserts that this phrase is also a hendiadys, meaning "utter chaos." He cites E. Jacob's *Theology of the Old Testament*: "where it [*tohu wabohu*] is met (Is. 34:11; Jer. 4:23), [it] denotes the contrary of creation and not merely an inferior stage of creation" (p. 4).

To which we reply: "No, it doesn't." For one thing, Jacob's statement makes no sense. There is no "opposite" or "contrary" of creation. There is only an opposite of order and life and fullness, which is disorder, death, and emptiness. Isaiah 34:11 and Jeremiah 4:23 do not speak of some opposite of creation itself but rather of the dissolution of the order of creation back to its original condition.

Moreover, Isaiah and Jeremiah are speaking to the situation after the rebellion of man, not to a situation of the good creation as it came from the hand of God. To import the nuances and connotations of these later passages back into Genesis 1:2 is hermeneutically impermissible.

Additionally, nothing in the phrase implies chaos. Is a lump of clay "chaotic" just because it has not yet been formed into a vase or a man? Is an empty room "chaotic"?

Waltke, however, has decided that the original world was in some *evil* sense dark and chaotic: "The Genesis account, however, teaches only that God brought the pre-Genesis darkness and chaotic waters within His protective restraints, not when or how they happened" (p. 4). In other words, God had created the universe at some earlier time, and it had fallen into chaos and darkness. Now, in Genesis 1, God is making it anew.

This is all based on reading into the phrase *tohu wabohu* meanings and connotations that it does not carry. There is nothing per se "negative" about the condition *tohu wabohu* as it originally came from the hand of God. Waltke is pushed to this "ruin-reconstruction" view of Genesis 1 by erroneously importing nuances from the use of this phrase in other contexts.

Now, is this phrase a hendiadys, or are two distinguishable aspects of the primordial creation in view? To answer that question we look first at the terms themselves, and then at the context of Genesis 1. The fact is that these two words are seldom found in Hebrew literature, so we must pay especial attention to the contexts in which they are found. Clearly they will not imply the same thing in a creation passage as they imply in a judgment passage.

The adjective *bohu* is found only three times, and only in conjunction with *tohu*. The latter is found twenty-one times. A survey of several passages will bring out the meaning.

In Deuteronomy 32:10, God is said to have found Israel in a desert land, in the howling waste of a wilderness, according to the NASB translation. Now, does this phrase imply emptiness or disorder? The context tells us. Verses 8–9 tell us that God separated Israel from the nations and set boundaries. God Himself was their boundary according to the second half of verse 10. Thus, the implication of *tohu* is that of boundarylessness, formlessness.

In Job 6:18, "the paths of their course wind along; they go up into *tohu* and perish." Again, the notion is that of formlessness. The winding, curling paths lead nowhere. Lack of structure is the idea. The same idea is in Job 12:24–25 and Psalm 107:40.

The lack of any boundary is also the implication of Job

26:6–7: "Naked is Sheol under Him and Abaddon has no covering. He stretches out the north over *tohu*, and hangs the earth upon nothingness." There are no boundaries between God and the parts of His creation.

Isaiah 24:10 uses *tohu* to mean confusion or chaos.

Isaiah 29:21 uses *tohu* to refer to confusing, misleading arguments.

Isaiah 34:11 uses both *tohu* and *bohu*: "He shall stretch over it the line of *tohu*, and the plumb line of *bohu*." In context, both chaos and emptiness are being discussed, so it seems likely that *tohu* alludes to the chaos and *bohu* to the emptiness.

Isaiah 40:17 says that God regards the nations as less than nothing and as *tohu*. Again, in context this seems to mean that the nations are not boundaried and measured off like God's own people, as the passage begins with verse 12 and concerns such boundaries and measurements. The same is true of the context of the word *tohu* in verse 23.

In Isaiah 41:29, the molten images are wind and shapelessness (not emptiness). The shaped idols have no shape. The same thought is found in 44:9.

Isaiah 45:18 reads:

> For thus says Yahweh
> The one creating the heavens is He.
> The one forming the earth and making her is He.
> He established her.
> Not *tohu* in His creating her.
> To be inhabited He formed her.
> I am Yahweh.
> And there is none other.

At first glance, it seems that *tohu* is parallel to "inhabited," so that here *tohu* means "empty."[18] If sheer emptiness were in view, however, other words would be better. I suggest,

[18] E. J. Young, *Studies in Genesis One* (Philadelphia: Presbyterian & Reformed Pub. Co., 1964) p. 12f.

in view of the use of *tohu* here, that it is not inhabitation by some sheer mass of people and animals that is in view but rather the kind of orderly inhabitation that the Bible presents as good. Not "*tohu*" but "formed."

In Isaiah 59:4, *tohu* is used for the confusion caused by lies and deception.

Finally, in the famous passage of Jeremiah 4:23, the prophet looks "on the earth, and behold, *tohu wabohu*." The ensuing verses speak first of chaos, as the mountains quake and move about, and then of emptiness, as the men and birds flee.

Now, what our survey has shown is that the traditional rendering of Genesis 1:2 is entirely correct. The earth was both unstructured and also empty.

Second, the context of Genesis 1 shows that *tohu wabohu* is not a hendiadys. The work of the six days clearly shows separate and distinct acts of forming and filling. God forms the world by dividing it into specific zones and setting up boundaries. He also populates it. These are two different things that take place as different actions by God. Thus, even if *tohu wabohu* were a hendiadys in some passages, it cannot be one here. The earth was (a) formless and also (b) empty, and God acted to change each of those states of affairs.

Contradictions in Genesis One and Two?

Waltke now turns to the process and progress of creation. The process he notes as the acts of God in bringing creation into its (initially) full and finished form. The progress he associates with parallels between the first three and the second three days of creation. We shall see as our studies proceed that this set of associations, which Waltke says goes back to Herder (c. 1750), does not really work.[19] In fact, as I shall argue later on, the seven days are structured

[19] See appendix B.

chiastically (that is, 1 and 7, 2 and 6, 3 and 5, and 4 in the center).

Now Waltke turns to the third part of his essay, the "genre" of Genesis 1. He quickly dismisses the notions that Genesis 1 is either a hymn or a liturgy or a myth. He then turns to the question of whether Genesis 1 is to be taken as history, and he answers that question "yes and no."

He rightly notes that Genesis 1 is linked to the history that follows it. Chapters 2:4–4:26 and 5:1–6:8 contain numerous allusions to Genesis 1. Genesis 1 is historical, he affirms, in the sense of saying God made everything to start with.

On the other hand, writes Waltke, the author of Genesis 1 "is just as clearly not giving us in his prologue a straightforward, sequential history" (p. 6). He continues by stating that Henry Morris is wrong to write: "The creation account is clear, definite, sequential, and matter-of-fact, giving every appearance of straightforward historical narrative." Waltke writes that "the text, however, is begging us not to read it in this way."

Now this is a bold claim. According to Waltke, it should be clear to any unbiased reader that Genesis 1 is not to be taken as a sequence of normal days. We may ask at the outset: If this be true, then why have the vast majority of commentators and theologians in the history of the Church read it that way? How could they all miss something so obvious?

With this in mind, let us look at the factors in the text that, according to Waltke, "beg" us not to take the passage as an historical narrative.

First, he writes, "such a reading creates an *irreconcilable contradiction between the prologue of Genesis and the supplemental creation account in Genesis 2:4–25*" (p. 7, emphasis his). Before looking at just what this contradiction amounts to, notice that Waltke has called Genesis 1 a "prologue" and Genesis 2 a "supplementary creation account." This in itself prejudices the discussion. To be sure, Genesis 1 is a prologue to the whole Bible, but Genesis 1–2 is also a prologue to the whole Bible, and so is Genesis 1–3. And so is Genesis 1–4. And Genesis 1–5. Ezekiel is a prologue to the Gospels. But Genesis 1 is far more than a prologue. Similarly, Genesis 2 is not merely a "supplementary creation account," save in the sense that the Church historically has understood it as an amplification of the sixth day.

Waltke lists a series of things that are said to have happened in this "supplementary creation account." First, "between the creation of man (2:7) and the creation of woman (2:18–25), God planted a garden (2:8); caused its trees to grow . . ." (p. 7). Waltke asks, "Are we to put our imaginations in fast-forward and see its trees as growing to maturity and bearing fruit" in a very short span of time? He asserts that when the text of Genesis 2:8–9 says God "planted" and "caused to grow," this implies normal growth, not an extraordinary quick growth. He contrasts such normal growth with the immediacy of Jesus' turning water into wine.

Well, what if this were true? Did Adam stand on the Edenic plateau for thirty years and watch the Garden grow up? If not, does Waltke also deny the historicity of Genesis 2? Was Eve not, in fact, made from Adam's side while he slept? Did two such people as Adam and Eve ever really exist?

According to Genesis 2, God made Adam and then planted the Garden-Orchard, obviously while Adam watched. Adam learned what it meant to tend the world by watching his Father. As for the trees springing up rapidly, what's so strange about that? If we compare it not with the miracle at Cana but with the budding of Aaron's rod (Num. 17:8), we can see that God does do "miracles of acceleration."

Thus, contrary to Waltke, everything in the passage indicates that the Garden sprang up very quickly, just like the grains and fruit trees of Genesis 1:11–12.

Waltke continues, second, by writing that after God planted the Garden he "caused a heavenly river to flow from the top of Mount Eden through the Garden whereupon it divided into four rivers flowing to the four corners of the earth" (2:10). But the text of Genesis 2 does not say this. It only says that a river was flowing out of Eden, etc. The river may well have been flowing since day 3 of Genesis 1. Indeed, it almost certainly had been.

Then, third, he writes that God "apparently, before he built the woman, formed the birds and animals (v. 19), and the man named them all" (v. 20). Supposedly this contradicts the account in Genesis 1, wherein the birds and beasts were made before man. Once again, however, there is no good reason to read the text this way. For one thing, only birds and wild beasts were "formed" and brought to Adam. This implies that the tame animals ("cattle") were already in the Garden with him. And this state of affairs tells us in what sense God "formed" the birds and beasts. The verb does not necessarily mean that God made the birds and beasts on this occasion, or even that He made a few extra ones for Adam to name. Rather, He "formed" them, pressed them together, in the sense of bringing them together in one place.[20] He collected them. They needed to be collected because they were wild, not domestic, animals. It is normally assumed that God did the same thing when the animals were gathered for the ark in the days of Noah. I regard this as the best way of reading the statement that God formed the animals on this occasion. But it is also perfectly possible to go with the more familiar sense of "formed" and read it as a pluperfect: that God *had* formed

[20] The verb *yatsar* appears first in Genesis 2:7–8, where God pressed dust into the shape of the first man. It is the verb regularly used for the work of a potter, which is pressing clay into shape. For a defense of this understanding, see Samson Raphael Hirsch, *The Pentateuch: Genesis,* trans. Isaac Levy (Gateshead: Judaica Press, [1963] 1989) p. 66.

the animals and then brought them to the man. That is, God had formed them earlier on the fifth and sixth days. Either way, there is no contradiction between Genesis 1 and Genesis 2 here, except in the mind of Waltke.

Waltke then quotes Gleason Archer's exclamation: "Who can imagine that all these transactions could possibly have taken place in 120 minutes of the sixth day (or even within twenty-four hours, for that matter)?"[21]

Well, anyone can imagine it:

6:00 A.M. – God makes the animals.
6:01 A.M. – God takes counsel with Himself to make man.
6:02 A.M. – God makes Adam. Forming him of dust takes one minute.
6:05 A.M. – After talking with Adam for a minute or so, God starts to plant the Garden.
6:10 A.M. – The Garden is completed.
6:11 A.M. – God puts Adam in the Garden.
6:12 A.M. – God warns Adam about the forbidden tree.
6:13 A.M. – Adam has breakfast.
6:30 A.M. – God reveals His decision to make Eve.
6:31 A.M. – God brings the animals to Adam to name. They are brought by "kinds," so not every specific species, let alone every individual, is brought. Let's say that it takes Adam eight hours to name them all, male and female, with a half-hour lunch break. (This is probably far too long at the time.) This brings us to:
3:00 P.M. – Adam takes a nap.
3:28 P.M.– Adam wakes up and meets Eve.
3:29 P.M. – God speaks to Adam and Eve (Gen. 1:28–30).
3:30 P.M. – We still have two and half hours to sunset.

Now, what's so hard about that?

Next Waltke explains that from time to time the Bible presents things in summaries and then expands upon them, so that the narratives are dischronologized. Of course. In

[21] Archer, *A Survey of Old Testament Introduction* (Chicago, IL: Moody Press, 1964) p. 192. "120 minutes" is surely a typographical error for "720 minutes," or twelve hours.

fact, the account of creation week runs all the way through the seventh day before going back and picking up the sixth day in more detail in chapter two. The fact that Bible passages are sometimes dischronologized does not mean that they are not historically accurate, or not to be taken as history.

Then Waltke turns to his second line of evidence that shows Genesis 1 is obviously not historical. He writes: "A straightforward reading of Genesis 1:4 and 14 leads to *the incompatible notions that the sun was created on the first day and again on the fourth day*" (p. 7, emphasis his). Now, how on earth does Waltke get this? We are clearly told that the Spirit of God was hovering over the earth on the first day, and then that light came forth. Rather obviously, the light came from the Spirit, who frequently appears in a Shekinah glory of light in the Bible.[22] We shall take up further arguments about days 1 and 4 as we proceed in this book.

Waltke becomes even more insistent when he writes:

> Furthermore, *verse 14 cannot be reconciled readily with verses 5, 8, and 13*. Our narrator begs us not to read him in a straightforward, sequential account by marking off three days (vv. 5, 8, 13), each with its own 'evening and morning,' before narrating that on the fourth day God created 'the luminaries . . . to separate the day from the night, and . . . to mark . . . days (v. 14). A sequential reading of the text lacks cogency. How can there be three days characterized by day and night before the creation of the luminaries to separate the day from the night and to mark off the days? Are we clueless?

Well, we can certainly see once again that Waltke thinks it is obvious that Genesis 1 is not to be read in the traditional way, but is he right? Well, no. We are told that on the first day, after God sent forth light, He distinguished night and day, evening and morning. This clearly means that there

[22] For a fuller discussion of this light, see chapter three.

was an alternation of darkness and light on the three days before the luminaries were made and appointed to take up the role of ruling day and night. There is nothing difficult or strained about reading the text this way. In fact, if we read it sentence by sentence, absorbing each statement as it comes, this is the plain and obvious meaning of Genesis 1. The sun replaced the glory-light on the fourth day. The cycle of night and day was in place before the sun was made. What's so hard about that?

Finally, Waltke offers as his third argument the assumption that Genesis 1 is obviously not historical narrative: "the language of our creation narrative is figurative, anthropomorphic, not plain." He asserts that the vantage point of the narrator is with God in heaven, and so Genesis 1 is designed to represent things taking place in that transcendent sphere. He quotes John Stek as observing, "What occurs in the arena of God's actions can be storied after the manner of human events, but accounts of 'events' in that arena are fundamentally different in kind from all forms of historiography."[23]

Now, such statements as these sound profound, but they have more to do with Barthianism than with orthodox Christianity. For one thing, Genesis 1 is about the creation of this world, not some other world. Regardless of "vantage point," it is not describing events in some transcendent realm. For another thing, the so-called transcendent realm of heaven is itself a created place, where the angels dwell with God, and where the saints now dwell with Him also. Is it really so radically different from the earthly realm that nothing can be said about it except metaphorically? What kinds of presuppositions would lead to such a notion?

Waltke concludes this section by writing, "To be sure

[23] H. Van Till, R. Snow, J. Stek, and D. Young, *Portraits of Creation: Biblical and Scientific Perspectives on the World's Formation* (Grand Rapids, MI: Eerdmans Pub.Co, 1990) p. 236.

the six days in the Genesis creation account are our twenty-four hour days, but they are metaphorical representations of a reality beyond human comprehension and imitation." To which we have to reply: Who says? Where is there even a hint in the narrative of Genesis 1 that this is the case? As we have seen, nowhere.

Waltke concludes his article with a few remarks about science, which are neither here nor there for our purposes. He concludes that Genesis 1 is a "literary-artistic representation of creation" (p. 9).

We conclude that Waltke has provided no reasons at all for taking Genesis 1 as anything other than a straightforward narrative of the first seven twenty-four hour days of the universe in which we live.

Chapter 3

The Framework Interpretation of Meredith G. Kline

Meredith G. Kline, "Because It Had Not Rained," *Westminster Theological Journal* 20 (1958):146–157.

Meredith G. Kline, "Space and Time in the Genesis Cosmogony," *Perspectives on Science and Christian Faith* 48:1 (March, 1996):2–15.

Meredith G. Kline teaches at Gordon-Conwell Theological Seminary and also at the Westminster Theological Seminaries (Philadelphia and San Diego). His works contain some interesting insights into the meaning of certain biblical texts, and as such his work is important. He is also creator of a new and, in the opinion of most, rather bizarre approach to the history of revelation and redemption.[1] It is as one of the foremost defenders of the "Framework

[1] Kline posits that history alternates between periods of "intrusion," which are like an extended Day of Yahweh in which God acts to enforce His theocracy, and periods of "common grace," during which God does next to nothing. In the former, blessings and curses are dispensed strictly according to merit; in the latter, there is no connection between blessings and righteousness and curses and sin. I should say that Kline's view alternates between periods of sheer rationalism and sheer irrationalism, and that since he cannot maintain this position coherently, he finds it necessary to mix the two. For a critique of this kind of thinking, the works of Cornelius Van Til are recommended.

Interpretation" approach to Genesis 1, however, that he interests us here.

Kline's Original Argument

The argument Kline presented in his original article, and which is repeated in his more recent one, is this: Genesis 1 says that on day 3 God created the plants, but in Genesis 2:5 we find that the plants had not been created because there was no man to till the ground; that is, the plants were created after man was created. In his new article, which we shall take as superseding his earlier one and thus reflective of his more mature thinking, Kline writes regarding Genesis 2:5, "Absent then were all plants, whether belonging to the unpeopled wilderness or to cultivated areas" (p. 12).

This, however, is precisely *not* what Genesis 2:5 says, nor is it what Genesis 1 says about day 3. Genesis 2:5 tells us that no "shrub of the field had been made" and no "plant of the field had sprouted" by the time of the sixth day. These events did not occur until after man was created. If that is so, then what kinds of plants were made on the third day of Genesis 1?

Genesis 1:11–12 tells us that two kinds of plants were made on the third day. The first was "grains seeding seed" (literally), and the second was "trees fruitbearing fruit." These two kinds of foods were given to Adam and Eve as food in Genesis 1:29. They are the kinds of plant food man encounters first, in the Garden-sanctuary at the center of the world, on the sabbath day. They were made first and already existed when man was made. They already existed for man to eat with God on the first sabbath. As we shall see, however, the grain did not exist yet in mature (food) form; only the trees had produced food. Thus, man's first sanctuary food was fruit, not grain.

Genesis 2:5 tells us that certain other kinds of plants

were not made on the third day.[2] By itself, this shatters the "modified day-age interpretation" of Genesis 1. The older "day-age interpretation" holds that each "day" was an age in the evolutionary development of the world, but this is obviously wrong since it would mean plants existed before the sun, moon, and stars. Thus, the "modified day-age interpretation" says that each of the six "ages" of Genesis 1 means that for some reason the item mentioned is highlighted in that age. Plants were around for an age; the mists cleared to reveal the sun for an age; then came an age of dinosaurs, fishes, and birds; and then came mammals and man. This may sound initially plausible, but Genesis 2:5 makes it impossible. We can hardly have only fruits and grains on the earth for millions of years before ferns, bushes, pine trees, and grass appeared!

Genesis 2:5 says that "no shrub of the field was yet in the earth." This clearly means that such plants had not yet been created. The word for "shrub" (*se'akh*) occurs only three other times in the Old Testament. Speaking of Hagar and Ishmael after they were driven out from Abraham, Genesis 21:15 says, "And the water in the skin was used up, and she left the boy under one of the shrubs." This associates shrubs with areas that are not "well watered throughout," as was the Garden of Eden (Gen. 13:10), and as is required for grain and fruit.

Speaking of trashy people, "whose fathers I disdained to put with the dogs of my flock," Job comments that they don't eat well: "Who gather mallow from the shrubs, and whose food is the root of the broom bush." Driven from the community for their crimes, "among shrubs they bray; under brush they huddle" (Job 30:1–7).

We can conclude that "shrubs" probably includes all plants that do not produce food in the form of grain or fruit. Some are indeed edible, but they are not the staple

[2] There is also a range of plants, like seaweed and other aquatic plants, about which we are told nothing.

form of diet, and they are not included as sanctuary food (bread and oil, and later, wine). These plants did not exist until after the six days of creation week were over. Their creation was suspended until after man was made, for a reason implied in Genesis 3:18. God waited until He saw whether man would sin or not. If man did not sin, the shrubs would have been one kind of plant; since man sinned, they grew up as "thorns and thistles."

Genesis 2:5 says that "no plant of the field had yet sprouted." This implies that such plants did exist and are indeed the same as the grains created on the third day. Such plants had been brought forth, but no second generation had sprouted. Genesis 1:11, "let the earth shoot forth shoots," uses *dasha'*, which implies growing up. Genesis 2:5, "had yet sprouted," uses *tsamakh*, which implies budding. The grains grew on the third day, but they had not sprouted buds until after the sixth. The grain plants had not yet sprouted their ears of grain.

Here again, I believe that the grains had not sprouted because it remained to be seen whether man would sin or not. Harvesting and winnowing grain is labor intensive, and Genesis 3:18–19 says that sinful man will grow and harvest it by the sweat of his nose.[3] God could have caused grain to sprout in a way that is not so labor intensive. Thus, the sprouting of the grain awaited the decision of man to sin or not to sin.

From these considerations we see that a careful reading of the text provides no hint of contradiction. Genesis 1 does not say that God created all plants on day 3. He only created fruit trees and grain plants. Genesis 2:5 does not say that there were no plants in the earth at the time under consideration. Rather it says that the remaining plants that would exist in the world had not been created and that the grains had not yet sprouted.

For a noted Hebrew scholar to make so elementary a

[3] Not "brow"; cf. Genesis 2:7, where the same word is used.

mistake is surprising, but it probably only indicates what happens to any scholar when he approaches a text with preconceived notions. He sees what he wants to see and ignores details that destroy his model. It is the more surprising, though, because other expositors, such as the noted Jewish commentator Umberto Cassuto, have taken the texts in roughly the same way I have presented them, and yet Kline completely ignores them, as if he were unaware of them! This is not good scholarship.[4]

Providence and Miracle

Mark D. Futato has summarized the thrust of Kline's original article thus:

> The article demonstrated that according to Genesis 2:5 ordinary providence was God's mode of operation during the days of creation. Since God's mode of operation was ordinary providence, and since, for example, light (day 1) without luminaries (day 4) is not ordinary providence, the arrangement of the six days of creation in Genesis 1 must be topical not chronological.[5]

We have shown that Kline's analysis of Genesis 2:5 is without merit. We must now comment briefly on this larger argument.

The argument is that since ordinary providence was operating during creation week, miracles could not have been. Neither Kline nor Futato put it that bluntly, but that

[4] A somewhat different answer to Kline is provided by Michael J. Kruger, "An Understanding of Genesis 2:5," *Creation Ex Nihilo Technical Journal* 11 (1997): 106-110. Kruger argues that the plants of Genesis 2:5 were those that required human cultivation, and that only the Garden of Eden is in view as regards these plants. I believe my interpretation does better justice to the terms employed in the text. Either way, there is no contradiction between Genesis 1 and 2.

[5] Mark D. Futato, "Because It Had Rained: A Study of Gen 2:5–7 with Implications for Gen 2:4–25 and Gen 1:1–2:3," in *The Westminster Theological Journal* 60 (1998):1. I take up Futato's essay in appendix D.

is the only possible understanding of what they have written. On the face of it, this is absurd.

No one has ever denied that ordinary providence operated during creation week. Gravity operated then, for instance. To say that God was operating using providence during creation week says nothing against His also employing what we would call miracles (exceptions to ordinary providence).

Let us consider another series of God's acts: the ten plagues on Egypt. Are we to suppose that because God was doing miracles during these weeks, ordinary providence was suspended? Gravity did not work? Plants did not continue growing? Or, to follow Kline's and Futato's reasoning, since ordinary providence did indeed continue working during the season of the ten plagues, therefore we must not see the plagues as discrete and miraculous events? Certainly *some* frogs came up from the Nile before and after the plague of frogs. This shows us, according to Kline, that the plague of frogs was not a special event. Thus, we should not take the ten plagues as a sequence of events. The arrangement of the ten plagues "must be topical not chronological."

Certainly, "light without luminaries" is not what we would call ordinary today. It may be quite ordinary to us after we have lived in the resurrection for a while. In the same way, light without luminaries was the "ordinary providence" for three whole days at the beginning of the world.

These observations are set globally against Kline's position, but he has an answer available. "Of course," he might reply, "these *other* aspects of providence, such as gravity, were in operation during creation week. But Genesis 2:5 says that the plants were not created until God caused it to rain, because plants need rain. Thus, Genesis 2:5 is giving us a completely different understanding of the creation of plants from Genesis 1:11–12." Lee Irons rehearses the argument this way: "Gen. 2:5 tells us that God would not create the vegetation until He had in place a normal providential mechanism for sustaining the vegetation, i.e., until He had caused it to rain."[6]

The argument seems to be that, according to Genesis 1, God caused the water to run off the earth on the third day and the plants grew up, but Genesis 2:5 says that mist/clouds/ground-water arose from the earth and watered the ground so that plants appeared. The events of day 3 are clearly miraculous: all the water disappearing from the ground in a few hours and plants almost instantaneously springing up. The description in 2:5 is of plants being watered by springs or clouds (the Hebrew word is obscure),[7] which is what we see in our normal experience—providence, not miracle, in other words.

It's hard to imagine all the waters running off the surface of the world in six hours, miraculously, and then clouds or springs coming up from the ground, and then plants growing up, all in one day. So, we're dealing with a symbolic day. That's the argument. Against it are:

1. If God can move all the water off the earth in a few hours, He can also make mist/cloud/springs appear in just a few hours. While Genesis 2:5 may *look* just like today's "ordinary providence," it does not have to be such.

2. But since Genesis 2:5 is not on the third day anyway and has nothing to do with the third day, the argument is nugatory to start with.

Kline's Newer Argument

Now we turn to Kline's new argument against a chronological reading of Genesis 1, as found in "Space and Time in the Genesis Cosmogony."

We must set out Kline's argument in some detail in order to deal with it. He begins by writing that "another line

[6] Charles Lee Irons, *The Framework Interpretation Explained and Defended* (published by the author, 1998) p. 25.

[7] See appendix D.

of exegetical evidence has come to fore in my thinking. It concerns the two-register cosmological concept that structures the whole biblical cosmogony" (p. 2). Kline's argument will be that just as there is, within the creation, a heavens above and an earth beneath spatially, so also there is a heavenly time and an earthly time. Since there is no question about the former, it is the latter that Kline must establish.

Kline rightly points out that God created two realms in the beginning: heaven and earth. Clearly, these two eventually were to become one, and that is what the history and maturation of humanity would lead to as a final eucatastrophe (good catastrophe). Moreover, as Kline points out, God set up within the lower (earthly) creation an upper and lower level, with the sky and its inhabitants called "heaven" and imaging the highest heaven within the earthly cosmos. Kline goes on to point out that the Tabernacle and Temple were also cosmic models, with the Holy of Holies as the highest heavens and the Holy Place and Courtyard as visible heavens and earth.[8]

Now Kline goes on from his general explanation of the two-tiered creation to a discussion of the six days. He advocates the notion that the first three days set out realms, while the next three set out rulers, kingdoms, and kings:

[8] Since I am reviewing this article here, I should point out two errors in Kline's otherwise fine discussion of these matters. On p. 3 he writes, "Taking its name from this above-section of visible space, supernal space (the above-section of the two-register cosmos) is then called 'heaven.'" Actually, it is the other way around: The visible heavens are called "heavens" because they reveal aspects of the invisible heavens. After all, the first use of "heaven" is in Genesis 1:1, so it is the original "heaven."

Second, on p. 4 Kline writes, "The Tabernacle and Temple . . . are made after the pattern of the upper register Temple revealed to Moses and Solomon." Rather, the Temple was revealed to David, who gave instructions to Solomon (1 Chr. 28:11–19). Solomon and all the later Temple-restoring kings are equivalent to the Bezalel who built the Tabernacle under Moses' instruction.

Day 1: Sky realm	Day 4: Sky rulers
Day 2: Upper and lower realms	Day 5: Birds and Fishes
Day 3: Earthly realm	Day 6: Earthly rulers

Without going into all the points he makes, I must raise questions about this approach. This is surely one way to look at Genesis 1, and it is not without value, but it is not the most comprehensive and valuable way of looking at it.

The first observation is that the birds and fishes of day 5 and the land animals of day 6a are not said to rule anything. They are only said to multiply and fill. Whatever else may be said about them in later biblical passages (some of which Kline references), nothing about ruling is said here. The parallel is not as exact as Kline would like it to be. Within the passage, the parallel for the filling and multiplication of birds, fishes, and animals is the filling of the earth with grain plants and fruit trees on day 3.

Moreover, birds are not said to dwell in the firmament or the sky, paralleling day 2. Rather, they are said to multiply on the earth (Gen. 1:22). They only travel in the sky—or more accurately, below the sky: "in front of the face of the firmament." Indeed, they nest and dwell on the earth and trees, which associates them more with day 3, and accordingly, the fishes with the seas of day 3. Indeed, the order (fishes and then birds) follows the order of day 2–3 (sea and then land/trees).

Third, I think it can easily be shown that the seven days of Genesis 1 are a chiasm. A chiasm is a literary style that has two elements. There is an *inclusio,* which means just what it sounds like: an inclusion. The first and last parts of the particular literary unit correspond to one another. Thus, for instance, Genesis 2:25 and 3:7 form an *inclusio* focussing on nakedness and shame:

> 2:25—And the man and his woman were both naked and were not ashamed.
>
> 3:7—And the eyes of both of them were opened, and they knew that they were naked; and they sewed fig leaves together and made girdles.

The second aspect of a chiasm is that the material within the *inclusio* is arranged as a series of inclusion-like statements, so that the second thing said is like the next-to-last thing said, and so forth. The central thing said is the pivot of the chiasm.[9]

Chiasm is an extremely common literary device in the Bible, occuring both in small paragraphs and also extending over whole books, with small chiasms often embedded within larger ones, but it is only in recent years that scholars and exegetes have become aware of how pervasively chiasm is found in the Bible. Thus, while recent commentaries and exegetical articles frequently take chiasm into account, earlier ones do not. So perhaps the failure of earlier expositors to detect the chiastic structure of Genesis 1 is understandable. Nevertheless, Genesis 1 is pretty clearly chiastic:

Day 1: Light
  Day 2: Firmament mediating between earth and God
    Day 3: Sea, Land, and Trees
  Day 4: Lightbearers in the Firmament (link to 1–2, 6–7)
    Day 5: Dwellers of Sea, Land, and Trees
  Day 6: The creatures who mediate between earth and God
Day 7: Sabbath

The connection between days 1 and 7 becomes much clearer later on in the Bible, as the Day of the Lord is linked with the sabbath. We shall have much more to say about the chiastic structure of Genesis 1 as we progress through the present book.

Fourth, not only does this outline do better justice to

[9] For a fuller discussion of chiasm, see appendix B. For a very good theological discussion of chiasm, see John Breck, *The Shape of Biblical Language: Chiasmus in the Scriptures and Beyond* (Crestwood, NY: St. Vladimir's Seminary Press, 1994). Also see J. W. Welch, *Chiasmus in Antiquity. Structures Analyses Exegesis* (Hildesheim, Germany: Gerstenberg Verlag, 1981) and *Chiasmus in the New Testament: A Study of the Form and Function of Chiastic Structures* (Peabody, MA: Hendrickson Pub., [1942] 1992).

the raw data, it also takes better account of what is said in verse 2, to wit: The earth was formless, empty, and dark. There are three "problems" to solve, not just two, and Genesis 1 solves them. The "kingdom and kings" approach to Genesis 1 does not take account of the fact that the entire passage is set up to "solve" these "problems." To wit:

Day 1: Darkness (light)
  Day 2: Formless (firmament)
    Day 3: Emptiness (grain and fruit plants)
Day 4: Darkness (lightbearers)
    Day 5: Emptiness (fishes and birds)
  Day 6: Formless (man the ruler/former/organizer)
Day 7: Darkness (God's judgment-light)

Thus, while Kline is certainly right to see heavens above and earth below as structuring the cosmos in Genesis 1, his attempt to show that this is the overarching concern in Genesis 1 is in error. The theme is not as prominent as he supposes. As we shall see, part of his argument against taking the days of Genesis 1 as normal earthly days is this supposed overarching concern with matters above and below.

Sacred Time

At this point, Kline makes the mistake of creating a false analogy between heavenly space and heavenly time. Just as heavenly space is different, so he supposes is heavenly time. (Remember, neither Kline nor I are discussing the eternity of God; rather we are speaking of the flow of time in the created heavens of the angels.) Kline writes, "Therefore, when we find that God's upper level activity of issuing creative fiats from his heavenly throne is pictured as transpiring in a week of earthly days, we readily recognize that, in keeping with the pervasive contextual pattern, this is a literary figure, an earthly, lower register time metaphor for an upper register, heavenly reality" (p. 7).

There are three global problems with this general argument, which I shall address before moving to Kline's particular contextual argument. First, Kline rightly argues that when God's Glory Cloud appears, it is the heavenly realm inserting into the earthly. But this means that God marches in earthly time along with His people. The Cloud parked in the Holy of Holies is experiencing earthly clock-history right along with Israel. Thus, even if there were two kinds of time, God chooses to come into earthly time and move with it. And since Genesis 1 has to do with the lightening, forming, and filling of the *earth*, it has to do with *earthly* time.

Second, there is no reason to think that heavenly time has a differently ticking clock from earthly time. There is no evidence in the Bible for such a notion, however it may be expressed. Quite the opposite: In the book of Revelation is it clear that heavenly time is the same as earthly time. The angels wait for Jesus' ascension. At God's command, they come down into the earthly realm and perform actions in human history. To be sure, most of the time statements in Revelation are symbolic, but it is clearly a symbolism common to the heavenly and earthly realms.

Third, Kline assumes that the bipolarity of space—heaven above and earth below—implies a bipolarity of time and days—heavenly days and earthly days. But this is to misunderstand completely the difference between time and space. Heaven is the spatial model for the earth, and it is spatially "above," or apart from, the earth. The first week is the temporal model for all weeks to come, but it is not "above" these other weeks; rather it is *before* all later weeks. The contrast is not between heavenly days and earthly days, but between the first days and later days, the first week and later weeks. Heaven relates to earth as archetype; the first week relates to later weeks as prototype.[10] The first week took the same length of time in both the heavenly

[10] See appendix F for more on this.

and earthly realms, and given how it is described in Genesis 1 (a sequence of normal days with evenings and morning), it took the same span of time as all later weeks. Heaven is a real place, and so is the earth. The first week was a real week, and so are all later weeks.

Now to the details. Kline's argument, in brief, is this: The alternation of day and night presupposes the creation of the sun, and so days 1 and 4 must happen at the same time, chronologically speaking. Since this is so, he argues, the events of Genesis 1 must all reflect intrusions of heavenly "days" into the earthly temporal realm. Therefore we should not take the "days" as chronological in an earthly sense.[11]

Kline begins, "Earthly time is articulated in the

[11] Kline's disciple Lee Irons explains how his mentor sees a "contradiction" between day 1 and day 4. He writes that on day 1 God separated light and darkness, day and night, and then He does so again on day 4. If the separation on day 1 was "good," "Why, then, does God need to discard that arrangement and replace it with a new one on day four?" (Irons, *Framework*, 25).

To this we can reply: The luminaries of day 4 give light on the earth, not on the heavens, while the light of day 1, positioned between heaven and earth, arguably shines in both directions. Thus, Irons is in error to write, "Exegetically there is no way around the stubborn fact that the divine purpose for the creation of light on day 1 and the purpose for the creation of the luminaries on day four is one and the same" (p. 25). Not so. The lights of day 4 are subsets and extensions of the light of day 1, and they only operate with reference to the earth below.

Irons quotes Kline, "Why would God . . . create a replacement cosmos to perform the very same functions already being performed perfectly well by the original system?" (Kline, "Space and Time," p. 9; Irons, p. 25). Again, this is because the later system is not the same as the earlier one but rather is a subset of it. The light of day 1 separates day and night in the whole cosmos, heaven and earth, while the luminaries of day 4 separate it only for the earth.

Moreover, there is no problem with God's setting up a system first and then passing part of it on to earthly representatives. That is, in fact, what He does in Genesis 1 and 2. His passing the light to the luminaries is exactly in line with the structure of God's actions elsewhere, and thus, it is not surprise.

astronomical phenomena that measure off and structure its flow" (p. 7). What Kline does not say is that the week is an exception to this astral measurement, and Genesis 1 is precisely a week. True, the day and the year and the month are measured by the sun and moon, but the week is measured only by God, angels, and men. The week, as a measurement of time, has its root in man's "position in the firmament" between heaven and earth. Man is lord of the week. The human week is not copied from the sun but from God's pattern of working in Genesis 1.

Ah, Kline says, but the human week consists of solar days. And so it does—now! Kline must show that from the beginning all days were solar days. He begins by asserting that day 4 must overlap day 1, for the alternation of day and night must be produced by the sun. He continues by arguing against various "day-age" notions, such as the sun being revealed only on the fourth day.

Then he comes to the only argument he can muster against a literal view of the days of Genesis 1. He writes,

> Some speculate about a supernatural light source, a manifestation of divine glory in space. But that distorts the eschatological design of creation history, according to which the advent of God's glory as the source of illumination that does away with the need for the sun awaits the Consummation. (p. 9)

If, however, we go back to Genesis 1:2–3, such a "glory-light" view seems quite natural. The Spirit entered the earthly realm and hovered over it. Then the Spirit gave forth God's glory-light for the first day. Kline's own study, *Images of the Spirit,*[12] shows that the appearance of the Spirit in history is accompanied by glory phenomena. He is forced by his position to make Genesis 1:2–3 the only exception to this observation.

[12] (Grand Rapids, MI: Baker, 1980). Reprint copies available from M. G. Kline, 163 Chebacco Rd., South Hamilton, MA 01982.

Moreover, a simple read of Genesis 1 would lead us to see that the sun was made to fit the preexistent day, not vice versa. The alternation of day and night already existed, and the heavenly bodies were set up to fit that preexisting pattern.

Kline, however, asserts that God's glory-light is eschatological, and he is right. The night does move to day. The night is not pitch black, for there are lesser lights in the sky, but such nights do move toward the Day of the Lord. And I suspect Kline would recognize such a motion in Genesis 1:2–3, from darkness to light. What he does not want to see is Genesis 1:3 as a typological revelation of the eschatological light. It must be, in his view, some lesser light.

Perhaps this is because that light is followed by another evening. Yet, when God appears in His glory-light in later history, such glorious appearances are also followed by evenings. The light is withdrawn. Indeed, Kline's own peculiar view of history alternates times of light ("intrusions") with times of relative darkness ("common grace"). Only at the full end will light be perpetual. Thus, there is no problem with seeing God's glory-light in Genesis 1:3, a light that is shortly veiled and that reappears twice before the sun is created.

Moreover, it is entirely appropriate that God initiate history with a revelation of where history is going. That is, it is entirely fitting that God reveal His glory at the beginning to set humanity in motion. This is clear from the fact that man was created later in the sixth day, so that his first full day was God's glory-sabbath. Man was to be given a taste of eschatological sabbath glory at the beginning to set him on his goal.

Agreeable to this, God appears in glory when He *initiates* covenants in the Bible. He puts the bright and glorious rainbow in the sky when He initiates the Noahic covenant. He appears as a pillar of glory-fire when He leads Israel from Egypt (Ex. 13:21–22). He appears in bright lightning flashes from His glory cloud at Mount Sinai, the point of full initiation of the Sinaitic covenant. And of course, Jesus is transfigured at the very point when He initiates the Church, revealing as the hymn says, "the glory that the Church shall share" (Matt. 16:13–17:8):

> O wondrous type, O vision fair:
> The glory that the Church will share,
> Our Lord upon the mount displays,
> The sun unequal to His rays.
> (Latin hymn, 15th c.)

Thus, contrary to Kline, everything in the immediate text and in biblical theology points to a revelation of God's own created heavenly glory-light on day 1. Nothing hints that the sun must have been made at that point.

Kline's conclusion, however, is: "Temporal recapitulation most certainly occurs at day four and hence there is no escaping the conclusion that the narrative sequence is not intended to be the chronological sequence." Since Kline's foundation is completely wrong, his conclusion does not stand.

This is Kline's argument, but he also makes a couple of other assertions. First, he says that "in the beginning" must refer to God outside of time and history, for it is from that situation that He made the universe. Quite so. But having made it, what indicates that there are two different kinds of time operating in it? From outside time God made time and heaven and earth. Nothing indicates two different flows of time. This is especially the case since Kline, rightly I think, argues that God's speaking into the earthly creation during the days of Genesis 1 is not from His eternal existence but from His (created) heavenly throne. Kline would have to show that angelic clocks run differently from human ones, and this he has not done. Whatever the case, the phrase "in the beginning" in Genesis 1:1 does nothing for his argument.

Secondly, Kline notes that there is a sense in which the

seventh day is unending. We shall "enter into" God's pre-existent sabbath according to Hebrews 4. Correct, but the seventh day is not said to have an evening and a morning either. There is no problem at all with the traditional view that we have six normal days followed by an unending one. Moreover, just because in one sense the seventh, sabbath day is unending does not in the least mean that in another sense, the seventh day of creation week was the length of a normal solar day. There is no rational justification for pitting the two against each other.

Evening and Morning

This brings Kline to an attempt to deal with the repeated phrase "and there was evening and there was morning," which is said regarding the first six days. This phrase is generally regarded as the hardest problem for both the Framework Interpretation and for the Day-Age Interpretation. Kline, however, simply dismisses the problem. He asserts: "The *imagery* of the evening and morning is *simply* a *detail* in the creation-week *picture*. This *refrain* thus functions as part of the *formularized* framework of the account" (p. 10; emphasis added). This statement, however, is precisely what Kline needs to demonstrate, not merely assert. Kline seeks to pass off the data as "simply a detail in the imagery of a picture."

He asserts that "the six evening-morning days then do not mark the passage of time in the lower register sphere" (p. 10). They were "upper register" days. But on what basis does Kline assert this? He has provided no credible evidence—indeed, no evidence at all—to suppose that there is any such thing as a different heavenly time. He asserts that the six days "are not identifiable in terms of solar days, but relate to the history of creation at the upper register of the cosmos" (p. 10). Well, even if so, so what? He has not shown that upper register time is any different from lower register time.

Moreover, this whole assertion strains at a gnat and swallows a camel. It is precisely the *earth* that is being lit, formed, and filled in Genesis 1. The evenings and mornings are measured out by light and lightbearers *within* the earth. The evenings and mornings are as much a part of the "lower earthly realm" as trees, fishes, and human beings. We have no reason to believe in an alternation of evenings and mornings in the upper heavenly realm. Evening and morning are, it seems, exclusively earthly phenomena. Thus, so are the days.

Kline states that "in the beginning" is timeless in some sense, and that the sabbath day is unending; therefore, the days bracketed by these two statements are not ordinary chronological days (p. 10). But, rather clearly, the six days are precisely ordinary chronological time. God initiates history "in the beginning" and ends it at the sabbath. What is in between? History! Clock time! The creation week typologically reveals the unfolding of history to us; it was initiated by God and consummated by His sabbath judgment and rest. Just as God appears as glory to start men off in their covenantal work (as we saw), so He also provides a microchronic sequence of history to show us where we are going. It is precisely history and chronological time that is revealed in the six days.[13]

Genesis 1 shows God initiating the world and then working with it for six days before entering into His sabbath and turning the project over to His servants. This is said to be a pattern for human work in Exodus 20:11. As a father patterns for his children, so God patterns for us. If the six work-days of Genesis 1 are not "lower realm" earthly days, then they don't have much relevance to the life of mankind.

And again, it is precisely the "lower realm earth" that

[13] On the temporal, rhythmical implications of the "evening and morning" refrain, see appendix A.

God is manipulating in Genesis 1. To assert that God is working in earthly space and using heavenly days is virtually a contradiction (assuming that heavenly days are any different).

Conclusion

We have seen that Kline's attempt to create a contradiction between day 3 and what is said in Genesis 2:5 is based on very poor exegesis. There is no contradiction.

We have seen that Kline's attempt to make the events of day 1 and day 4 the same chronologically is also devoid of foundation; it goes against biblical theology.

We have seen that these are the twin pillars of Kline's argument for a nonchronological "framework" approach to Genesis 1. This is by his own statement (p. 2). Without these two pillars, Kline's position falls by his own hand.

Finally, nothing else Kline has noted along the way provides any evidence for a framework view.

It appears, thus, that the framework approach to Genesis 1 is devoid of any sound foundation.

The fact that the blocks of events are called "days" could, by itself, arguably be evidence of the "invasion of history by God's glorious day-ness," analogous to the various "days of the Lord" in the Bible. In fact, we can readily grant that this is one aspect of the theology of Genesis 1. But that the days are sequentially numbered, that they have mornings and evenings, and that in context the sun is said to measure the length of these very days after the fourth day, demonstrates fully that the events of Genesis 1 are chronologically sequential and that the days are of short and ordinary duration.

Chapter 4

Gnosticism Versus History

Throughout history, the Christian Church has had to guard against the heresy of gnosticism. Gnosticism is not an ordinary heresy, because it does not manifest itself as a set of defined beliefs. Rather, gnosticism is a tendency: the tendency to replace the historic facts of Christianity with philosophical ideas. Gnosticism is the tendency to de-historicize and de-physicalize the Christian religion. Gnosticism transforms history into ideology and facts into philosophy. Gnosticism tends to see religion as man's reflections about God and reality instead of as God's revelation of Himself and His Word to man. As a *tendency*, Gnosticism has always plagued the Church, and it is alive and well today, openly in "liberalism," and in a more concealed fashion, in "evangelicalism."[1]

Gnosticism rears its head in orthodox circles whenever systematic theology runs roughshod over biblical theology (the study of the unfolding history of the covenant in the Bible). It comes whenever abstract theological language (like catechisms) overwhelms the concrete pictures and symbols (like the Proverbs) God chose to use in the

[1] For an illuminating if incomplete study of gnosticism in recent centuries, see Philip J. Lee, *Against the Protestant Gnostics* (New York: Oxford, 1987). Lee's critique is inadequate because, as something of a Barthian, he is himself a gnostic.

Bible to communicate His truth; whenever the ritual of the Lord's Supper becomes a means of devotion and contemplation rather than an action performed in God's presence. Whenever the Supper is restricted from small children because they have not reached some "age of reason." Whenever the sequence of the covenant renewal in worship is ignored and only the performance of certain "elements" is considered important. Whenever the body is regarded as unimportant, so that we no longer need to kneel in worship or greet one another with a holy kiss.

For our purposes, the gnostic tendency is the tendency to downplay history, so that the cross becomes an idea more than an event. The gnostic tendency in Protestant theology makes it easy for theologians to dismiss the chronology of the Bible, asserting without any evidence that it contains gaps, and focussing only on the supposed ideas contained in such passages as Genesis 5 and 11. The intimately time-grounded character of biblical revelation is rather easily set aside by the gnostic.

Because gnostic thinking is generally hidden from view, a series of illustrations will help the reader to see how pervasive it actually is. For many readers, I suspect, the discussion that follows will seem odd, for the gnostic tendency is very much with us all.

Biblical religion affirms that God entered human life as a real human being in the incarnation of Jesus Christ. It also affirms that Jesus' physical body was resurrected in a transfigured but still physical form and that it abides with Him forever. But there has always been a tendency to deny this. Early Christian "docetists" did not like the idea that God incarnated Himself in "lowly matter," and thus they said that Jesus was a merely "spiritual" being. Others were willing to say that the Son of God "humbled Himself" to take on material flesh, but He gave it up at His resurrection, or He will give it up at the end of history. All of this is predicated on the notion that there is something bad about "matter;" it is a denial of the goodness of creation and of human bodily existence. In authentic Christianity, the "spiritual body" is not an immaterial body but a physical body energized by the Holy Spirit in a new, fuller way than before. Moreover, there was nothing humiliating about the incarnation of the Son of God. God made a beautiful creation, and for the Son to take on human flesh is like a man putting on a beautiful garment he has made. The only thing humiliating about the incarnation was that the Son entered into a humanity that bore the effect of sin: death.[2]

God's affirmation of the material world is seen in the fact that He uses physical water to introduce people into His kingdom, and by the fact that we eat Christ's flesh and drink His blood in the Lord's Supper. Many Christians, however, cannot embrace such physical ideas. Water baptism, is thus reduced to a mere symbol instead of a powerful communication from God, and so are the bread and wine of the Supper. Such a reduction was not the view of the Protestant Reformers, who sought to correct the magical views of the Papal Church without denying that God really acts through such material means.

By the nineteenth century, however, the heirs of the Reformers were no longer willing to abide their starkly materialistic views. Calvinistic theologians like Charles Hodge viewed Calvin's doctrine of the union of believers with Christ's physical humanity in the Lord's Supper as an "uncongenial foreign element" in Calvin's thought, having "no root in the system."[3] Another Calvinist, Robert Dabney, rejected Calvin even more strongly.[4] Calvinistic theologian Benjamin B. Warfield wrote against what he called "sacerdotalism," the idea that God communicates saving

[2] Note: He did not take on sinful flesh but flesh that was subject to the consequence of sin.

[3] [Charles Hodge], Review of [John Nevin's] *The Mystical Presence*, in *Princeton Review* 20 (1848):251f.

[4] See Peter J. Leithart, "What's Wrong with Transubstantiation? An Evaluation of Theological Models," in *The Westminster Theological Journal* 53 (1991):295–324.

grace through created means.[5] Such views are commonplace today, but they are fundamentally wrong and were not the views of the Reformers.

God created the universe in such a way that it is designed by Him as His means to communicate with man. Does anyone want to say that God saves people apart from His Word? But the Bible is a physical book, and when we read it, physical light passes between our physical eyes and the pages of the book, stimulating our physical brain. When we hear the Word read, physical vibrations in the physical air rattle three physical bones in our ears and stimulate our physical brains. All of this is thoroughly physical and material. They are the means God has appointed to bring us near to Him as God's Spirit uses these physical things.

Thus, if God also uses water, oil, bread, and wine to communicate His presence to us, what is strange about that? Nobody is magically "regenerated" by water baptism, any more than he is magically saved by merely hearing the Word read aloud. But God has appointed these as His instruments, and those who are saved are saved by means of them. Of course, God is free to make exceptions, but these are the normal means He has appointed. The gentle caress of water is the normal way He puts His loving hands on us and takes us into His arms, as a mother gathers up her child. But Warfield wants to get as far away as possible from such physical, material things and wants only to speak of God's "immediate operations on the soul." What is this, if not a radically gnostic tendency?

Thus, what do we see? Instead of a real shower of water from above in baptism, we get a few drops. Instead of a good munchable piece of bread, we get a tiny bit of cracker. Instead of a good slug of alcohol, which makes real peace-inducing impact on the body, we get a sip of insipid grape juice. And anointing the sick with oil, as commanded by

[5] Benjamin B. Warfield, *The Plan of Salvation* (rev. ed., Grand Rapids, MI: Eerdmans, [1918] 1973) pp. 52ff.

James 5:14, has almost disappeared entirely.

Evangelicals read repeatedly in the Bible that they are to greet one another with a holy kiss (Rom. 16:16; 1 Cor. 16:20; 2 Cor. 13:12; 1 Thess. 5:26; 1 Pet. 5:14). Why is this command repeated so often? Could it be because the men of the apostolic church didn't want to do it any more than modern men want to? But evangelicals read right past these commands and gnostically convert them into a command to say hello to one another.

Evangelicals hear God command in Psalm 95, "O come, let us worship and fall down, let us kneel," but they don't do it. They only fall down and kneel inwardly. For some reason (!) they think that such "inner kneeling" is all God really wants. God does not care what our bodies do, it seems. They read Psalm 150, which commands music with trumpets and cymbals, but they are satisfied with organs, which might suffice for the trumpets, but not for the cymbals. The more radically gnosticized traditions in evangelicalism feel that singing without musical instruments is more "spiritual."

In fact, the whole progress of history in the Bible is often understood in pagan terms as a movement from the material to the "spiritual," from the external to the internal. Thus, the people of the Old Testament were "primitives" and "children," and God appointed for them "carnal, earthly" physical rituals and the like. After the coming of the Spirit at Pentecost, however, we are "spiritual," and so God no longer comes at us through such "lowly" means. It somehow escapes the minds of those who argue this way that sound waves, as we have seen, are thoroughly "carnal and earthly." But more importantly, such people are reading the Bible in pagan, Greek terms. The movement from the old to the new is indeed a movement toward the spiritual, but it is not a movement toward the nonphysical. Rather it is a movement toward a life characterized by a greater fullness of the presence and power of the Holy Spirit of God, energizing our physical, carnal, earthly bodies. Water coming on us in baptism, and our taking in bread and wine, are as "external" as anything that Israel was commanded to do under the Law. The Church is every bit as physical as the land of Israel, because the Church is made up of human beings who are made of soil.

We could go on and on illustrating this anti-material tendency, this fear of the "drag" of the physical world, as if matter rather than sin were man's problem. There is a whole history here of fear of the arts, fear of sexuality, fear of literature, fear of rich food, rejection of enthusiasm in worship, of hand-raising, of clapping—all such fear is completely foreign to the Bible. All of this comes from the influence of Greek philosophy.

If downgrading the material world is one part of the gnostic tendency in evangelicalism, a tendency to eternalize time is the other. The Bible is filled with chronological information, and it clearly presents an unbroken chronology from the creation of the world to the Babylonian exile. Nobody in the Church ever questioned this until the late nineteenth century. It has become commonplace now, however, to hear that the Bible is not really concerned with chronology, that there are "gaps" in the biblical chronology as it stands, and so forth. Indeed, the nineteenth century became an age of gap theories as far as evangelicals were concerned: Gaps were inserted between Genesis 1:1 and Genesis 1:2, into the chronologies of Genesis 5 and 11, into the chronologies of the kings of Israel and Judah, and into the seventy weeks of years in Daniel 9. Such a cavalier approach to a text that abounds in detailed chronological information is only possible when men have already begun to think that chronology and history are not all that terribly important.

Similarly, the New Testament writings frequently speak of certain events as drawing near, as being "at hand," as coming "soon," or coming "on this generation." All of these time markers used to be taken seriously and were understood to reveal events that were going to take place in the first century, soon after Jesus' ascension: a conversion of many people, a falling away of many into apostasy, a great persecution at the hands of Jews, apostates, and Romans, and the destruction of Jerusalem in A.D. 70. When we turn to twentieth century evangelical writings, however, and especially to those of Calvinists, we find that these time-markers have been somehow eternalized. God is always "near"; the events are always "at hand"; "this generation" is always the generation of judgment; etc. The events "near at hand" are also simultaneously "far off," and thus predictions about first century events can be transferred to the events of the end of human history in the future.

It has become very easy for twentieth century evangelicals, and especially Calvinists, to downplay the time groundedness of biblical revelation, and it is no accident that the Framework Interpretation is most common in Calvinistic circles. (I need to add that I am myself located in the Calvinistic Presbyterian milieu.) Modern evangelical expositors are very quick to say that certain passages of the historical books of the Bible are "dischronologized." To be sure, some are, but without extending this discussion into a whole series of arguments and illustrations, I submit that such dischronologizations are far less frequent in the text than is often believed.

A telling statement by a Calvinistic church historian illustrates the pervasiveness of gnostic tendencies in the nineteenth century, of which we are the heirs. What we call the Apostles' Creed is the great anti-gnostic statement of the early Church, though we don't know when and by whom it was written. At the center of it lies a whole series of purely historical statements: "born of the virgin Mary, suffered under Pontius Pilate, was crucified, dead, and buried. He descended into sheol. On the third day, He rose again from the dead. He ascended into heaven, and sits at the right hand of the Father." Notice the specific historical and chronological markers "under Pontius Pilate" and "on the third day." These statements were pointed directly against the gnostics, who said that the history did not matter. The only thing that mattered, according to the gnostics, were the ideas contained in the story of Jesus.

Now comes the Scottish church historian William Cunningham and his *Historical Theology*. According to him, the Apostles' Creed "is not entitled to much respect, and is not fitted to be of much use, as a summary of the leading doctrines of Christianity."[6] Why is this? Because for Cunningham, the important doctrines are the more timeless and theoretical ones. The fact that the Apostles' Creed pits the world's only history-grounded religion against all others does not even register with him. The Apostles' Creed is a "very inadequate and defective summary of the leading principles of Christianity"[7] because it does not go into such matters as predestination, justification by faith, and the two natures of Christ. For Cunningham, "doctrines" and "principles" have nothing to do with the recounting of historical events.

Now, does this make Cunningham a gnostic? Does he deny that these events happened? No, of course not. In a sense, he assumes the history really happened. But the history *as history* seemingly plays no part in his understanding of the Christian religion. The coming of the Kingdom of God through a series of historical events is not the foundation, the bedrock of his faith. Rather, a series of ideas about God and man have moved into first place in his thinking. Those ideas are true enough, but they mean nothing if God has not brought us into His Kingdom through these historical events. This fact Cunningham does not see, and he does not see it because the gnostic *tendency* has blinded him to its importance.

Such a down-playing of the importance of history is laced into the warp and woof of evangelical thinking, espe-

[6] Cunningham, *Historical Theology*, 2 vols. (London: Banner of Truth Trust, [1862] 1960) 1:90.

[7] Ibid., p. 92f.

cially since the nineteenth century. It is for this reason that nonhistorical readings of Genesis 1 find such ready acceptance in evangelical circles. The reading of the Bible as a series of pictures has replaced the reading of the Bible as the history of the coming of the Kingdom.

For instance—and this kind of thing goes back long before the Reformation—the narratives of the Bible are usually taken as moral tales rather than as stages in God's development of the human race. Jacob's story is the story of a bad man who was punished by God until he became a good one. The story of David and Bathsheba shows us that God does not like adultery. So does the story of Samson and Delilah. Note that such moral messages would be valid whether the stories ever really happened or not. It is no accident that after centuries of this kind of reading of the historical parts of the Bible, liberalism arose to claim that these stories never really did happen.[8]

Without any difficulty, one can see in the background the influence of such completely pagan writings as Plutarch's *Lives of Famous Greeks and Romans*. Plutarch, as a pagan, writes biographies as static character studies. The biblical narratives are, unlike Plutarch's, stories of historical transformations.

Similarly, there is a long tradition of reading biblical history as nothing more than a revelation of the doctrines of systematic theology. The stories are read to teach election, or justification by faith, or the two natures of Christ, etc. Once again, it would not matter if the stories ever happened or not.

Along these lines, we find that the evangelicals camp in the New Testament epistles, especially the Pauline letters. Here is where we do indeed find doctrine and morals for

[8] For an illuminating if very detailed discussion of just this problem, moralism versus historical reading, as it played out in the Netherlands in the early twentieth century, see Sidney Greidanus, *Sola Scriptura: Problems and Principles in Preaching Historical Texts* (Toronto: Wedge Pub., 1970).

the Church, and thus there are thousands of commentaries and probably millions of essays and articles on these books of the Bible. But one will search a long time to find a decent commentary on Judges, Nehemiah, or Esther, for the few that exist only use them as moral and doctrinal tales.

Ritual is a series of actions, in a flow of time, that encapsulates the larger life of man. True ritual keys a person into God's way of living in history. But not only is ritual regarded with grave suspicion in the evangelical churches, biblical rituals are studied only as snapshots of the work of Jesus. Similarly, the tabernacle of Moses, the temple of Solomon, and Ezekiel's visionary temple, each of which is described over the course of many chapters in the Bible, are studied (when they are studied at all) as only so many pictures of Jesus and the Church. Nowhere are they discussed in terms of their consciousness-transforming impact on the developing life of God's human community in time and history. The question is never asked, let alone answered: "How did the presence of these structures and rituals change the people from an old kind of people into a new kind of people over the course of centuries?"

It might be thought, yea hoped, that the development of "redemptive historical theology" in Calvinistic circles provides a corrective to this tendency, and to some slight extent it has. But in the hands of men like Meredith G. Kline, it does not. Kline sees the history of the Bible as bouncing back and forth between periods of "intrusion" and periods of "common grace." In "intrusion" periods, God draws near, punishing sin and rewarding obedience swiftly, while during "common grace" periods God remains far off and there seems to be little if any relationship between cause and effect in human history. Such a scheme not only badly misreads the sequence of covenants in the Bible, it is also patently unhistorical. Biblical history is a record of how God gradually develops the human race through various experiences toward our glorious destiny. It is a history of maturations through crises. Some maturations are deformations and lead to judgments; others are progressive and lead to greater maturity for humanity. Maturation and development, however, play virtually no role in Kline's approach to biblical history. For him, the only categories at play in the narratives are obedience and disobedience, sin and grace.

From what we have seen, the tendency in the evangelical reading of biblical history—and other branches of the Church are no better—has been to convert history into pictures. The stories are illustrations of moral matters or of doctrinal matters. To be sure, moral and doctrinal matters do factor into the historical narratives, yet the overall meaning of biblical history is God's development of His daughter into a bride for His Son. But after centuries of such merely illustrative and pictorial readings of the Bible, it can come as no surprise that evangelicals readily take to a merely pictorial way of reading Genesis 1.

Biblical history is a history of transformations in time. Jacob is transformed from one kind of man into another, a new kind of man. Israel is transformed by the Sinaitic Law, with its rituals and tabernacle, into a new kind of nation. There is no historical narrative anywhere in the Bible that is not a narrative of a transformation, and the historical progress of all the narratives is a history of progressive transformations. If this fact were even slightly understood, it would be obvious that the seven days of Genesis 1 are a series of transformations in time. It would be no surprise, for instance, that the light of day 1 transforms into the luminaries of day 4. It would never occur to any reader of Genesis 1 that days 1 and 4 are the same day![9]

[9] The theory of evolution and the modern evolutionary view of the universe are in fact grounded in a Christian view of time. In a sense, such theories are far more Christian than many evangelical views of how to read the Bible. Of course, these evolutionary theories are in

Gnosticism and the Framework Interpretation

By now I hope it is obvious that the gnostic tendency to convert historical events into mere ideas is manifest in the so-called "Framework Hypothesis/Interpretation" view of Genesis 1. The Framework Interpretation converts the six days of Genesis 1 into six big ideas. According to the Framework Interpretation, the events recounted in Genesis 1 never happened; rather, Genesis 1 is simply describing the cosmic order using the literary device of six "days."[10]

It is interesting to note that the Framework Interpretation has been thoroughly refuted over and over again, and yet it has more adherents today than ever before. G. C. Aalders of the Free University of Amsterdam pointed out in 1932 that (1) in the text of Genesis 1 there is not a single allusion to suggest that the days are to be regarded as a merely stylistic device, and that (2) Exodus 20:11 presents God's activity as a pattern for man, and this fact presupposes that there was a reality in the activity of God that man is to copy. As E. J. Young of Westminster Theological Seminary pointed out in his book *Studies in Genesis One*,[11] no one bothered to answer Aalders. Young himself went on for fifty pages refuting the Framework Interpretation, and until very recently nobody has tried to refute Young.[12]

error, and they are a perverted application of the Christian way of looking at time and history. But such theories were not possible before the coming of the Christian view of time as transformation. It is a sad thing that this fundamental Christian insight is put to use more often by non-Christians, who misuse it, than by Christians, who need to reclaim it and use it properly.

[10] Lee Irons vociferously denies this charge in his *The Framework Interpretation Explained and Defended* (by the author, 1998), which is a defense of Meredith Kline's particular approach. We shall take up this version of the Framework Interpretation later in this present chapter. For now, I reply that my charge is sound as regards how the Framework view is usually presented.

[11] (Phillipsburg, NJ: Presbyterian and Reformed Pub. Co., 1964).

[12] Irons's attempt in *The Framework Interpretation* is the only real effort I know of.

Recently, Kenneth Gentry has summarized the exegetical arguments against the Framework Interpretation as follows:

(1) "Day" is qualified by "evening and morning" (Gen. 1:5, 8, 13, 19, 23, 31), which specifically limits the time frame.

(2) The very same word "day" is used on the fourth day to define a time period that is governed by the sun, which must be a regular day (Gen. 1:14).

(3) In the 119 instances of the Hebrew word "day" (*yom*) standing in conjunction with a numerical adjective (first, second, etc.) in the writings of Moses,[13] it never means anything other than a literal day. Consistency would require that this structure must so function in Genesis 1.

(4) Exodus 20:9–11 patterns man's workweek after God's original workweek, which suggests the literality of the creation week.[14]

(5) In Exodus 20:11 the plural for the "days" of creation is used. In the 702 instances of the plural "days" in the Old Testament, it never means anything other than literal days.[15]

The Framework Interpreter can try to have his cake and eat it too, if he wants. He can say the days are our normal 24-hour days, but that the entire passage is symbolic, so these are symbolic 24-hour days. We can answer this contention by adding two other arguments of a more global character.

[13] Gentry includes Genesis as a writing of Moses, which it may well not have been. Gentry's point is still valid as far as it goes.

[14] To this we may add Exodus 31:15–17.

[15] Kenneth Gentry, *The Greatness of the Great Commission* (Tyler, TX: Institute for Christian Economics, 1991) p. 9.

First, there are several other places in the first five books of the Bible where we have seven "panels" of things. These seven-step passages cover the same seven aspects of creation as the seven days of creation, but they do so without using the word "day." For instance, in Exodus 25–31, we find seven speeches from Yahweh telling Moses how to build the Tabernacle. The Tabernacle is an architectural model of the world.[16] Each of God's seven speeches is introduced with the phrase "Then Yahweh spoke to Moses, saying," or some variant of this phrase (Ex. 25:1; 30:11, 17, 22, 34; 31:1, 12). Allowing for the fact that the Tabernacle is a symbolic cosmos, we can see the seven speeches of Exodus 25–31 covering the same ground as Genesis 1. For instance, the third speech (Ex. 30:17–21) concerns the laver, the sea in the Tabernacle, corresponding to day 3 in Genesis 1. The sixth speech (Ex. 31:1–11) appoints the man who will build the Tabernacle, corresponding to day 6 when man was created. The seventh speech (Ex. 31:12–17) concerns the sabbath, day 7.[17]

Now, what is important for our purposes is that the book of Exodus does not say that God made these seven speeches to Moses on seven consecutive days. Moreover, there is no "literary device" of "days" employed in Exodus 25–31, or in any of a half-dozen similar passages, even though the same seven "cosmic features" are set forth. Clearly, if its author had wanted to, he could have written

[16] In brief, during creation week God made a home for humanity. During human history, encapsulated in the building of the Tabernacle, humanity makes a home for God. At the end of history, the total world of heaven and earth will be fully finished and God will dwell with man in it forever.

[17] For a full discussion of this and several other seven-section passages, see my monograph, *The Tabernacle: A New Creation*, Biblical Horizons Occasional Paper 5 (2nd ed., June, 1993, available from Biblical Horizons, Box 1096, Niceville, FL 32588) and the literature cited there; and also see my book *Covenant Sequence in Leviticus and Deuteronomy* (Tyler, TX: Institute for Christian Economics, 1989).

Genesis 1 without saying anything about "days." The contrast between Genesis 1 and Exodus 25–31 shows that the "days" are *not* a mere literary device.

Second, the Framework Interpretation has to hold that the events recounted in Genesis 1 never happened. Quite apart from the matter of "days," Genesis 1 makes a whole series of claims that the Framework Interpretation says are false.

Let's be clear about this: We are discussing what the text claims happened. Genesis 1:7 says that an event happened in which God made a "firmament" and separated waters above the firmament from those below. The Framework Interpretation says that this event never happened.

Genesis 1:9 says that God gathered all the waters on the earth into one place and the dry land appeared. The Framework Interpretation says that as an event, this never happened. Perhaps it happened as a long process but not as an event.

Repeatedly throughout the chapter, the text claims that God said things. These are events. We might interpret Genesis 1 and suppose that since human beings were not on the scene, God did not "speak" in audible tones. We might even say that these phrases mean that He "put forth His Word," and thus they refer to the Second Person of the Trinity. The point, however, is that the text claims that God *did* these things, *said* these things, as *discrete actions*. The Framework Interpretation says that God never did these things, that no such individual acts ever occurred. According to the Framework Interpretation, all Genesis 1 means is that God's Word (or "wordness") lies behind everything that came into being over the course of who knows how long a time. The Framework Interpretation denies that there was a certain time in history when God said "Let there be light," and another, different event in history when God said, "Let there be luminaries."

To put it simply, Genesis 1 clearly claims that certain events took place, and the Framework Interpretation says that those events simply did not take place. The Framework Interpretation denies the specific claims of the text: The text as it stands is in error; these things never actually happened. All we are supposed to learn from the text, according to the Framework Interpretation, is the *idea* that God made everything and ordered it.

This is a very interesting way to read the Bible! Let's apply it to John 20. John 20 says that Jesus' body was not physically in the tomb on resurrection morning and that He physically rose from the grave. But we "know" from modern science that dead people don't rise! Maybe John 20 doesn't really have to be taken with "wooden literalism." Notice, for instance, in verse 12 that two angels sat in the tomb, one at one end of the slab and one at the other. What this means is that the death of Jesus is the "mercy seat" where God meets with men, for in the Tabernacle two cherubim stood on either end of the "mercy seat." Now that we have the *idea* from this verse, we no longer have to believe that it ever really *happened,* at least according to the interpretive methods of the Frameworkers.

Or consider John 20:15. Mary Magdalene saw Jesus and thought He was the gardener, for the tomb was in a garden. Well, here is the new Eve, restored from her sins, encountering the New Adam in the new garden of the new covenant. That's the *idea.* But did she really see and touch the physical body of Jesus? Who knows? and who cares? asks our hypothetical Frameworker. The point of the resurrection narratives is not to tell us about historical events but to make us understand God's word to us, which perhaps is: "Don't worry; be happy!"[18]

Now, I don't know any evangelical Frameworkers who

[18] We can perform this trick with any story in the Bible. For instance, once we realize that Jonah represents sinful Israel, that the sea represents the gentile world into which they will shortly be exiled, and that the big fish represents Assyria, which Jonah's preaching will prepare as a protective haven for the exiles—well, then, we certainly don't need the actual story of Jonah's living in a big fish any longer, do we?

would want to apply their methods to John 20, but what is to stop someone else from doing so? Evangelical Frameworkers want to have both the events of John 20 as well as the theology. In fact, most of them would see that the theology of John 20 depends on whether the events really happened: If Jesus did not really rise from the tomb, then His death cannot be our "mercy seat," and He cannot offer Himself as our new Gardener-Husband. When it comes to Genesis 1, however, they want the ideas without the events.

Genesis 1 makes claims about historical events just as surely as does John 20. If the claims of Genesis 1 are in error, then there is no reason to think the claims of John 20 are true. If the Bible is the inerrant Word of God, then what it claims happened really happened, and that is just as true for the creation as it is for the resurrection.

The Later Klinean View Revisited

The Klinean version of the Framework Interpretation, as defended by Irons,[19] is sensitive to our charge. Irons insists that the Klinean version of the Framework Interpretation does not deny the specific events of Genesis 1, that it only denies that they happened in the order presented by the text. It is only the days, not the events in the days, that are not historical, or better, not earthly.

Thus, God might have made light, the firmament, and the stars all at one time, or one right after the other in three seconds. Maybe He did these things instantly and modern science is completely wrong about the evolution of the cosmos. God might have made the fish before the plants and the birds after the beasts. The events, therefore, really happened, whether instantly or over millions of years. What did not happen was a week of 168 hours.

This is because the days are heavenly days, while the

[19] Op. cit.

actions are earthly actions. We have already discussed this at some length in chapter three above, but we will take it up again in this context: Clearly days 4–6 are earthly, solar days, measured by the sun. This implies earthly days: The sun was set up to fit the preexisting day-night cycle, not the other way around. Moreover, God has entered the earthly creation through His Spirit on day 1 and is working within the earthly creation. This also implies earthly days. Third, what evidence is there that heavenly days travel at some different rate from earthly days?

Fourth, and this is a new point: Let us assume that the six days of Genesis 1 are not the same as the days measured by the sun. They are the original, heavenly days, super-days as it were, and the solar day is an earthly copy. The sun was set up on the fourth super-day to regulate earthly days, but the super-days of Genesis 1 were heavenly days, not earthly days. If the days are heavenly days, what does this mean? Are there evenings and mornings in heaven, alternations of dark and light? True, day and night are characteristics of earthly solar days, but in Genesis 1 they are characteristics of the supposedly heavenly days as well. Yet, everything in the Bible points against such a notion: Heaven is created as a fully formed and filled place of perpetual light, while the earth is growing from darkness to light, from formlessness to form, from emptiness to filling. The earth is growing to become like heaven, which means heaven is already at the point earth will eventually reach: full of light with no darkness at all (Rev. 21:25: "there shall be no night there").

It will not do to say that the "evenings and mornings" apply to the earth while the "day" applies to heaven. The text is clear: "there was evening and there was morning, a second (etc.) day." The day, supposedly the heavenly day, is described as having evenings and mornings, as moving from darkness to light. I submit that this is not possible as regards heavenly days. On the face of it, there are no evening-morning days in heaven because there are no nights in heaven. Accordingly, the days in Genesis 1, which include nights, are not heavenly days.

Fifth, even if somehow there are days with (or without) evenings and mornings in heaven,[20] and even if they are much longer than earthly days, we still have a sequence of days in Genesis 1 and no permission to jump around from day to day as regards the events. Now, Kline and his followers believe that they have permission to jump around among the days of Genesis 1 because they think they have proved that the sun must have been made on day 1 along with the light. We have seen that this is without foundation, but assume for a moment that their argument is sound. It proves too much, for in such a case there are no days (plural) at all. It is all the same day in heaven (since day 1 = day 4), and all the same day in earthly history as well: a heavenly "moment" (perhaps) translated into an earthly period of undetermined length, both of which are "days." In that case, the days are not a set of successive heavenly days (for there is only one heavenly day) but a mere literary framework.

What does the biblical material lead us to believe about days and daytime? Well, to begin with, God is light and in Him is no darkness at all; therefore, light is an attribute of God. Light is called day; therefore, dayness is an attribute of God. God extends His eternal dayness into the cosmos, but since the cosmos travels in time, His eternal dayness takes the form of specific days.

Now, Genesis 1:1 tells us God created two spatial realms, heaven and earth. The Klineans assume from this that God also created two time-flows, two kinds of days, one heavenly and one earthly. This is a confusion of the characteristics of time and space. Moreover, there is zero

[20] Job 1:6–7 implies that there is a succession of days in heaven, for Satan appeared on a particular day. But are there nights? Not likely, as we have seen. Rather, the 24-hour periods in heaven are fully lit all the time by the glory of God.

biblical evidence to support this notion. Everything in the Bible indicates that the succession of days, as experienced in heaven, does not include nights or evenings, because heaven was created perfect. The successive days on earth proceed from evenings to mornings as a type of the progression of history from primordial darkness to the everlasting light-time of the New Jerusalem.

On the first day of Genesis 1, the light was positioned between heaven and earth, which were not separated by any firmament. Thus, the evening and morning, the darkness and then light, was present to both heaven and earth. Since heaven was lighted by God's glory at that point, the darkness did not reach *into* heaven, but only *unto* it. But darkness (evening) was over the earth. Then light came, morning, and day.[21]

There was another evening, beginning the second day. Then, during the daytime of the second day, God walled off heaven from earth with the firmament. After that event, the Spirit-light no longer shone upwards *unto* heaven, nor did the ensuing darkness. After the creation of the firmament, the night-day cycle of days was exclusively earthly.[22]

On the fourth day, the Spirit passed on this duty to the newly-created sun, while the veil of the firmament was expanded outward to form a huge tent of stars, within which the earth is now situated.

These are the days of Genesis 1. They are cosmic, earthly days, because they start with darkness and move toward light. There are also days in heaven, which move at the same rate as earthly days, because God did not create two kinds of time when He created two kinds of space.

[21] The fact that evening must precede morning, and that the phrase "there was evening and there was morning, a second (etc.) day," must refer back to the preceding events, which will be shown later in appendix A.

[22] The undying light in heaven is also a work of the Spirit, but for the Spirit to be operating in two places at once is no problem since the Spirit is omnipresent.

Or, to put it another way, the two sequences of time are in temporal succession: first week and later weeks.

What About 2 Peter 3:8?

The oft-quoted statement in 2 Peter 3:8 that "with the Lord one day is as a thousand years, and a thousand years as one day," points to the Day of the Lord, not to some kind of "heavenly days," as does the passage to which Peter refers from Moses' psalm, Psalm 90:

> You turn weak man back to dust,
> And You say, "Return, sons of Adam."
>   For a thousand years in Your eyes are like a day,
>   Yesterday that has gone by,
>   And a watch in the night.
> You sweep them away.
> They are sleep.
>   In the morning, like the new grass, he sprouts.
>   In the morning he springs up and sprouts;
>   By the evening he is withered and dry.
> Indeed, we are consumed in Your anger,
> And by Your indignation we are terrified.

God's Day for Adam lasted almost a thousand years (930 years). God's Day for the New Adam lasts a full millennium (Rev. 20:4, 6). None of these passages is intended to indicate that such Days of the Lord always last precisely a thousand years!

Thus, we may not assume that human history is going to last precisely seven thousand years, as some of the early Church writers did. Nor may we argue, as the crudest form of the Day-Age Interpretation does, that the seven days of Genesis 1 lasted a thousand years each, so that plants grew on the earth for two thousand years before there were any insects to fertilize them.

Moses and Peter are using the word "day" symbolically. They are not trying to tell us about the length of supposed heavenly days or any such thing. It involves a very unsound hermeneutical procedure to read such later symbolic usages of "day" back into Genesis 1 without warrant. "Day" means "light-time," and every Day of the Lord, however long it may last, is a time of light.

Two Test Cases

But let us turn to two other seemingly historical events in the Bible and apply to them the hermeneutical principles of our Frameworker brethren. The first to which we turn is the ten plagues visited on Egypt.

First of all, we note that twentieth-century historians of the ancient world cannot find any evidence of a vast host of people leaving Egypt at the time the Bible says it happened. Moreover, according to the text of Exodus, all the Egyptian crops and cattle were destroyed, along with the Egyptian army and a large number of Egypt's sons. Modern "scientific" archaeology and history find no such event. Therefore, we have to look at the text of Exodus anew. Maybe these events never really happened. Maybe they are just a "true myth," providing archetypical "ideas" that undergirded God's relationship with Israel.

Well, do we find any indications in the text that the ten plagues are only a story, that they never really happened? Yes, we do. According to Exodus 9:6, all the livestock of Egypt died in the fifth plague, but according to 9:19, there were still more livestock to be killed in the seventh plague. Also, according to Exodus 8:24, the insects of the fourth plague destroyed all of Egypt, clearly including the plants, while in 9:31, the flax and barley were destroyed later on in the seventh plague, and then in 10:15, the locusts of the eighth plague ate all the remaining plants. This is a much clearer "contradiction" than anything found in Genesis 1. And to these we may add that repeatedly Pharaoh says he will let the people go, but then he changes his mind. How likely is this?

Well, since we have found such clear indications that

these plagues are not to be taken as real history, do we find a literary framework to posit as some kind of alternative? Certainly. There are three groups of three plagues, and then a tenth. The first plague in each cycle begins with a command to go to Pharaoh in the morning. The second in each cycle begins with a command simply to go to Pharaoh. The third in each cycle is not announced to Pharaoh at all. The first three plagues are brought by Aaron's staff, while the last three are brought by Moses' hand. Etc. So, we have a clear literary structure.

Of course, traditional expositors have suggested ways around the "contradictions" in the historical narrative of the ten plagues, but if we are going to let the interpretation of Genesis 1 be our guide, we are not authorized to get around these contradictions. Rather, we must let them be indicators that these events never really happened, at least not the way they are recorded. Clearly, the fifth and seventh plagues happened at the same time, and the fourth, seventh, and eighth happened at the same time. Thus, the passage does not intend to teach us a chronological sequence of events.

What then? Perhaps the sequence of ten plagues only took place in heaven; heavenly plagues as opposed to earthly plagues, as it were. Maybe the firstborn died early on, and the locusts came after. Or maybe none of these events, as events, happened at all: The plagues on Egypt were not historical events; they are a foundational and archetypal myth for the nation of Israel, just as the six days of Genesis are a foundational and archetypal myth for the whole universe.

Now let us turn to the resurrection of Jesus Christ. Repeating our Genesis 1 procedure, we note first of all that "scientific" historians can find no evidence that Jesus rose from the dead. Josephus says nothing about it, and neither does any other "unbiased" source. So, maybe it never happened. We must inspect the text anew.

Do we find contradictions that indicate that the resurrection never happened? Of course we do! The four gospels are in obvious conflict with one other regarding the events of Easter morning. Of course, traditional expositors try to harmonize these four accounts,[23] but we should let the contradictions stand as they are, for they indicate to us that we are not dealing with what we think of as history at all.

So, seeing that there are contradictions in the text, do we find literary structures that indicate the real meaning of the text? Certainly. In John, as I've already mentioned, Jesus' tomb is presented as a Holy of Holies with the slab on which He lay as an Ark-cover with two angels at either end. Moreover, Jesus appears as Gardener in a new Edenic garden in John. Thus, John is giving us theology, "ideas," not history.

I trust the point is clear. If we approach the Bible the way the nonhistorical interpreters of Genesis 1 want us to, the Christian religion gradually disappears into gnosticism. By the same token, if we take other passages of the Bible in their obvious historical sense and resolve seeming contradictions in the way the Church has always done, then we must do the same with Genesis 1.

The Framework Interpretation and its brethren import to the Bible a hermeneutic completely alien to the Christian religion. Our faith is based in facts, historical facts: the acts of God in history, in creation, redemption, and new-creation. The faith of the gnostic is in ideas about eternal matters.

Conclusion

I have charged that the Framework Interpretation, as usually presented, betrays the influence of gnostic thinking, the downgrading of history, time, and event in favor of ideas.

[23] For a good treatment, see John Wenham, *Easter Enigma: Are the Resurrection Accounts in Conflict?* (Grand Rapids, MI: Zondervan, 1984).

The Klinean Frameworkers seek to avoid this charge by maintaining that they still affirm the events of Genesis 1, but not the sequence of events as presented. But the essence of their position makes a hash of history and sequence. They pit the literary structure of Genesis 1, as they conceive it, against the temporal flow of Genesis 1, supporting this belief by calling attention to supposed contradictions and difficulties in Genesis 1 that upon inspection are simply not present there. The sequential flow of events in Genesis 1 is perfectly coherent, and there is no biblical basis for disturbing it. It is only the pervasiveness of a gnostic, a-temporal orientation in post-Enlightenment thinking, that renders such an approach credible.

Chapter 5

The Anthropomorphic Days of C. John Collins

C. John Collins, "How Old Is the Earth? Anthropomorphic Days in Genesis 1:1–2:3," *Presbyterian* 20 (1994):109–130.

C. John Collins, "Reading Genesis 1:1–2:3 as an Act of Communication: Discourse Analysis and Literal Interpretation," in Joseph Pipa, Jr., and David Hall, eds., *Did God Create in Six Days?* (Oak Ridge, TN: Covenant Foundation, 1999) pp. 131–151.

Dr. Collins's 1994 essay has been widely accepted in evangelical Presbyterian circles as an attractive alternative to the traditional view on the one hand and the Framework Interpretation on the other. His 1999 essay presents a refinement of his arguments. Our purpose now must be to examine Collins's arguments to see if in fact they provide sound reasons to reject the historic Christian understanding of this passage. Inescapably this will entail our covering some of the same ground we have already plowed, simply because some of the same arguments are presented.

At the outset it must be noted that Collins is very insistent that the six days of Genesis 1 take place one after another in historical sequence. Since he does not believe Genesis 1 requires 24-hour days, it might seem that he is positing a Day-Age Interpretation, and in fact his position is similar to it. In his 1999 essay he summarizes his approach as "*analogical (or 'anthropomorphic') days*—days are God's work-days, hence of unspecified relation to time as we experience it (but 'broadly consecutive' and 'historical')" (p. 146). In essence, Collins suggests that the days are sequential, but probably rather long, and overlapping to some extent. He argues that God chose to do His world-building work over the course of six periods of time, that can be called "days," to set an example for His images, who are also to work six days and rest on the seventh. But Collins objects to making these "days" ordinary "human 24-hour days." He argues that the text, rightly read, would not lead us to such a conclusion. Let us now examine his case, beginning with his 1994 essay.

Collins begins his earlier essay with general remarks about the history of interpretation and the role of science in challenging our traditions. We shall address these matters in chapter six of the present book. For now, we turn to Collins's interpretation of Genesis 1 and the biblical material in general.

Section four of Collins's essay, as well as an appendix to it, is devoted to an exploration of Church history to show that earlier theologians and exegetes did not always hold with a literal Six Day view of Genesis 1. It is true that a few pre-modern commentators did not, but not many, as Collins points out.

Collins moves on to express general agreement with E. R. Thiele's *The Mysterious Numbers of the Hebrew Kings*, published originally in 1965, which attempts to shorten the chronology of the book of Kings to make it fit data from the Assyrian King Lists.[1] Collins then cites W. H.

[1] In fact, Thiele's "solution" to the problems involved in putting together the chronology of the Kings of Israel and Judah is fraught with major problems of its own. See the devastating discussion in O. T. Allis,

Green's famous (or infamous) essay that argues for "gaps" in the chronologies of Genesis 5 and 11. Green arbitrarily asserts that the chronological statements in Genesis 5 should be read as follows, for example: "And Seth lived 105 years and became *the ancestor of* Enoch. And Seth lived 870 after he became *the ancestor of* Enoch, and he had sons and daughters" (Gen. 5:6–7). This gnat-straining and camel-swallowing way of reading the simple Hebrew verb "fathered" puts a gap between each of the patriarchs in Genesis 5 and 11—except that it won't work for Adam's fathering Seth (5:3 with 4:25), nor with Lamech's fathering Noah (5:28–29), nor with Noah's fathering Shem, Ham, and Japheth (5:32), nor with Terah's fathering Abram, Nahor, and Haran (11:26–27). Such a totally preposterous misreading of the text never occurred to anyone in the entire history of the Church before the late nineteenth century. Collins quotes B. B. Warfield's approval of Green's odd notions: "It is to theology, as such, a matter of complete indifference how long man has existed on earth."[2] Given Warfield's gnostic inclinations, however, his despising of biblical chronology is no great surprise.[3]

Finally, on p. 117, Collins arrives at Genesis 1. He begins, "It is simplest to take Gen 1:1–2 as a heading, as the NIV does: God called all things into being 'formless and

The Old Testament: Its Claim and Critics (Phillipsburg, NJ: Presbyterian & Reformed Pub. Co., 1972). On the unreliability of extra-biblical sources, especially the Assyrian King List, for ancient chronology, see Peter James, et. al., *Centuries of Darkness: A Challenge to the Conventional Chronology of Old World Archaeology* (New Brunswick, NJ: Rutgers University Press, 1993), esp. chaps. 11 and 12.

[2] Warfield, "On the Antiquity and the Unity of the Human Race," *Princeton Theological Review* 9 (1911):1–25.

[3] For a consideration of Green's and Warfield's numerous errors, and their repetition by Francis A. Schaeffer, with a criticism of the entire notion of gaps in biblical chronology, see James B. Jordan, "The Biblical Chronology Question: An Analysis," *Creation Social Sciences and Humanities Quarterly* 2:2 (Winter 1979) and 2:3 (Spring 1980). A photocopy of this essay is available from Biblical Horizons, Box 1096, Niceville, FL 32588.

empty,' and the rest of the chapter is six 'days' of structuring and filling" (p. 117). (Actually, the world was also dark, and the six days deal with three areas, not just two.)

In his 1999 article, Collins expands on his understanding of Genesis 1:1–2. These represent "an unspecified length of time prior to the beginning of the first 'day'" (p. 144). Collins argues that because the verbs in verses 1 and 2 are in the Hebrew perfect, and the narrative sequence of Hebrew imperfect verbs does not begin until verse 3, the account of the building up of the earth does not start until verse 3. We can just as well, however, take it that the Hebrew perfects are the start of the narrative chain, as is often the case. Building on his assumption, Collins argues that Genesis 1:3ff is only concerned with the lower earth and has nothing to say about the highest heavens. As he puts it, the focus is only on "this terrestrial ball" (p. 136). Thus, he argues, Genesis 1 is not presenting a cosmogony (origin) of the entire universe and its structure but is only concerned with planet earth as man's home.

There is a major problem with this assumption, and Collins does not address it. On the second day God took some of the earthly waters up above the firmament, and this can only mean they were taken into the angelic heavens. Since the stars were placed in the firmament, the waters must be beyond the stars. Thus, when heaven is opened in the Bible, we see an ocean there (Ezek. 1:22; Rev. 4:6). Accordingly, the events of Genesis 1 are indeed concerned with the total cosmology of existence, angelic heavens included. It is not just "sky and land" that are in view. Thus, contrary to Collins, the events of Genesis 1 do indeed concern the entire cosmos, and the angelic heavens as well. They are not merely concerned with planet earth.

Along these same lines, Collins wants to remove the creation of the sun, moon, and stars from the fourth day, thereby preserving an exclusively "terrestrial ball" focus for the work of the six days. He points out that the Hebrew word for "made" in verse 16 can also mean "prepared" or even "appointed." Continuing, he writes, "Further, the expression in verse 14 'let there be' need not denote their origin so much as their purpose: 'let lightbearers in the extended surface of the sky be for the purpose of' marking the progress of the liturgical calendar" (1999, p. 135). This way of reading the events of the fourth day is defended at some length by John Sailhamer, and I shall take the matter up in detail in chapter seven. For now, repeatedly the word "make" occurs in this passage having the meaning "make," not "prepare" or "appoint" (1:7, 25, 26, 31; 2:18), so why not here? What reason is there, in the text itself, to give it a different connotation in this one place?

To summarize: Collins's understanding is that God made the angelic heavens and the entire starry universe "in the beginning." Exactly how He did it, the text does not say and is not concerned with. Then Genesis 1 describes the preparation of planet earth. On the first day, God appointed a separation of light and darkness for the earth. These (evidently) had already been in operation, but now they take on a special meaning. On the second day, God appointed a blue sky over the earth, which again had already been in place, but now it receives a special meaning. At least, this seems to be Collins's meaning, and why he wants to exclude the angelic heavens and the outer cosmos from consideration as far as actual "making" and "changing" are concerned.

But if this is what he intends, he has a problem: Did men already exist before the sixth day and only receive a special appointment on that occasion? It is pretty clear that Collins does not believe any such thing. Moreover, if these are only days of appointments, why not see them as six ordinary 24-hour days?

On the other hand, if these are days in which God actually makes new things, like plants, animals, and men, on what basis do we say that He did not also actually make (not just appoint) light (day 1), some sort of physical firmament boundary (day 2), and the stars (day 4), and *in that sequence*, since Collins affirms that Genesis 1 is an historical sequence of events?

In other words, it involves a lot of special pleading, in terms of hidden presuppositions, to assert that God's making things means "making" on some days, and only "appointing" on others. This is not a coherent way of reading the text.

Returning now to Collins's original essay: He writes, "The simplest explanation for these six days is that they are anthropomorphisms: that is, they are 'God's days'" (p. 117). The days are analogous to our days. On these days God works like a human being. He does things that human beings do, such as working over the course of six days, resting on the seventh day, working in the daytime and not at night, etc. With all of this we can completely agree, but without drawing Collins's conclusions from it. All of this is quite true, but it in no way argues against the normal 24-hour day interpretation.

Collins's reply will be that there are a couple of other factors that indicate that these days are not of the same quality as human days. One is that the sixth day is pretty full, and it is hard to believe that Adam watched God plant the Garden, named the animals, and had an afternoon wife-making nap, all on the same day. We have dealt with this already in chapter two. There was plenty of time in a 12-hour day for Adam to have done it all and still have had lots of time left over.

Collins also points out that the seventh day does not seem to end, and therefore it is not a model for human days. Well, this is only a problem if we want it to be. Certainly, God has rested from His world-building work ever since the seventh day, and in that sense it continues. God does do other things, of course, so in another sense He continues to be active. Moreover, Genesis 1 is not merely a record of creation; it is also a typology of history, and the final sabbath will be endless. These facts do not hint in the least that the days are any other than ordinary days.

More globally, Collins argues that the various things that take place during creation week would take a lot of time if they happened in our world today, such as all the water running off the earth and the trees growing up all on one day (the third), and the planting of the Garden of Eden. Quite true, but this does not imply that God did not act more rapidly on these occasions. As a human being, I can type fast or slow, walk slowly or run fast, etc. So can God. Aaron's rod blossomed overnight (Num. 17), showing us that when God wants to, He can work fast. Similarly, it was certainly exceptional for vast numbers of frogs to come up from the Nile during the second plague on Egypt, but we don't draw from this that the plague took place gradually and not swiftly, as it is recorded to have done. There is nothing "unanthropomorphic" about God's rapidly blowing out the firmament veil to form the starry cosmos on the fourth day. God can work fast or slow, just as we can.

Collins adds in his 1999 essay that the language used in Genesis 1 is "high" language, not ordinary language, and this should direct us away from taking the narrative as "ordinary" (p. 141). His point is that the original author did not intend this passage to be read as ordinary history but as something perhaps more like liturgical language. This observation can be granted as at least partially true, but the following must also be born in mind. First, the *entire Bible* is written in a kind of exalted prose style, not just Genesis 1. It is all "high" language: "stylized," "majestic," and "patterned." For obvious examples, read Genesis 24 and note the stylized repetitions, and Leviticus 1, and John 1, and any of the psalms. Second, while Genesis 1 does speak of the "greater light" rather than of the "sun," it also uses quite "ordinary" language such as "stars," "fruit trees," "men and women," and so forth. Thus, the style of language used in Genesis 1 does not in any way indicate that it is to be read in some "unordinary" way as contrasted with the rest of the Bible.

Collins concludes his 1994 essay with this: "The seven

'days' of the creation week are an anthropomorphism to describe God's activity. If we wish to specify their relationship to time as we know it, perhaps we may view them as successive periods of undefined length (with perhaps some overlap)" (p. 120). Several observations:

First, if these "days" are simply an exercise in anthropomorphism designed to point to something ineffable, then they need have no relationship to "time as we know it" at all. They are nothing more than a literary figure. I don't understand why Collins perceives a need to retain the idea of a sequence of such "days" as eons or anything else.

Second, "time as we know it" is the only "time" there is, because God is eternal. Genesis 1 describes God's actions in time, and it does so in the plainest language imaginable. Collins has provided no basis for thinking that some other kind of "time" is in view here.

Third, how can these "days" be of undefined length, when the fourth day and those after it are measured by the sun? It is clear from Genesis 1 that these days are normal solar days. And, since *the sun was made to fit the day rather than the other way around,* it is also clear that the preceding days were of the same length.

Last, the notion of overlapping days, which Collins merely suggests as a possibility, is excluded as a possibility for three reasons. One, the repeated phrase "and evening happened, and morning happened, on *n*th day," indicates that the work of that day was finished on that day. Two, the repeated phrase, "and it was established," indicates a completion of the work mentioned. Three, the repeated phrase, "and God saw that it was good," also indicates a completion of the work mentioned. Thus, while it is true that a human being may begin a work on one day and complete it later on, it is also true that a human being can finish a particular project on the same day he starts it, and this latter is what Genesis 1 indicates as regards God's works.

Concerning Anthropomorphisms

Simply saying that the days of Genesis 1 are anthropomorphisms or are days analogous to human days is not enough, because everything we know about God we know analogically and anthropomorphically. This fact follows from the doctrine of creation. There is nothing outside of the creation that God worked with in order to make the world, and therefore His personality is fully revealed in everything He has made. It cannot be otherwise. Moreover, since human beings are images of God, man is a theomorph. Every aspect of human life is a copy of something in God. Accordingly, whenever we see God do anything at all, we see Him doing something that is like something in human life. Or, to put it simply, God always acts anthropomorphically, as far as our perceptions are concerned. We cannot perceive Him and His actions in any other way.[4]

Of course, there are aspects of God that are not copied in human life, but in the nature of the case, we *cannot* understand them. They have no analogy in creation or in human life and experience, and they never will. Everything we know, we know *as* human beings, *as* theomorphs. It is not possible for us to stand outside of what we are and know other things about God.

Thus, when we read that God puts forth His mighty arm, this means that there is in God a capacity for action that is copied in human life in the form of putting forth an arm. There is a capacity in God of which the human arm is a created analogue. It would make no sense to us if God said, "I shall quibanque Myself." God must use the languages He created for human beings to use, if we are to understand Him, and since God made these languages, they are perfectly suited for His purposes.

The human mind was created to understand God the

[4] For a biblical defense of this doctrine, see my book *Through New Eyes: Developing a Biblical View of the World* (Eugene, OR: Wipf & Stock, [1988] 1999) chap. 2.

way a perfect glove fits the hand. Romans 1:19–20 tells us that we understand God perfectly; it is just that, being sinners, we don't like what we see and thus suppress our knowledge. There is no "understanding gap" between God and His creation.

Now, there is a long and sad history in Christendom of not understanding this fact very well. We are told that the Creator must "accommodate" Himself to our finite understanding and "lisp" to us like children. He must "condescend" to us. He must "overcome the distance" between us and Him. He must "descend to our level" in order for us to understand Him. Such language presupposes that God and man are on a continuum, with God at the big end and man at the small end, so that the big God has to make himself small in order to talk to us. But God does not need to do that, because the difference between God and man is not a matter of bigness and smallness but of Creator and creature. God created us with the capacity to understand Him exactly as He intends us to. There is no "problem" that He must overcome in order to reach us.

What is this tradition—which is only one side of the tradition, I hasten to add—really saying? It seems that God did such a crummy job of creating the universe and humanity in the first place that He is now faced with the problem of communicating with us. God did such an imperfect job of designing human languages, images of His eternal Word, that He now must overcome the problems in those languages. He did such a bad job of designing the human mind and person that He now must add rituals and sacraments in order to get through to us, which we would not need if only He had done a better job in the first place. Is *that* what Christians believe?

No, no. A thousand times *no!* Of course we can believe no such thing. There is no metaphysical or epistemological "distance" between the Creator and His creation that He must "overcome." The creation is perfectly designed to know and interact with the Creator. The problem between man and God is a matter of sin, not of "distance."

Sadly, many theologians write as if the Bible contains some anthropomorphisms as well as some nonanthropomorphical language. Anthropomorphisms, it is held, are God's "condescending language" to us, which we are to overcome as we mature. This notion is a denial of the doctrine of creation, for no matter how much we grow throughout eternity, we shall never stop being theomorphs who view God anthropomorphically. Every bit of the Bible, as well as all human language, is completely anthropomorphic. There cannot be, for human beings, any other kind of language. Nonfigurative, nonsymbolic language is every bit as anthropomorphic as figurative, symbolic language is. To deny this is to assert that men can become God.

Anthropomorphic language exists because man is like God. Thus, to describe God in human terms is completely accurate. It is not some kind of inadequate or second-class kind of language; it is the only kind of language that exists for human beings, and the only kind that will ever exist, for we shall never cease to be human beings. We confess that God, as Creator, is also beyond anything that we can imagine or say, and this prevents us from thinking that God has a physical arm or a physical body like a man. But to know God *directly,* to know God *as He is in Himself,* we would have to *be* God ourselves, and the lust to become God is original sin.

The only thing in Genesis 1, and in the whole Bible, that is not anthropomorphic is the act of creating out of nothing, which is something only God can do and is something we cannot understand at all. Just try to think about it. There is nothing outside of God that provoked Him to decide to create. And there is nothing lacking in God that would make Him want to create the world, for the three Persons of God experience perfect communication and love with each other and need nothing else. There is nothing in human experience like this totally free and uncaused act of creating. Everything we do as creatures has some kind of causation behind it, but God's act of creating is completely uncaused in any human sense. God simply decided to do it, and that is all we can say about the act itself. For this reason, the verb "create" is never used in the Bible except with God as its subject. Only God creates, and there is no analogue in human life to this. When we speak of human creativity, we are speaking of our ability to rearrange and transform the world God made, and this activity is not analogous to God's creative acts but to His acts of changing things He has already created. It is analogous to the other acts in Genesis 1 but not to the creative acts.

Thus, *of course Genesis 1 is anthropomorphic language!* And of course the days of Genesis 1 are anthropomorphic days! The fact that Genesis 1 is anthropomorphic says nothing one way or another about whether the days are long or short, or whether they are a mere literary framework or an actual sequence of events.

Now, there is another kind of "accommodation" in God's communication with us, which is radically different from what we have been considering. It stems from the fact that we mature in time, from babies to youths to adults to elders, on and on forever and ever. God speaks and writes to us in language fitted to our stage of maturity.[5] This is *mostly* what is meant in the traditional theological discussions of God's accommodation to man, but unfortunately it is almost always mixed up with the errors we have been considering.

Now, is there something inadequate or problematic about God's speaking more simply at the beginning of the Bible, with more complexity as the Bible moves along, and climaxing in the book of Revelation? No, there is not. At

[5] A useful discussion of this, though much confused at points, is Jacobus de Jong, *Accommodatio Dei: A Theme in K. Schilder's Theology of Revelation* (Kampen, The Netherlands: Dissertatie-Uitgeverij Mondiss, 1990).

each stage the revelation is perfect and communicates perfectly. God designed it that way. He did not build any imperfections into His plan of historical development. Later revelation in the Bible never contradicts earlier revelation, though it expands and deepens it.[6]

Consider. If I say, "The sun rose at 6:01 this morning," that statement is perfectly true and communicates perfectly what is meant. I can also say something more precise, like: "At exactly 6:01:49 A.M., Greenwich Mean Time, the horizon of the earth dropped to reveal the upper tip of the sun as observed from 41°14'22.18" latitude and 55°21'45.44" longitude." This second statement is more *precise*, but not more *true* than the previous one. We understand the first statement perfectly well.

Similarly, in Genesis 1, God could have said that He made the firmament at the fourth hour after daybreak, the sixteenth minute, and the thirty-fourth second, on the second day. That would be more precise, but not more true.

Genesis 1 is not "scientifically precise," but it is not untrue for that reason. We know what a day is, for Genesis 1 defines it as a "time of light," and further as a whole period having and evening and a morning. We know what kind of "day" that is: It is an ordinary, "24-hour" day. We know this because the length of the day is said to be meas-

[6] And, to reiterate, neither does human sinfulness mean that God has to make some special "condescension" to communicate with us. We understand God perfectly. We just don't like what we hear Him say. Contrary to what many theologians say, we do not cease to be the images of God because we are sinners. We are perverse images, but the image of God is the definition of what a human being is, and even in hell, sinners will still be human beings, and thus still images of God. Also, contrary again to many theologians' beliefs, we do not cease to be in covenant with God when we sin. We are still in covenant, and still connected to God by covenant, but we are under the negative, curse side of the covenant. The connection is still present, because it cannot be otherwise. We cannot cease to be creatures, we cannot cease to be images of God, and we cannot cease to be covenantally related to God one way or another.

ured by the sun, and since the sun was made to fit the day rather than the other way around, we know that the first three days were of the same length. The passage is perfectly clear about this.

Is the whole chapter, then, a figure of speech? That is theoretically possible, but we dare not assert that it is such without biblical warrant and evidence. Where do we find any such evidence? Not in the so-called "contradictions" in Genesis 1, because there aren't any. Not in any later passage of the Bible, because no such passage exists. The only references to the length of creation week and to the lengths of the days compare them directly to the ordinary human week and days (Ex. 20:11; 31:17).

If we are to try to draw on "ordinary human experience," as Collins suggests, and say that the events of Genesis 1 are not what we usually see going on—well, what would we expect? This is, after all, the creation of the world and of the universe, which is not something we see going on every day! Moreover, using this criterion, we would have to say that women don't ordinarily grow out of the ribs of men, that people don't ordinarily live nine hundred plus years, that serpents don't ordinarily talk, etc. If we introduce a hermeneutical principle of casting doubt on anything unusual in the Bible, where do we draw the line? People don't ordinarily come out of tombs, either.

Conclusion

Thus, we gladly grant what Collins wishes: that there are lots of anthropomorphisms in Genesis 1. Indeed, we insist that the entire passage is anthropomorphic and that God is presented as working in the same way as a human being works. The question is: So what?

The passage clearly presents God as choosing to work over the course of a week of seven days, days that have regular evenings and mornings. Either this is just a poem, a literary figure, or else it is a description of what God actually did. Collins seems to want to have it both ways, but his position, as presented, provides no justification for doing so. Either Genesis 1 is a merely literary figure or it is a narrative of actual events. If it is the latter, then we need to take it at face value: God made the world in seven days, as a model for His images, human beings. Nothing hints that these days were anything other than days of ordinary length, the kinds of days measured by the sun as the fourth day states, and the attention called to evenings and mornings proves that they were of ordinary length.

Chapter 6

The Questions Posed by "Science"

Dr. Collins begins his earlier essay, discussed in chapter five, with a brief statement of the Day-Age view and then a brief statement of the Six Day view, focusing on the challenge to that view posed by modern "science." He ends this discussion by writing: "Two crucial points are at stake here: first, the principles of Bible interpretation; and second, the validity of scientific method" (p. 111). With this statement we can heartily agree.

Collins is not wrong to begin by mentioning modern science. If we trust God and His Word, we shall not be afraid to look back at it to see if we have interpreted it rightly. The challenge of modern science to the Bible motivates two responses that are not mutually exclusive. One is to rework the data and examine the premises of modern science, with a view to bringing it into line with biblical teaching. The other is to ask whether traditional approaches to creation and chronology are actually justified by the text of the Bible.

"Science" and Natural Revelation

Collins provides one paragraph on science and natural revelation, and what he states there is problematic. Perhaps I can be pardoned for observing that it appears to me that occasionally he writes as a trained scientist who is so immersed in science that he does not fully perceive the nature and limitations of scientific inquiry. Our procedure will be to examine critically what he states before providing some wider comments on the subject.

Collins asks, "Does the creation speak truly?" We can reply to this very general question with a very general answer: Of course it does, but is the creation designed to speak by itself? The answer to that second question is clearly no. The creation does not "speak" at all, actually. Rocks, trees, birds, and stars do not communicate linguistically. The information that is contained in the creation must be put into words by human beings, and since human beings cannot exist without language, human beings are always interpreting the creation linguistically.[1]

Human beings are living words and live in a linguistic environment because they are images of God, who is Word and who lives in an environment of eternal communication. Since God created the universe, His linguistic interpretation of it is absolutely correct; we think His thoughts after Him.

There are special event-revelations that are connected to special word-revelations, and there is the general revelation through nature that is connected to general language. The special event-revelations (i.e., miracles) cannot be understood without special word-revelation (i.e., the Bible). The Bible explains the miracle, not vice versa. (For instance,

[1] As one reader of this manuscript pointed out, all creation images God in a sense, and God is Word, so therefore creation is in a sense God's speech. Speech, however, requires breath, which in this case is the Spirit, who entered the creation at the moment of creation. It is through the Spirit that the creation speaks. The Spirit entered humanity when man was created (Gen. 2:7), and so it is through mankind that the creation speaks. The speech of creation consists of human language, not of something else.

For a fuller discussion of "natural revelation," see my study "Twelve Avenues of Revelation," serialized in the *Open Book* essayletter Nos. 30–34; available from Biblical Horizons, P.O. Box 1096, Niceville, FL 32588.

a "New-Ager" might admit that Jesus rose from the dead but would deny the interpretation the Bible places on that event.) The miracle is context; the Bible is explanation. Similarly, nature is context, while language is explanation.

Thus, the idea that either special or general events and phenomena have "messages" that "speak" to us needs to be probed very carefully. Psalm 19 is often referred to in this regard, and Collins mentions it. Supposedly this psalm says that the creation in general is somehow communicating information. If we look at the text, however, and consider it as ancient people would have, we come up with something quite different. The heavens are declaring things because the constellations of the zodiac reveal certain truths in symbols. What they reveal is the same thing the law of God reveals, as the parallel with the second half of the psalm indicates. The former is for the gentiles, from the Noahic covenant (the zodiac being a form of the rainbow, perhaps); the latter is for the priestly people. Thus, Psalm 19 is not speaking of some kind of general revelation through nature, but rather it alludes to a symbolic system that was put in place at some point in history.[2]

Romans 1:20 tells us that information about God is clearly revealed in the creation, and this statement is more general than Psalm 19. Even here, however, the text does not say that the creation somehow "speaks" to man. The creation provides evidence of God's presence, but apart from man's putting language onto the evidence, the evidence is mute.

All of this is not to do away with the reality of "natural revelation," but it is to say that the matter of natural or general revelation involves subtleties that need to be

[2] For a discussion of astral revelation and imagery in the Bible, see my book *Through New Eyes: Developing a Biblical View of the World* (Eugene OR: Wipf & Stock, [1988] 1999), and my monograph *Behind the Scenes: Orientation in the Book of Revelation*. Biblical Horizons Occasional Paper 19 (2nd ed., May, 1999; available from Biblical Horizons, Box 1096, Niceville, FL 32588).

considered. We cannot simply say, "The creation speaks truly," because in fact it is man who speaks, and man is a willing slave of the father of lies. Man seldom speaks truly.

Collins on Science

Turning then to Collins's own presentation: Referring to Psalm 19:1–2 and Romans 1:18–20, he asks,

> How could we be "without excuse" unless the created realm speaks truly? How could we justly be held accountable for not receiving a message that was not sent? This implies that properly done science will not mislead us (provided that the material world is rightly viewed in the light of special revelation—and taking account of our own subjectivity). (p. 112)

With this statement we can have no objection. We can ask, however, whether Collins has drawn out all the relevant implications of his statement.

Collins follows with this: "It also implies that the 'appearance of age' idea, being deceptive, would be unlikely to commend itself to a biblical author" (p. 112). This statement is a gigantic red herring drawn across the reader's eyes and nose. What is deceptive about the creation of something with an appearance of age? It would be deceptive *only if we think we can deduce the age of something by looking at it*—and that is the whole question.

Consider the creation of the Primordial Atom at the time of the supposed Big Bang 25 billion years ago. If you had been there one second later, could you tell how old it was? Looking at it, you might think it was 25 billion years old, or infinitely old. You see, as far as this question goes, it does not matter when or how God created the universe, because one second after He created it, you could not tell how long it had been there.[3]

[3] For a humorous and penetrating conversation between Adam and Eve on this subject, see Jeffrey J. Meyers, "The First Sabbath Conversation," in *Christendom Essays. Biblical Horizons* 100 (December,

Second, there is nothing in the least deceptive *if God goes to the trouble of telling you about the matter*—which in fact He has done, in Genesis 1.

Collins expands on his comment in a footnote:

> Perhaps it is possible to argue that special revelation must override the apparent evidence of our senses. Thus, we "know" that the universe is young because "the Bible tells us so." However, (a) this begs the question, does the Bible say so . . . ; (b) this view undermines the truthfulness of nature's testimony, which Paul presupposes in Rom. 1:18–20. (p. 112, n. 17)

Yet, we must "override the apparent evidence of our senses" all the time in life, especially in the world of modern science and technology. My senses tell me that the earth is flat and still and that the sun goes around the earth. My senses tell me that a friendly-looking lion in the zoo wants me to pet him. My senses tell me nothing about the way my computer works. Anyone who has ever observed a court case involving many witnesses knows that people's observations and senses can be very incorrect; what people think they saw may not be what happened at all.

Moreover, our senses tell us nothing about the history of the cosmos. Our senses react to pain and light and sound, but they have nothing to do with grand philosophical cosmogonic schemes. It is not the "apparent evidence of our senses" that Genesis 1 may "override" but rather the highly rarified philosophies of our sin-twisted reason.

Genesis 1 is clearly presented as a week of miracles, exceptions to what we usually see going on in the world. It is analogous to Jesus' converting water into wine at the wedding in Cana. The "evidence of our senses" would say that the wine had been made the usual way, over a long course of time. We are told otherwise. The same is true regarding the events of the creation of the world.

1997; available from Biblical Horizons, P.O. Box 1096, Niceville, FL 32588).

Truly or Clearly?

Collins says that the "message" of creation is truly sent, so that we are without excuse. That is not quite the question, however. The "message" may be *truly* sent, but not *clearly* sent. Now, as regards the revelation of God through the creation, it is truly and clearly manifest.[4] As regards other kinds of information, however, the matter is otherwise.

What Romans 1:20 says is that information about *God* is clearly manifest in the creation. It does *not* claim that other kinds of information are clearly manifest—"It is the glory of God to conceal a matter; it is the glory of kings to search it out" (Prov. 25:2). This is true not only of biblical theology, but also of the world of created nature. People used to think that air travelled through our veins, until such "kings" searched the matter out and discovered otherwise. Collins, however, is trying to use Romans 1:20 and Psalm 19 (on his interpretation) to say that *other kinds of information* are "clearly revealed, so that we are without excuse." This is not correct. The Bible does not say this at all. It is information about God, not about dinosaurs or sedimentary stratification, that is said to be clear. It is information about God, not about carbon-14, that leaves us without excuse. Collins has, it appears, completely misapplied these texts.

Essentially, Collins is saying that the creation is giving *clear* information about its history that seemingly contradicts the traditional understanding of Genesis 1. We must say that this is *prima facie* highly questionable. (1) Unlike the prophecy of Zechariah, Genesis 1 is a very easy passage to read and understand. In terms of clear versus cloudy, Genesis 1 is definitely on the clear end of the scale. (2)

[4] Cornelius Van Til has shown that just as Scriptural revelation is necessary, authoritative, sufficient, and perspicuous, so also is revelation through the creation. See "Nature and Scripture," in *The Infallible Word: A Symposium by the Members of the Faculty of Westminster Theological Seminary* (Philadelphia: Presbyterian & Reformed Pub. Co., 1946).

The Bible nowhere says that God is clearly giving information about the creation through the creation. It says that He reveals Himself clearly. It does not say that nature yields her secrets easily. (3) As a matter of fact, nature does not yield her secrets easily. Therefore, to use the cloudy and questionable "witness of nature" as a challenge to any reading of the Bible is not likely to be a fruitful enterprise.

What Is "Science"?

Now, this is virtually all Collins says about science in his essay, and because of that, it may well be unfair to impute to Collins the errors in thinking that we shall now discuss. From what he has written, however, it appears that Collins thinks that natural revelation indicates an ancient universe and earth, so that the constructs of cosmology that are current in the late twentieth century A.D. are to be taken as facts to be reckoned with—or perhaps better, that these constructs are close enough to the truth that the traditional interpretation of Genesis 1 needs to be reconsidered. Regardless to what extent Collins may be caught up in it, this entails a very common and serious error in thinking.

To begin with, we have to distinguish between "science" as technique and "science" as construct. We can use electricity without understanding it at all. A physicist may know more about it, but does he understand it fully? Yet he can use it. Engineers and inventors can do great things with the natural world.

We move into a completely different realm, however, when we enter the world of science as construct, what is sometimes (prejudicially?) called "pure science" as opposed to "applied science." A "scientist" can spin an elaborate theory about why things work they way they do, but that is nothing more than a theory. We know as Christians that one dimension of the way things work is that God works them that way and that another dimension is that God's agents, the spirit angels, work them that way. God and His angels are at work in the flow of electricity, for example. Now, this fact does not exhaust what can be said about electricity, and perhaps our present understanding of the flow of electricity is quite correct and will not need adjustment in the future. Then again, we may find that our present theory does need revision.

This is, or should be, far more obvious when it comes to things of which we have no direct experience. We have only begun to scratch the surface of an investigation of the first inch of the foyer of the outer universe, for instance. Yet, with supreme confidence modern scientists project theories about how the universe works, as if they already had all the facts needed to form a final theory. On the surface of it, this is ridiculous. I personally remember when the first quasars were discovered. What else remains to be discovered?

Indeed, we only finished mapping the surface of the globe a century or so ago. What is really under the ice of Antarctica? And what things lie in the depths of the sea? We have little knowledge of these things.

The amount of erroneous and prejudiced misinterpretation of data is vast. A couple of thousand years ago a few refugees lived in caves in France for a short time, and this fact has been turned into the myth that human beings lived in caves for millennia! Why should any thinking person accept such a notion? Because of carbon-14 dating? But C-14 dating is extremely subjective and frequently misleading.[5]

We may ask: In a hundred years, will anyone still believe that you cannot go faster than light?[6] In a hundred

[5] See Douglas F. Kelly, *Creation and Change: Genesis 1:1–2:4 in the Light of Changing Scientific Paradigms* (Ross–Shire, UK: Mentor–Christian Focus Publications, 1997) chap. 8.

[6] Every physicist knows that gravitational force "travels" almost instantaneously and thus is "faster than light." For a summary of recent discussions, with bibliography, and much evidence that Einstein was wrong, see Tom Bethell, "Rethinking Relativity," in *The American Spectator* 32:4 (April, 1999):20–23.

years, will anyone still believe that the red-shift in the spectra of stars is caused by their rapid movement away from us in an "expanding universe"? Why on earth should anyone, especially thinking Christians, commit themselves to the temporary notions of "scientific" theories, knowing that a century ago nobody believed such things, and knowing that we have only just begun to explore the outer universe?

A scientific construct is just that: a construct. It may be quite helpful. It may be the best we can do at present. It may be a step along the way to a better understanding, or it may be a blind alley. But when it is obvious that scientists are dealing with only a very few facts, and there is a great deal more to be learned, there is no earthly reason to accept any such construct as the final word.[7]

This, however, is what many evangelicals do. They assume that today's constructs are the last word, and they believe the Bible must be reinterpreted in light of them. This is an utterly preposterous procedure.[8]

Now, it is to Collins's credit that he does call attention to this matter: "On the other hand, it is important to keep in mind the limitations of science as a tool of knowledge. Confident pronouncements are imprudent when we do not even know how much we know!" (p. 123).

Science and Dominion

There is more to be said about science, however. What human beings look at with the eye, human beings have mental dominion over; but information that comes through the

[7] A good treatment of science as construct is J. P. Moreland, *Christianity and the Nature of Science* (Grand Rapids, MI: Baker, 1989).

[8] For example, see Hugh Ross, *Creation and Time: A Biblical and Scientific Perspective on the Creation-Date Controversy* (Colorado Springs, CO: Navpress, 1994), and Howard J. Van Till, *The Fourth Day: What the Bible and the Heavens Are Telling Us About the Creation* (Grand Rapids, MI: Eerdmans, 1986).

ear, we don't have dominion over. People can say things to us that we don't want to hear, while we can close our eyes to any sight we don't want to see. This fundamental distinction informs the biblical hostility to all iconic worship; a silent statue or picture can never challenge or rebuke us.

Now, information once given through the ear enters the mind and can be examined with the eye of the mind, and we can have dominion over it. Thus, while the Word of God comes to us initially as challenge and rebuke, once we have heard it, we can meditate upon it—and even abuse it or dismiss it. Science is concerned with information that has come through the eye or else through the ear and that we can reflect upon.

What science cannot deal with is time, because God alone is Lord of time. God is eternally active and infinite, and as a result, the future always brings new things into play as God does new things, revealing new aspects and implications of His being and plan, bringing forth new things that were hidden and embedded in the creation at the beginning. Thus, it is simply not possible to imagine the future accurately. When men imagine the future, they imagine something very much like their own present, only more so in some particular way: more money, more steam, more sexual license, more computers, etc.—thus, it is amusing to read the science fiction written a century ago, or fifty years ago. For this reason, the biblical pictures of the future are always presented in symbols that point to future realities that cannot presently be described. Ezekiel, for instance, is shown a picture of the Restoration Era sanctuary in the form of a huge Temple and City (Ezek. 40–48), but these were not actually built; rather, they pointed to the Spiritual realities of the period after the Babylonian Exile.

If the future cannot really be envisioned, then it cannot be controlled, which means the believer lives a life of faith and obedience, not of planning and dominion. Human dominion is exercised toward the lower world, the world of science; history, however, must be accepted as authored by God and lived by faith.

Because men cannot control the future, they deny it. Human beings exist, after the Fall, in a war with time. They want to escape time, to escape the unsettling changes of the future. The works of Mircea Eliade explore this phenomenon in some depth. All pagan religions seek to "eternalize time" and thereby escape God's ordination of the future. They all look *back* to a golden age, which they can understand, because if they were to look to the future, they would have to bow before their Creator.[9]

A "spatial" mode of thinking is very much present in Western Civilization, especially since the so-called Enlightenment. After all, science works: It brings good things, such as light bulbs and velcro. Science can be understood. Science is under human dominion. Science is free of the "messiness" that is involved with the understanding of history. Thus, the exploration of space and place and dominion over the creation have become the models for *all* human inquiry, as the various works of such thinkers as Herman Dooyeweerd and Eugen Rosenstock-Huessy have pointed out.

This mode of thinking has greatly affected theology and Christian religion. One effect has been to assist the widespread belief that we are living at the end of history and that Christ must come soon, a belief that has distorted the thinking of Christians for several generations. The fact that this belief is shown false decade after decade has not lessened its credibility, because men like to believe that no significant changes are to occur in the future; in fact, Christians will be "raptured" so as not to have to go through any such changes. Biblical prophecy is repeatedly reinterpreted in terms of contemporary events, phenomena, and

[9] The "golden age" of pagan thinking exists in the ur-time, a time different from ours, a time that is really heavenly and eternal in nature—very much like the "heavenly days" of the Klinean Frameworkers.

devices. Another legacy of this mode of thinking is the notion we have already examined, that nothing new remains to be discovered that will significantly alter current scientific constructs.

Still another effect of this mode of thinking is the notion that the way things are now is the way things have always been. Virtually all historical fiction, for instance, projects modern Western-type people back into historical times. The characters in such fiction think and act like modern people. Few are the authors who are able, or even willing, to try and think like people in other cultures.

Yet, if the future is unpredictable and certain to be different from our expectations, it follows that the past is quite different from the present. There is absolutely no "scientific" basis for the notion that the way things are now is how they have always been, and that is true whether we are considering the character of human society, the psychology of human beings, the behavior of animals, or the way the universe runs. Clearly things were different during the first two thousand years of human history in one respect at least: People lived much longer lives. It may well be that the universe functioned somewhat differently under the angelic administration of the Old Creation, before the change in the world in A.D. 70, when that creation was fully superseded by the humanly administered New Creation. It may well be that the "natural revelation" that impelled men to sacrifice animals under the Old Creation will impel men not to do so under the New.[10]

The only way we can know anything about the past is through historical study, in the broad sense: the study of the present-day relics of the past. For instance, we may know that right now there is a certain amount of carbon-14 that lodges itself in plants and then deteriorates, but we cannot know if the identical same conditions were in place

[10] I only offer these as possibilities, and please note that I write "*somewhat* differently."

in 1000 B.C.[11] We may know that right now the solar system has a certain configuration, but are we certain that it had exactly the same configuration four thousand years ago? Do we know that the earth turned on its axis at precisely the same rate four thousand years ago as today?[12]

Now, it may be a good working hypothesis to assume such continuities, though we cannot be certain of them. Indeed, we should assume a general kind of continuity based on God's faithfulness to His covenant. If, however, we have good evidence from the ancient world that things were different, we need to take that into consideration. For instance, it seems that comets were quite a bit more plentiful in ancient skies than today; the ancients had them categorized into as many as thirty different kinds.[13] It is also conceivable that comets did indeed appear as warnings of catastrophes in the ancient, angelically-governed skies, which is what all the ancients believed. Are we certain they were wrong?

Or again, the Bible (in Job) speaks of dinosaurs. Indeed, dragons and great lizards are found in stories all over

[11] "Unfortunately, [Carbon-14] calibration is not a simple matter—the amount of Carbon-14 in the atmosphere fluctuated greatly in the past, at times falling and then rising again significantly within a single century. . . . A notably complex period is the 'first-millennium B.C. radiocarbon disaster.' Between 400 and 800 B.C. the calibration curve is essentially flat, with calendar dates within that range all equivalent to a radiocarbon date of around 500 B.C." Peter James, et.al, *Centuries of Darkness: A Challenge to the Conventional Chronology of Old World Archaeology* (New Brunswick, NJ: Rutgers University Press, 1993) p. 325.

[12] The earth undergoes small shifts in its rotation as a result of tidal and other forces. See the various studies of astronomer Robert R. Newton of Johns Hopkins University, such as *Ancient Astronomical Observations and the Accelerations of the Earth and Moon* (Baltimore, MD: Johns Hopkins, 1970) and *The Moon's Accelerations* (Johns Hopkins, 1979).

[13] For citations from ancient authors, see Bruce J. Malina, *On the Genre and Message of Revelation: Star Visions and Sky Journeys* (Peabody, MA: Hendrickson Pub., 1995) pp. 112–116. My reference to this book is by no means to be understood as an endorsement of its general thesis.

the world. If all these people just coincidentally made these things up, it is curious that what they made up corresponds, at least generally, with bones not unearthed until the nineteeth century. But we moderns assume that (a) ancient people were primitive and stupid, and so they did not know what they were talking about when they spoke of great dragons; and (b) that our dating methods are sound. The bones "say" that they are millions of years old, so we ignore the testimony of the Bible and of other ancient literature.

The point of all this is that the past is not subject to the kinds of controls and observation that science requires. Interpreting the past involves guesswork to a far greater degree than observational science, and thus there is far more room for presuppositions and assumptions to play a role.

Which brings us back to Genesis 1. Is there any real evidence that the earth is older than the Bible seems to say it is? Is there any real evidence against the traditional view of Genesis 1? No. All there is against the idea of a recent creation is a series of scientific constructs, all based on the examination of present states of affairs. When science tries to speak of past or future things, it moves rapidly into constructs that are very much open to challenge.

Nature and Parable

There is, however, a further matter that needs to be discussed, and that is the parabolic character of revelation. Jesus states in Matthew 13 that He spoke in parables to enlighten the righteous and to confuse the unrighteous. What is said of the parables is true, in a wider way, of the entire Word of God. Those who study the Bible apart from faith are invariably and inescapably led to wrong conclusions, as the Jehovah's Witnesses and Higher Critics demonstrate. To take a pregnant example: God revealed His power and nature to Pharaoh in a whole series of extraordinary miracles, yet Pharaoh did not perceive the reality of the situation at all.

If creational revelation is truly revelation, then it partakes of this same parabolic character. We should not, and must not, expect the creation (nature) to "speak clearly" to the unbeliever. Like the written Word, the "natural Word" of God will mislead the faithless. Ultimately, such distortions come about because of the sinful heart-orientation of man, but it is important to understand that the creation is designed in such a way that it does not yield its character—its secrets so to speak—to unbelief. The fact that unbelieving "science" does not perceive the true nature of the universe is, thus, not surprising, and when Christians operate on the same premises as unbelievers, they will not perceive it aright either.

As the various works of Stanley Jaki demonstrate, true science arose in Christian civilization for the reason that only Christians can understand creation rightly. Not all do, of course, but only Christians and those working in a Christian framework are able to do so. The rejection of Christian worldview in "modern science" naturally leads to radical misreadings of the book of nature. Creational revelation is no more "neutral" than the Bible.

Collins seems to start with the assumption that God will not mislead any who look at the creation, but since God has said that He will and does mislead people through His Word, Collins's assumption needs refinement and/or alteration.

Natural Revelation and Sin

Finally, the point needs to be made that sinful man will instinctively misinterpret the data of creation. Sinful man is motivated at the root of his being to distort anything that forces him to come face to face with God. If the creation took place suddenly and recently, God cannot be avoided. The supposition of long evolutionary ages pushes into the shadows any god there might be. Such a god does not speak or act directly; he (it) just sets things in motion.

The degree to which our modern scientific constructs are the result of this overwhelming desire to evade God is evident when we compare those constructs with the testimony of the Bible.

Nor are such distortions always the relatively innocent actions of a deep-rooted dread of God. The considerable amount of sheer fakery that goes on in scientific research has finally begun to receive attention. Such fakery results from the desire to prove a theory, the need to "publish or perish," the lust for fame, but it also results sometimes from a desire to squelch anything that might give aid and comfort to the creationist enemy.

One aspect of this sinful suppression of natural revelation is, perhaps, preeminently important for our consideration, and that is this: Sinful man wants to ascribe to nature the power to make and remake the world. This is because Adam placed himself in subjection to a beast in the beginning, thereby making the lower creation his god. "Mother Nature" and "Natural Law" thus replace the Creator in the thinking of sinful man. The universe becomes self-creating and self-maintaining.

The other side of this is that God and His direct interaction with the cosmos and with humanity is denied, or pushed far, far into the background. Now, practically speaking, the result of this is that sinful man asserts that exceedingly long time processes are necessary for any creative (positive) change in the world and in humanity, and this occurs in the face of pervasive evidence to the contrary.

Some examples will clarify. A couple of years ago, a large hurricane washed away most of the sand dunes in the area of Destin, Florida, very near to where I live. Reports said that it would take a century for the dunes to rebuild. In fact, we already have many high dunes, and the rest of the beach is rapidly recovering. It will take no more than a decade for the beach to look as it did.

Twenty or so years ago, it was said that Lake Erie was virtually dead because of pollution. It would take centuries, maybe millennia, for it to recover, we were told. But only a few years after pollution reform, it was once again abundant with life.

We are told that it takes a long time for civilizations to form and grow. In fact, revivals of religion have produced virtually instantaneous changes in cultures, while wholesale apostasies have destroyed civilizations overnight. Tribal people usually shift from being peaceful villagers to being roaming warriors every few generations, but you would not know it from the way they are usually presented.

I recall a television special about a tiny group of people living in the jungle of Indonesia (I think that was the place; maybe it was the Philippines), called "the gentle Tasudai" (I'm not sure of the spelling). The reporters told us that anthropologists believed these people had lived in isolation from the rest of humanity for thousands of years. There were only about twenty or thirty of them, and they gave evidence to my eyes of being quite feebleminded. I believe these people had probably left some other tribe or village about half a century earlier, and had lived in the woods since. That's just common sense. But it is not what sinful man wants to believe.

In short, the world changes far more rapidly than modern historians, anthropologists, paleontologists, biologists, and geologists maintain it does. They maintain these huge spans of time in the face of the evidence because their belief in the immanent power of nature to be self-creating requires it. Belief in the necessity of huge spans of time is a way of suppressing the evidence that God and nature work together rapidly; it is a way of suppressing the fact of God. Substituting long spans of time for the power of God is a way of evading and suppressing man's innate knowledge of God and his fear of God's judgment. Compared to other world religions and cultures, biblical religion and only biblical religion insists on a short time span for the world and for human cultures.

Conclusion

I have wandered rather far from Collins's modest remarks about the challenge of science to biblical interpretation. I have done so in the interest of showing, however briefly and cursorily, that the challenge of science is nowhere near as impressive as many evangelicals seem to think it is. These studies have repeatedly shown that Genesis 1 cannot rightly be interpreted other than the traditional way, and such is the major concern of our studies. These remarks on science have been by way of an extended footnote.

Chapter 7

The Limited Geography Interpretation of John Sailhamer

John Sailhamer, *Genesis Unbound: A Provocative New Look at the Creation Account* (Portland, OR: Multnomah Press, 1996).

Dr. John Sailhamer is Professor of Old Testament at Western Seminary in Portland, Oregon. Sailhamer is an evangelical, Bible-believing Christian (as are all those with whom we are interacting in this book). He is a respected scholar who has served as Professor of Old Testament and Semitic Languages at Trinity Evangelical Divinity School and also on translation committees for two recent Bible translations.

In *Genesis Unbound*, Sailhamer advocates the notion that the creation account in Genesis 1 is a record of the preparation of the Garden of Eden, which he maintains is the land of Canaan, not a record of the preparation of the whole earth. *Genesis Unbound* is courteously written and undogmatic; Sailhamer is setting forth his interpretive hypothesis for the larger Christian community to examine.

In brief, Sailhamer proposes that Genesis 1:1 tells us that God created the heavens and the earth at some time in the past. We don't know when, and it might have been millions or billions of years ago. Then Genesis 1 continues by telling us that in the recent past, God spent six 24-hour days working miracles to prepare the land of Eden (Canaan) and its Garden for Adam and Eve to live in. Thus, Sailhamer's thesis offers a new and interesting resolution of the conflict between modern science and biblical revelation.

Sailhamer points out that his approach is not quite brand new. He writes, "The medieval Jewish commentator Rashi understood most of the account of Genesis 1 as a direct reference to God's preparation of the promised land." He goes on to point out, though, that the Rashi had an axe to grind. This was the time of the crusades, when the question of who had the right to Palestine was crucial. The Rashi wanted to make the case that God created the promised land (Eden = Palestine, for him) and gave it to the Jews (Sailhamer, p. 215).[1] According to Sailhamer, the Rashi was followed later on by the eminent Puritan-era scholar John Lightfoot (p. 216).

A fuller discussion of the history of this view is desirable. I don't have the resources to check out the little information Sailhamer provides, but my Jewish commentaries make no mention of this approach. The lengthy (2232 pp.) ArtScroll Tanach Series commentary on Genesis does not mention it, though it summarizes what all the preeminent rabbis, including the Rashi, have to say about every topic.[2] The great orthodox Jewish commentator Samson Raphael Hirsch makes no mention of this view, and neither does the great modern Jewish commentator Umberto Cassuto.

Now, Sailhamer does not imply that his view is found commonly in Jewish commentaries. It appears, however, that nobody but the Rashi and possibly Ibn Ezra (Abraham ben Meir) ever held this view. Certainly the rabbinic community over the ages has not been impressed with it, since

[1] RASHI is an acronym formed from the initials of RAbbi SHlomo Izchaki, or in English, Rabbi Solomon ben Isaac, 1040–1105. Thus, "the Rashi" is "the Rabbi Solomon ben Isaac."

[2] See Meir Zlotowitz, *Bereshis: Genesis: A New Translation with a Commentary Anthologized from Talmudic, Midrashic, and Rabbinic Sources* (Brooklyn: Mesorah Publications, 1977).

they don't even take it up as a possibility.

There are two ways we can proceed in dealing with *Genesis Unbound*. One is to take up a few crucial arguments presented in the book and discuss them. The other is to take up the book at length. I have opted for the latter, because Sailhamer's approach is new, different, and intriguing, and I think will prove attractive.

Sailhamer takes Genesis 1 literally as a series of miraculous events over the course of six days. He does this by limiting the geography of Genesis 1 to Eden-Palestine (which he equates). Since, according to him, Genesis 1 is not concerned with the creation of the universe, there is no apparent conflict between most modern scientific hypotheses and the Bible.

Moreover, Sailhamer is a noted scholar. His arguments will look very good to those not equipped to think them through. His book is popularly written, presented in friendly paperback rather than intimidating hardcover, with footnotes carefully hidden from view in the back of the book, and published by a respected and well-distributed evangelical publishing house. The opening pages of the book contain (carefully guarded) statements of recommendation from numerous evangelical scholars. For all these reasons, I think a detailed analysis is warranted.

Also, covering Sailhamer's book in detail allows me to set forth some detailed arguments that I shall build upon in the next chapter, which contains what I submit is an accurate reading of Genesis 1. Thus, the present critical discussions form a transition to my positive presentation in chapter eight.

In the Beginning

After two introductory chapters, Sailhamer begins his exposition of Genesis 1 with chapter three, entitled "In the Beginning." He argues that the word "beginning" does not mean a point of time but a period of time. From this he argues that the "beginning" may have lasted millions or billions or even googols of years before the work of six days that follows in Genesis 1. Let us now consider his arguments.

He writes:

> The Hebrew word *reshit*, which is the term for "beginning" used in this chapter, has a very specific sense in Scripture. In the Bible the term always refers to an extended, yet indeterminate duration of time, *not* a specific moment. It is a block of time which precedes an extended series of time periods. It is a "time before time." The term does not refer to a point in time but to a *period* or *duration* of time which falls before a series. (p. 38, emphasis his)

As evidence for this, Sailhamer points to Job 8:7, where "beginning" refers to the earlier part of Job's life before disasters overtake him. Also, he points out that the first year of a king's reign is counted from the official beginning of the year, and he states that the time between the death of the previous king and that official date is the "beginning" of the new king's reign.

Sailhamer also argues that if a particular point in time were meant by "beginning" in Genesis 1:1, a different word would have been used: "The author could have used a Hebrew word for 'beginning' similar to the English word 'start' or 'initial point' (for example, *rishonah* or *techillah*)" (p. 41).

Finally, Sailhamer softens his argument just a bit when he writes, concerning a point-beginning, "Such a concept, however, is not likely to be connected with *reshit*, the Hebrew word actually used in Genesis 1:1" (p. 42). That is, a point-beginning might indeed be connected with *reshit*, but it is "not likely."

Now, what shall we make of this? At the outset I think it is significant that none of the numerous exegetical commentaries available to me make any mention of this matter. Nor do Hebrew lexicons and theological lexicons. It does not seem to have occurred to anyone else that *reshit* has to mean a period of time rather than a point of time. By itself, of course, this does not make Sailhamer wrong, but it does mean that the burden of proof is on him to make his case. Unhappily, it seems that the popular style of his book has excluded the kind of extended technical argumentation that is precisely needed at this point.

First, while *reshit* is sometimes used for a period of time at the beginning of something, it is also used (contrary to Sailhamer) for a point-beginning, as in Deuteronomy 11:12, ". . . a land concerning which Yahweh your God is caring for her continually. The eyes of Yahweh your God are on her from year's beginning even to year's end." The (lunar) years in Israel had a definite beginning on the first day of the first month and a definite end on the last day of the last month.

Thus, it is context that determines the precise nature of the "beginning" spoken of. In Genesis 1:1, the "beginning" is the creation "out of nothing" of the cosmic heavens and earth, as Sailhamer himself argues. Moreover, Sailhamer himself argues that "create" is a unique, instant act of God (pp. 247–250). Thus, it would seem that the "beginning" in Genesis 1:1 has to be a point of time, not a period of time.

Now, while I did not find Sailhamer saying it in these precise words anywhere in his book, it seems that his view is this: During the age of "beginning," God did a number of miraculous instant actions. At some point, for instance, God "created" the animals (see his chapter fourteen). Thus, a Sailhamer-esque paraphrase of Genesis 1:1 might be, "During the beginning period, God created all the things in heaven and on earth." As I have pointed out, however, we have as yet found no compelling reason to insist that the "beginning" must be a period of time.

Second, while *reshit* can be used for a period of time at the beginning of someone's life or reign, I do not find any place where it clearly refers to the year zero of a king. The few times it is used for the "beginning" of the reign of a king, nothing indicates that this precise time period is in view (Jer. 26:1; 27:1; 28:1; 49:34). In fact, as Sailhamer has to admit, Jeremiah 28:1 speaks of the fourth year of Zedekiah as part of the "beginning" of his reign. Now, Sailhamer makes a great deal out of his argument here. He says that the "beginning" of the king's reign is an indeterminate period, which is followed by numbered years. He makes this an analogy to Genesis 1, an indeterminate period followed by numbered days. But there is no evidence I can find that the Bible uses "beginning" this way with regard to the kings—quite the opposite: Zedekiah's fourth (numbered) year was within his beginning period. Sailhamer provides no citations to support his assertion. Thus, I submit that he is simply wrong in this argument.

Third, Sailhamer is correct that if all Genesis 1:1 wanted to say is that God created the heavens and earth at a point in time at the beginning, *rishon* or *techillah* would have been better. But that does not mean that *reshit* was used to indicate a period of time. In fact, unlike these other two words, *reshit* can also mean "first" in the sense of "chief," "the principal thing," or "firstfruits." Now, it would be wrong to translate Genesis 1:1 as "The chief thing God created was the heavens and the earth," because the preposition "in" tells us that we are speaking of time. But it seems clear that the author of Genesis 1:1 wants us to understand that not only did God make the universe at the beginning of time, but also this act was the fountain from which everything else flowed. Thus, *reshit* rather than one of the other words was used.

Let me expand on this observation. *Reshit* is used, I suggest, because of its connection to firstfruits. The firstfruits were brought before God on the Sunday after Passover, the same day as God created the heavens and earth (Ex. 23:19; Lev. 2:12; 23:9–14). Exodus 20:9–11 says that God worked for a week to set a pattern for His image, humanity. The law of firstfruits tells that the first part of our labor, done on the first day of the week, so to speak, is to be given to God. Only after we have given the first part to God may we eat of the rest of the harvest of our labors. This, I submit, is the true analogy to Genesis 1:1. Man acknowledges God's supremacy by giving God his firstfruits. Man's firstfruits signify the whole "heaven and earth" produced by man, God's image. Note that Adam was created on the sixth day, and the next was the sabbath. His small works of the sixth day were his firstfruits, which he should have dedicated to God on the seventh. Specifically, he should have dedicated Eve to God instead of to Satan, which he did by standing silently and letting the serpent seduce her. Eve, coming from Adam's side, was his firstfruit. The heavens and the earth, made by God in the beginning, was His firstfruit. Man offers his firstfruits to God. God the Father offers His to His Son, and the Son offers His back to the Father. Indeed, by creating the world and then putting humanity in charge of it, God amazingly offers His firstfruits to *us!* The use of *reshit* in Genesis 1:1 sets up this understanding and fully accounts for why *reshit* rather than some other word is used here. Thus, one dimension of Genesis 1:1 would be "As the firstfruits of His creation, God made the heavens and the earth." This, however, is a secondary implication of the use of *reshit* in Genesis 1:1, because the preposition "in" clearly implies time and temporal sequence.

To sum up, *reshit* is not used in Genesis 1:1 because the writer wanted a word that implies a period of time. Rather, it is used because the writer wanted a word that implies firstfruits.

Finally, if Sailhamer were correct that "in the beginning" refers to a period of time, I really don't see why that time cannot include the six days as well. As mentioned above, Sailhamer does not prove that a "beginning" is a time before a numbered sequence. Thus, on *his* presuppositions, I submit that the "beginning" might just as well include the six days—in which case the six days are at the beginning of time.

In conclusion, Sailhamer argues that the word translated "beginning" always refers to an indeterminate period of time before other events. We have seen that this is not the case. He also argues that if a point of time were meant by "beginning" in Genesis 1:1, certain other words would be better. We have seen that this would be true *if* all Genesis 1:1 meant to communicate was the idea of an instant beginning. In fact, however, the author chose *reshit* because of its broader nuances of meaning. Finally, since it is the creation "out of nothing" that is being spoken of in Genesis 1:1, there really can be no doubt that an instant event, the first event in time and history, is in view.

The Land

Sailhamer begins chapter four of his book with a discussion of the word for "earth" or "land" used in Genesis 1, the Hebrew word *'erets*. What he argues is that the "earth" in Genesis 1:1 refers to the whole cosmos apart from the angelic heavens. Then in verse 2 he argues that the meaning of "earth" shifts to a particular land, the promised land, which is Eden.

He begins by warning us not to read Genesis 1 in modern terms. The "earth" in Genesis 1 is not planet earth as opposed to the other planets and the sun and stars. Rather, the "earth" in Genesis 1 is the habitable land, as opposed to the seas (and, I might add, to the wilderness). The word *'erets* or "habitable land" can be used for the whole world or for the particular land of a particular people. With all of this we have no quarrel.

Then Sailhamer gets to his main thesis, which is that the "earth, land" of Genesis 1:2ff refers to the particular land of Eden, which he submits is also the promised land, today called Palestine. He presents four arguments.

First, he says that "the close relationship between the first two chapters of Genesis supports a localized view of the 'land'" (p. 50ff). He states that Genesis 1 and 2 are about the same events and have the same setting but are from differing perspectives. No argument is presented for this; Sailhamer simply asserts it at this point. In chapter eight of his book, however, Sailhamer presents his arguments; we shall get to them in due course. For now, let us allow Sailhamer to direct the flow of presentation, with one comment: It is certainly correct that Genesis 1 and 2 are quite closely related and are parallels. But I shall argue that the parallel is not one of identity but of analogy: The microcosm of Genesis 2 is a copy of the macrocosm of Genesis 1.

Second, Sailhamer argues that the original land was west of Babylon, and thus was Palestine. He starts in Genesis 11:1, where the whole "earth/land" had the same language. The next verse says that as "they" journeyed east, they came to Shinar and built Babel there. Sailhamer believes that those who built Babel, the "they," are the same as "the whole earth/land" of verse 1. But there are good reasons not to agree with him here. Just four verses earlier, in 10:30, we read of certain Hebrews who moved east. Ignoring the chapter break, which is not part of God's Word but was added by men, we can easily see that those who were journeying east were these Joktanite Hebrews. Arriving in Shinar, they joined with Nimrod's Cushites and built Babel (10:8–10).

Genesis 11:1 means that all human beings descended from Noah; all people on the earth had the same religion[3] and the same language ("set of words"). The Hebrews were representatives of the human race, being the direct carriers of the religion-bearing responsibility assigned to Shem (9:26; 10:21). The rebellion of these Hebrews at Babel had consequences for the whole race of mankind, just as Adam's original sin did. It is in this context that God calls

[3] "One lip," usually mistranslated "language"; the Hebrew *shaphah* means "religious confession," not simply language as such.

a faithful Hebrew, Abram, to carry on the task of Shem and Eber (Hebrew).[4]

Sailhamer proposes that the "whole earth" of 11:1 is a "whole land of people," and these people moved east to Babylon. Where did they come from, he asks? Well, to the west is Palestine, so that is where they originated. He then goes back to Genesis 3:24 and 4:16 to show that movement away from God is signified by and originally manifested as eastward movement. Now, this is very true, but it does not in the least indicate that the movement is away from Palestine, or that Palestine is Eden. The Ark landed, after all, in the mountains of Ararat, which are not in Palestine. Thus, what area these people came from as they journeyed east cannot be ascertained. But even if we could be sure that they came from the region of Palestine, that would not show that the pre-flood land of Eden had the same location.

Third, Sailhamer says that one of the major themes of the Pentateuch (the first five books of the Bible) is God's gift of the promised land to His people. If we really grasp this, he says, it will make sense that Eden was that same land. Moses has the promised land in view as he writes Genesis 1–2, Sailhamer assumes. But this is highly unlikely. Genesis 1–11 does not concern the priestly people of Israel, who are given the promised land, but the universal history of humanity. To be sure, the promise of a garden-land is important in both histories, but that they must be the same location is not important. Noah planted a vineyard after the Flood, a new version of the original Garden planted by God. Was this in Palestine also, or in the region of Ararat?

Moreover, we must challenge the notion that "Moses wrote Genesis with the Sinai covenant in view." Sailhamer

[4] For an extensive discussion of this matter, see my essay, "Babylon and the Babel Project," in *Studies in the Revelation* Nos. 11–12 (1996; available from Biblical Horizons, P.O. Box 1096, Niceville, FL 32588).

spells out this view on page 87, where he asserts: "The writer of the Pentateuch wrote Genesis 1 primarily because he wanted his readers to understand something about God and the nature of the covenant He made with Israel at Mt. Sinai. At the center of that covenant was the promise of a homeland for His people (Deut. 5:32–33). Already in the first chapter of the Pentateuch the author directs the readers to God's concern for that land." I can only assume that by "the writer" Sailhamer means Moses.

Yet nowhere does the Bible ever say that Moses wrote Genesis. It was part of the corpus of five books that Moses put in the Tabernacle, but he is never said to have been its author. I suggest that Joseph wrote Genesis. Moses may have edited it somewhat, but the likely author is Joseph, as I've argued previously. And who can say I am wrong?[5] There is no evidence either way. Thus, we must not assume that Genesis was written at Mount Sinai, or that the Sinaitic covenant was directly in view in the writing of Genesis. There is simply no reason to believe such a thing.

And even if Moses did write Genesis, we have no grounds for assuming that he wrote it with the Sinaitic covenant directly in view. To be sure, the history recorded in Genesis lays the foundation for later events (though it is well-rounded and complete in itself, ending with the entire world coming to Joseph for food and thus presenting a very positive picture of a restored Edenic food-garden, the kingdom of God). And certainly, *if* Moses wrote Genesis, the later events would be in the back of his mind. But to assert that Mount Sinai is in the foreground of the meaning of Genesis is to assert something for which there is simply no evidence.

Fourth and finally, Sailhamer says that later passages of Scripture assume that Eden is the Promised Land. He begins

[5] Joseph probably used earlier records in composing Genesis, which then was the Bible for the Hebrews while they were in Egypt, a Bible full of promises for them to grasp and pray about. See chapter two for a fuller discussion of the authorship of Genesis 1.

with a very serious misinterpretation of Jeremiah 27:5–6, which reads:

> [5]I have made the earth/land, the men and the beasts which are on the face of the earth/land, by My great power and by My outstretched arm, and I give it to the one who is upright in My sight. [6]And now I have given all these earths/lands into the hand of Nebuchadnezzar king of Babylon, My servant, and I have given him also the wild animals of the field to serve him.

Now, Sailhamer rightly points out that "all these lands" refers in context to Edom, Moab, Ammon, Tyre, and Sidon in Jeremiah 27:3. But he also asserts that "the earth/land" of verse 5 must refer to the land of Israel. If it referred to the whole earth, he argues, it would be an error, for surely God did not give the whole earth to Nebuchadnezzar.

Yet verse 5 does not say that the whole earth is to be given to Nebuchadnezzar. It only says that God disposes of the earth and gives it to whomever He pleases. In fact, "the one who is upright in My sight" must ultimately be Jesus, and He does indeed receive the whole earth. In other words, verse 5 establishes the principle that God is Lord over all the earth, and verse 6 says that certain parts of the earth, certain lands, are given to Nebuchadnezzar.

Moreover, contrary to Sailhamer's argument, verse 7 immediately goes on to say this: "And all the nations shall serve him, and his son, and his grandson, until the time of his own land comes; then many nations and great kings will enslave him." So, it would seem that in a sense God *did* give all the lands of the earth to Nebuchadnezzar—at least all the earth on the horizon of the chosen people of that time.

Thus, Sailhamer's attempt to force Jeremiah 27:5 to refer to the land of promise, and also to Eden and also to Genesis 1, is completely without foundation. It is not the land of Judah that is in view at all, rather it is the whole earth.

Sailhamer also refers to the promises that the people will "return to Eden" after the exile (Is. 51:3; Ezek. 36:35; Joel 2:3) as evidence that Eden and the Promised Land are in the same location. But this is to mistake symbolic language for literal, historical language. Exodus 15:17 says that the Promised Land is a new Eden planted by God, but that does not mean that the Promised Land is in the same location as the original Eden.

Conclusion: Sailhamer has failed to present even a prima facie case for thinking that the location of Eden was the same as that of Canaan. For all I know, of course, they might have been the same, but our author has given us no sound arguments for making such an identification.[6]

The Edenic River(s)

Sailhamer returns to the matter of Eden and Palestine in chapter six of his book. He argues that the four rivers of Genesis 2:10–14 form the boundaries of the land of Eden and that these are also the boundaries of the Promised Land (p. 72). There are two problems with this.

First, the Promised Land extended only to the Euphrates River on the east, but the Tigris is mentioned also in Genesis 2:14, and it is to the east of the Euphrates. The area between the Euphrates and the Tigris was *not* part of the Promised Land.

Second, the text of Genesis 2:10 specifically states that the four rivers were *not* the boundaries of Eden or of the Garden of Eden. "And a river was flowing from [the land of] Eden to water the Garden, and *from there* it divided and it became four headwaters." These rivers carried Edenic waters *out* of the Garden to four locations, signifying we may suppose the four corners of the earth.

Thus, it would seem that the land of Eden *cannot* be

[6] I must say, however, that linking Eden with Canaan makes a whale of a lot more sense than trying to link it with Mesopotamia, which is what is most often done. For an example of this kind of thing, see appendix D.

the same as the Promised Land. If we draw back the present lines of the Tigris and Euphrates to a common source, we wind up in the region of Ararat, whence Noah began the second world. This would seem to be the location of Eden as well, on high ground whence rivers arise and down from which they flow.

An Eden in Ararat or Turkey receives further evidence from the other two rivers. Sailhamer says that the Pishon, which is mentioned first, cannot be located because the land of Havilah whither it flowed cannot be located for certain. But there seems to be little doubt but that Havilah is somewhere in Arabia, likely in the Sinai Peninsula, due south of Canaan. This emerges from Genesis 15:18 and 1 Samuel 15:7, because the land of Shur is on the east side of Egypt. Accordingly, the Pishon is the Jordan river before it was stopped up by the Dead Sea at the destruction of Sodom and Gomorrah. It was while in Havilah that Israel found the bdellium-colored manna and the gold and onyx used to built the Tabernacle and the High Priestly garments (Gen. 2:12; Ex. 25:7; 28:9–12; Num. 11:7).

Similarly, since the Gihon went down to Cush (Ethiopia), it ran parallel to the Jordan and east thereof. This river no longer seems to exist after the Flood.

At any rate, if we draw lines from the Jordan northward to where it would intersect the lines drawn from the Tigris and Euphrates, we come to Turkey, Armenia, or the region of Ararat.[7] I cannot, of course, be absolutely certain of the region of Ararat, but it is certain that Sailhamer has not successfully made a case for the land of Eden being the land of promise.

Moreover, one might just as well make a case for Lebanon as Eden. The garden in Canticles is clearly an extension of the original Garden, a restoration and a historical advancement and transformation thereof. I don't think any-

[7] For more on this, see my book *Through New Eyes: Developing a Biblical View of the World* (Eugene, OR: Wipf & Stock, [1988] 1999).

one disputes this. In Canticles 4:15, we read of "a garden spring, a well of living water, and streams from Lebanon." Trace the Jordan northward and you immediately come to the mountains of Lebanon. As Eden was the source for the river in the Garden, so Lebanon is the source of the river in Solomon's garden. A study of the relationship of Lebanon to Solomon's garden in Canticles will only confirm this analogy. The same kind of relationship is seen in Ezekiel 31:3–9. Now, I am not arguing that Lebanon was the location of the original land of Eden. I am only pointing out another and different symbolical-literary association with Eden that is found in the Bible. If we are going to follow Sailhamer's mistaken attempt to turn these symbolic associations into geographical verities, Lebanon is as good a candidate as Canaan.

I may add that in this chapter and the ones that follow (chapters six and seven), Sailhamer points out some significant correlations between the land of Eden and the promised land, and between the Garden of Eden and the Tabernacle. There are many, many such correlations, but they are thematic and theological, not geographical. It is abundantly clear that the promised land is a new Eden and the Tabernacle courtyard a new garden, but these relationships say absolutely nothing about historical geography. They are irrelevant to Sailhamer's case. To be sure, these correlations can fit his case, but they fit just as well without his attempt to link Eden and Canaan geographically.

Heavens and Earth

Back to chapter four of his book: Sailhamer argues that ordinarily the word "heaven" means "sky." This is quite true. He then argues that the phrase "heavens and earth" is a unit and means "the whole universe." Granting his point for the sake of argument, we then follow him to the assertion that since God made heavens and earth in Genesis 1:1, He also made the sun, moon, and stars then, because they are in the heavens (pp. 57–58). Later on, he will argue that

God also made all plants and animals in Genesis 1:1, "in the beginning period."

I see two major problems with this. First, if Sailhamer wants to say that God made everything during the "beginning period," then that must include man as well. Accordingly, the man put into the Garden (Canaan) in Genesis 2 may have been a special man, but there were already men around. Ah, but it turns out that Sailhamer wants to make an exception for mankind. He wants to say that God made everything except man during the "beginning period." But there is absolutely no way Sailhamer can have it both ways. If God made the first man on the sixth day, then He made the first fish on the fifth day, and the sun on the fourth day. If God made "everything" during the "beginning period," then man was also made then. Exegetically and logically, Sailhamer has no grounds for making man an exception to his scheme.

Second, Sailhamer seems to think that the heaven of Genesis 1:1 is the same as the heavens where the sun is located. But Genesis 1:8 says that there is a second heaven, the firmament heaven, and verse 14 says that the sun is located in this second heaven.

Moreover, if Sailhamer is correct, so that the heaven created in Genesis 1:1 is just the sky above, then what about the angelic heaven? When was it made? That there is such a place, and that it is not the starry universe, is clear from many passages of Scripture, and it has always been assumed that its creation is given in Genesis 1:1.

Yet it seems that Sailhamer would want to include the angelic heaven in Genesis 1:1, since he tells us that the phrase "heaven and earth" means "everything." But if the angelic heaven is in view in Genesis 1:1, then nothing is implied about the sun, moon, and stars, for these are not part of the angelic heaven.

The traditional view is quite clear and simple. In Genesis 1:1, God made the angelic heavens and the cosmos. This original "earth" was undifferentiated, but God acted to separate this original "earth" into sky, sea, and land/earth. We now have two heavens and two earths: the original angelic heaven and the new sky-heaven within the cosmos, and the original cosmic earth and the new land-earth within the cosmos. These parallels emerge from a simple reading of the text. After the fall of man, we also have two seas: the sea within the cosmos, and the abyss of hell. Thus, we can diagram it this way:

HEAVEN	
	sky – heaven
EARTH	land – earth
	sea – deep
ABYSS	

Sky, land, and sea are parts of the EARTH that correspond to the greater HEAVEN, EARTH, and ABYSS.

In conclusion, Sailhamer seems confused about what the original heavens and earth included. Did they include the angelic heaven or not? Is the later sky-heaven part of the original heaven or part of the original earth? Perhaps Sailhamer will be able to untangle this for us as we go along. At this point, his case is more and more unconvincing.

Formless and Void

Let us move on and see if Sailhamer can rescue his thesis with other information and arguments.

In chapters five and twenty-one of his book, Sailhamer argues that the phrase "without form and void" is a mistranslation. He states that this mistranslation goes back to attempt to accommodate the biblical account with pagan notions of a primeval chaos. The pagans believe that originally there was an unformed mass of material in existence, which the gods or the demiurge then worked over to bring the present ordered cosmos into existence. Sailhamer thinks that many early translators were operating with this kind of thinking in their background and that they set in motion an erroneous tradition of translation that still warps our English versions today.

Sailhamer asserts that the Hebrew phrase *tohu wabohu*, rendered "without form and empty," actually means nothing more than "wilderness." And as such, the reference is to a particular spot on the earth, which God makes into the fruitful land of Eden. So, what is the nuance of the term in Genesis 1:2? Sailhamer and some commentators take it as defined by the following term, with which it is paired. *Bohu* means empty. So the phrase means "very empty" or "a total wilderness."[8]

The big problem with this approach, which Sailhamer does not even mention, is that Genesis 1 rather obviously follows an outline set up in 1:2. The earth is formless, empty, and dark. This sets up the discussion that follows, to wit:

First, God takes care of the darkness problem by creating light.

Second, God takes care of the formless problem by separating waters above and below and putting the firmament between them, and then by separating land and sea. These actions take place on days 2 and 3a and are linked not only thematically but by the fact that the situation is not pronounced good until the second act of forming is completed on day 3a.

Third, God takes care of the emptiness problem by creating grain plants and fruit trees on day 3b.

Fourth, God refines His solution to the darkness problem by creating the sun, moon, and stars on day 4.

Thus, days 2–4 take up in series the three problems outlined in 1:2. Then, days 5–7 show God blessing various parts of the world He has organized.

Accordingly, the passage itself explains what is meant by *tohu wabohu*, and it means just what the traditional translations say it means: formless and empty.

There is no need to see the original formlessness of

[8] For a full discussion of this error, see chapter two.

the earth as a primeval chaos. There was already some shape to the creation, because the land was under water, and there was some kind of space above the water even then. For God's purposes, however, the world was without form, or formless.

This formlessness seems to have particular relevance to the sea. Originally the sea covered the land. Then God took part of the sea into the angelic heaven and put the rest of it below the land (i.e., lower than the land).[9] The filling seems to have particular reference to the land (day 3b), and the lightening seems to have particular relevance to the heaven or sky (day 4).

Now I really do have to complain against Sailhamer here. Virtually every discussion of Genesis 1 takes up the "forming and filling" aspects of the passage. True, few seem to see that there are three problems, not just two, in Genesis 1:2. But apart from that, Sailhamer has to know that the usual interpretation distinguishes the problems of formlessness and emptiness—yet he does not discuss this interpretation at all. He simply leaps to the conclusion that a "wilderness" is all that is in view, and then he uses this to argue for his notion that only the land of promise is in view in Genesis 1.

Thus, Sailhamer does not make a case for his position at all. He simply asserts it. He ignores the strong case against it. Even though this is a popularly-written book, there is simply no excuse for this omission.

In conclusion, Genesis 1 as a whole makes very clear that the traditional translation, "formless and empty" is quite correct. Sailhamer's contention that nothing more than an empty wilderness is in view here is without foundation.

[9] On the firmament and the heavenly sea, see the discussions later in this chapter and in chapter eight and appendix C.

Narrative Relationships

In his chapter eight, Sailhamer states that "the relationship between Genesis 1 and 2 follows a common pattern seen throughout the further narratives of the primeval history (Gen. 1–11). The author often links two distinct narratives to reflect a specific textual strategy. For example, after a narrative with a general description of an event, the author often attaches one which gives more detail about the same event. Having described the dispersion of the nations 'according to their languages and countries' in Genesis 10, the author attaches the story of the city of Babylon (Tower of Babel) in Genesis 11:1–9 to explain the origin of their different languages" (p. 91). Sailhamer then argues that the general description in Genesis 1 is followed up with a "closeup" description of creation in Genesis 2.

Now, Sailhamer's general statement is correct. We do indeed see in the Bible sometimes a more general summary of an event followed by a more detailed narrative. The problem with his assertion is that Genesis 2 may be specifying Genesis 1 in a way different from what Sailhamer asserts. Traditionally (and correctly, I submit), Genesis 2 is seen as an expansion of the sixth day of Genesis 1. Thus, by itself, Sailhamer's observation does nothing to prove or even hint that his view of Genesis 1 is correct.

Now as a matter of fact, Genesis 2–3 does recapitulate Genesis 1, but this occurs at a microcosmic level. What Genesis 1 says about the entire earth is repeated with reference to man, Eden, and the Garden. This can be seen in that the structure of the two passages is the same, the second building on the first. To wit:[10] Genesis 2:4 is parallel to Genesis 1:1.

[10] A discussion of these parallels can be found in Jacques B. Doukhan, *The Genesis Creation Story: Its Literary Structure*. Andrews University Seminary Doctoral Dissertation Series 5 (Berrien Springs, MI: Andrews University Press, 1978). I do not entirely agree with Doukhan's arrangement.

In Genesis 2:5–7 we find that the earth is said to be empty of plants and shrubs "of the field." That is, the earth is formless, because the distinction between garden and field has not yet been established, and void because of the absence of these plants. The earth is also covered with water, in the form of streams that water "the entire surface of the ground." Then, as God made light in Genesis 1:2, so God makes man to be light-bearer and governor in Genesis 2:7.

On day 2, God set up the firmament to separate waters from waters, and on day 3 He made the land appear and put food-plants on it. Genesis 2:8–14 speaks of the Garden and its food-plants, and of the land that arises in the center of the world. (Since the rivers flowed out of Eden to water the whole earth, Eden is the highest point on earth.) Thus Genesis 2:8–14 *seems* to be a recap of day 3.

Actually, however, we should see the Garden of Eden as the place where man the light-bearer is placed, so that the Garden corresponds to the firmament heavens that were set up on day 2, and into which the sun, moon, and stars were placed on day 4. Later on in the Bible, the Garden-sanctuary is associated with the firmament.[11] The Garden is between the Land of Eden and the rest of the world, since the river arises in Eden, and thus the Edenic Plateau was higher than the Garden. Similarly, the firmament is between the highest heaven and the cosmos.

So, Genesis 2:5–7 recaps day 1, 2:8 recaps day 2, and 2:9–14 recaps day 3. Then in Genesis 2:15–17 God puts the man in the Garden of Eden to dress it and to guard it. Guarding involves separation and distinction, since the man has to know what to guard against. He must guard his own heart against disobedience, and as we shall see, he must guard the Garden against invasion. God tells him to distin-

[11] I have set out many of these associations in *Through New Eyes*. See also Vern S. Poythress, *The Shadow of Christ in the Law of Moses* (Phillipsburg, NJ: Presbyterian & Reformed Pub. Co., 1991).

guish between the ordinary trees and the two special trees and between the special tree that might be eaten (the Tree of Life) and the special tree that is forbidden (the Tree of the Knowledge of Good and Evil).

Thus we see in Genesis 2:15 the same themes as day 4. Man is clearly *over* the Garden, in the same way as the lightbearers are over the earth. The lightbearers are to govern day and night, and the man is to dress the Garden. The lightbearers are to separate light and darkness, and the man is to distinguish between obedience and disobedience, between friend and enemy.

On day 5, God made the fish and birds to dwell in the seas and on the land, corresponding to day 3. He also gave them the first command recorded in Genesis 1. In Genesis 2:16–17, we have God's command to Adam.

Day 6 is equivalent to Genesis 2:18–24. On day 5 God created sea creatures and birds. On day 6a He made the land animals, and on day 6b He created man. Here in Genesis 2:18–24 God brought beasts and birds, representatives of the two days, before the man. When none proved suitable as a mate, God created woman. Thus we move from animals to humanity once again.

This brings us to the seventh day. In Genesis 1 God rested on the seventh day. Genesis 2 brings out the notion that God rested not only because He was finished but also because He had turned the administration of the world over to a steward. He turned the Garden over to Adam and Eve and departed.

It is clear that God departed, because after our first parents sinned, He returned. Genesis 2:24 also points to God's departure when it says "for this reason a man will leave his father and mother and cleave to his wife." We are so used to seeing this sentence as an aphorism that we fail to take note of it in context. Adam's father is God. There is a sense in which Adam leaves God as earthly father and sets up his own household in Genesis 2:24. God continues, of course, to be Adam's heavenly father. This is a point of tension in the passage, because now the question comes: How will this young man fare now that he is on his own, captain of his own family and in charge of the Garden? It is the same question that parents ask themselves when they give their children away in marriage.

Now, if we examine the acts of "Yahweh God" in Genesis 2, we can see even more closely the parallel literary structure that this passage bears to Genesis 1. The two passages are parallel chiasms:

1. Garden formless, empty, given light-bearer (man), 2:4–7
   "And YHWH God formed man"
   Spirit hovered, made light // breathing into dust, made man

   2. Garden-sanctuary, 2:8
      "And YHWH God planted a garden"
      Parallel to firmament

      3. Trees grow out of land, 2:9; centrality of land, 2:10–14
         "And YHWH God caused to grow"
         Reverse parallel to land and trees of day 3

4. Man established as ruler, 2:15
   "And YHWH God took the man and put him"
   Parallel to luminaries "put" and established as rulers on day 4

      5. Commands, regarding trees, 2:16–17
         "And YHWH God commanded the man"
         Parallel to command on day 5

   6. Community, 2:18–24
      "And YHWH God said"
      Parallel to community of man and animals, man and wife

7. Sabbath sin and judgment, 2:25–3:23
   Parallel to sabbath, day 7

Now, these parallels establish a far closer association of Genesis 1 and 2–3 than Sailhamer himself seems to recognize. Yet, these parallels also clearly separate the two passages as to their referents. The light and lightbearers of Genesis 1 become the man in Genesis 2–3. The firmament of Genesis 1 becomes the Garden of Genesis 2–3. From these facts, and the others, we can see that the links Sailhamer seeks to forge between Genesis 1 and 2–3 are the wrong links.

Presenting humanity as lightbearers in the firmament, who are mediating between heaven and the world, is implied in the Genesis 1 account. As we have seen, Genesis 1:2 announces three "problems," to wit: the earth was formless, empty, and dark. The formlessness of the world is taken care of by the two great separations of days 2 and 3a. The emptiness of the world is taken care of by the trees and grains of day 3b. The darkness of the world is taken care of by the initial light of day 1 and then by the lightbearers of day 4.

Now, the lightbearers culminate all three "answers." They separate the day and the night (form); they fill the sky (fill); and they govern (vv. 16 and 18). They are signs of rulers.

When humanity is made, God tells them: Be fruitful and multiply and fill the earth (filling); and subdue it (forming); and rule over it (lightbearing, analogous to lightbearers of day 4). Human beings are thus just like the lightbearers. Moreover, as we have seen, the sixth day corresponds to the second, so that humanity is like the firmament. It is only a very slight move to see that multiplied humanity is, accordingly, like the lightbearers of the firmament.

Thus, the account in Genesis 1 has already set up an analogy between humanity and the lightbearers in the firmament. All Genesis 2 does it make it more explicit. Genesis 2 is an expansion of the sixth day. On that day, God recapitulated the work of the six days but in a humaniform fashion. "Man in garden" is a microcosm of the macrocosmic "man in world."

The Covenant God

In chapter nine, Sailhamer argues that the God of Genesis 1 is the same as the covenant Yahweh God who brought Israel out of Egypt. For him this is further evidence that Genesis 1:2ff deals with God's putting man into a specific land, Eden, which for him is Canaan also.

Here we must make two observations. First, of course it is the same God. And, since the only God there is also is the covenant God, we can certainly see covenantal aspects in Genesis 1.

Second, however, Sailhamer completely overlooks the implications of the fact that Genesis 1 speaks only of "God," while the name "Yahweh God" appears throughout Genesis 2–3. The name "Yahweh God" is the name given by God in a peculiar way to the people of Israel at the exodus from Egypt (Ex. 6). The name was known earlier, of course, but not given in its full meaning until the exodus.

So, there is indeed a link between the exodus to Canaan under Yahweh God and Yahweh God's putting Adam into the Garden of Eden. Adam made an exodus from wherever he was originally, in 2:7, into the Garden (2:8, 15).

But the fact that "Yahweh God" is *not* used in Genesis 1 certainly indicates a contrast. If "Yahweh God" is the "land-covenant name" of God, then its absence from Genesis 1 is significant. Genesis 1 is *not* presenting God as the "land-covenant" God but as the "cosmos-covenant" God. In terms of this distinction, we have a macrocosmic name for God in Genesis 1, and a microcosmic name for God in Genesis 2. We have God's covenantal relationship to the cosmos *apart from man* in Genesis 1, and His covenantal relationship to the cosmos *through man* in Genesis 2. This is the fairly obvious relationship between Genesis 1 and 2–3 that Sailhamer overlooks, does not deal with argumentatively, and he has said nothing to dislodge.[12]

[12] Of course, there are more nuances of distinction between "God" and "Yahweh God" in the Bible than the ones we are considering here.

Once again, Sailhamer has just sailed through the passage, presenting his position without even taking notice of the common and well-nigh universal interpretation that he is discarding. His hammer simply misses the anvil of argument completely.

When Was Man Created?

On page 106, Sailhamer presents his argument that mankind was not made during the "beginning period" of Genesis 1:1 but on the sixth day of the "special land-making" work of Genesis 1:2ff:

> Were it not for the rest of Genesis, particularly the genealogies in chapters 5 and 10, we would be correct to include human beings among the creatures which inhabited the earth at this time. The genealogies of Genesis, however, tell us clearly that all human beings on earth are descendants of the man and woman created on the sixth day of the week which follows. We are forced by the logic of the text to exclude humans from the world created "in the beginning."

While I certainly agree that all humanity are descended from Adam and Eve, I don't see how this can be asserted on Sailhamer's premises. If he were correct, the genealogy of Genesis 5 would only concern the human beings set up in the original land. The post-Flood genealogies are not at issue, since they deal with humanity after the world-wide Flood. Maybe the "daughters of men" that the "sons of God" intermarried with in Genesis 6 were pre-Adamic humans. How can Sailhamer know? Genesis 5:1–6:8 does not state anywhere that all the human beings on the whole earth were descended from Adam. Of course, that is assumed—but again, how can Sailhamer know?

Now, if we take the traditional view of Genesis 1, we know for a fact that the only two human beings on the whole earth were Adam and Eve, who were created on the sixth day. But with Sailhamer's view, these were two human beings created and put into the special land. Nothing indicates that there were not other human beings already in existence. Moreover, Sailhamer's assertion that everything in heaven and earth was made "in the beginning period" can hardly exclude such a pre-Adamic humanity.

The First Day

For Sailhamer, the first day starts in Genesis 1:2, not Genesis 1:1. Now, in a further attempt to substantiate his position, he creates a problem in Genesis 1 where none exists. He asks (as others have) how there can be light on the first day if the sun was not created until the fourth? As we have seen in chapters two, three, and four, there is no problem here at all. When the glory cloud of God appears in the Bible, it is always refulgent with light. The hovering Spirit, who is always associated with the manifestation of God's glory, is the Source of the light on days 1–3 of Genesis 1.

Sailhamer solves this nonexistent problem by asserting once again that the universe, including the sun, had been around for a long time. Since (for him), Genesis 1:2 only concerns the forming of the Edenic land, "let there be light" just means "let the sun rise." Well, if Sailhamer's interpretation were correct, then his interpretation of "let there be light" would be possible. But as we have seen, Sailhamer has utterly failed to persuade that "in the beginning" refers to a long period of time, or that Genesis 1:2ff has to do only with the promised land.

The Second Day

A more significant problem of interpretation surrounds day 2 of Genesis 1. Sailhamer takes up the second day in his chapter eleven. Sailhamer says that the "firmament" is simply the sky and the waters above the firmament are clouds. If Genesis 1:7 said that the waters are "within" the firmament, the reference might be to clouds. But the text says that the waters are "above" the firmament.

What the "firmament" is in Genesis 1 is a hard problem and can only be addressed by taking into account much that is found later in the Bible. Even in Genesis 1, however, we can see what the most likely interpretation is.

In the beginning, God created the angelic heaven and the cosmic earth. From Genesis 1:1–2 we see a four-tiered universe. Lowest was the land. Over the land was the sea. Over the sea was some kind of dark space. And over the dark space was the angelic heaven. There was no boundary between the angelic heaven and the cosmic earth.

On the second day, God established a boundary between the angelic heaven and the cosmic earth and took part of the sea up into the angelic heaven. The notions that the "waters above" are simply clouds in the sky or a water canopy over the whole world will not withstand close inspection. Since the sun, moon, and stars are located "in" the firmament, the waters "above" the firmament must be "beyond" the visible universe. Thus, the waters above cannot be clouds or a vapor canopy, both of which are under the stars. Moreover, whenever the angelic heaven appears to men in the Bible, it is as if a curtain had pulled back and the angelic heaven is revealed as being very near at hand. Later passages of Scripture picture the angelic heaven as having a sea in it (Ezek. 1:22; Rev. 4:6).

Thus, the firmament is some kind of "dimensional barrier" between the angelic heaven and the cosmic earth. Neither the angelic heaven nor the firmament (its far side, anyway) can be reached by a spaceship.

Further study will reveal that the firmament is not only a shell-like barrier or curtain between heaven and earth but also a chamber between the two. The highest heaven is equivalent to the Holy of Holies in the Tabernacle. The firmament heaven is equivalent to the Holy Place (and notice the seven astral lamps in the Holy Place, symbolically linked to the sun, moon, and five visible planets).[13]

[13] For a fuller discussion of the firmament, see chapter eight and appendix C.

Taking water from the earth up into heaven is a prophetic type of taking baptized people from earth up into heaven.

Setting aside such details, however, it is clear that the waters "above" the firmament cannot be clouds, and thus Sailhamer's exegesis cannot stand. Removing water from the earth into the angelic heavens, beyond the stars, is clearly a much more cosmic action than merely putting clouds above the land of Eden. Thus, the events of the second day by themselves alone completely destroy Sailhamer's thesis.

Not Good?

Since Sailhamer has ignored the programmatic character of Genesis 1:2 for the passage as a whole, he is left with a question about why God did not pronounce matters "good" at the end of the second day. He submits that the "land" was not yet good for humanity at that point, since water still covered it. We can say the same thing for the midpoint of the third day, however, since there were not yet any plants on the "land" at that point. Yet God calls matters good before setting in the plants. Thus, I don't think Sailhamer's explanation carries any water at this point.

Rather, as we have noted already, God is working to take care of the three "problems" set out in Genesis 1:2—darkness, formlessness, and emptiness. The second day and the first half of the third day deal with the problem of formlessness, and that is why God does not pronounce things "good" until the end of the second half of the third day. Only then was the forming work completed.

The forming work in Genesis 1 takes the original structure of the world into a new structure, which has a wonderful balance and symmetry. Here is the end product:

I. ORIGINAL HEAVEN
- A. Highest Heaven
  - 1. Angelic heaven
  - 2. Heavenly sea as floor of heaven, above firmament

II. ORIGINAL EARTH
- A. Firmament Heaven
  - 1. Far side: right "under" the angelic heaven; stars
  - 2. Near side: the blue sky
- B. Earth
  - 1. Land
  - 2. Sea

Notice first of all that the resulting configuration of the Highest Heaven and the Earth is the same: dwelling place with sea underneath (below) it.

Second, notice that the firmament is called "heaven," which means that the firmament displays within the original "earth" (cosmos) the nature of the Highest Heaven. The stars in the firmament are related to the angels and their realm, while the blue sky at the lower end of the firmament is by means of this configuration related to the heavenly sea.

All of this is the forming work that God originally had in mind and in terms of which the original creation was relatively "formless." I may add that this is precisely the cosmic configuration seen in the Tabernacle:[14]

Highest Heaven – Holy of Holies
- Cherubim
- Blue cherubim veil (waters)

Firmament Heaven – Holy Place
- Lamps (stars)
- Second blue veil (blue sky)

Courtyard – Earth
- Altar of earth raised up
- Third blue veil at entrance (lower waters)

[14] For more on the cosmic imagery of the tabernacle, see Jordan, ibid., and Poythress, ibid.

The Third Day

In chapter twelve, Sailhamer discusses the third day. He states that "in Hebrew, any 'pool' of water—regardless of size—is called a 'sea'" (p. 126). I don't know where he gets this. It is not evidently true. A sea in the Bible is a large body of water.

In a note he refers to the Bronze Sea in the Temple of Solomon. The Bronze Ocean, mounted on a pedestal (of bulls), represents the waters above the firmament, the heavenly ocean. It is not a pool.[15]

Sailhamer goes on to say that the gathering of the waters "into one place" clearly does not refer to the oceans but to the various seas and lakes of Palestine, which are gathered into that one place. But it is a fact that there is only one world ocean. The continents are but large islands in this one world sea. Sailhamer has several seas in one place, but the text indicates one large sea. Rather clearly, a world-wide order rather than a localized one is in view.

Sailhamer goes on to say that only fruit trees were made on the third day, by which I take it he means that of the trees, only fruit trees were made. For him, this means God specially planted these trees in the land of Eden. But the text clearly says that grain plants as well as trees were made on the third day. Sailhamer should have discussed why, in terms of his interpretation, Genesis 2 only mentions trees in the Garden while saying nothing about the grains.

Sailhamer then goes on to challenge the traditional view, asking what the animals and birds and fishes were supposed to eat if the only vegetation in the world was fruit trees. The answer is, of course, grain plants. (Aquatic vegetation does not come into view in Genesis 1–2. When it was made

[15] On the cosmic and societal symbolism of the original laver, the bronze sea, and the laver stands of the Temple, see James B. Jordan, *Chariots of Water: An Exploration of the Water-Stands of Solomon's Temple*. Biblical Horizons Occasional Paper (April, 1991; available from Biblical Horizons, Box 1096, Niceville, FL 32588).

we are not told, but clearly it was there for the fishes to eat.)

Then Sailhamer says that since God planted fruit trees in the Garden in Genesis 2, that planting is to be identified with the planting on the third day. But Sailhamer can only make this association because he has completely ignored the grains. It seems to me that Sailhamer is so enthralled by his thesis that he is simply blind to certain matters in the text.

The Fourth Day

Chapter thirteen deals with the fourth day. Sailhamer generates some nonexistent problems that supposedly show that God did not make the sun, moon, and stars on the fourth day. He writes:

> But does the text actually say that the sun, moon, and stars were created on the fourth day? I don't believe it does. Yet if the text *did* say those heavenly bodies were created on the fourth day, a major problem would confront us. How could the universe—which includes the sun, moon, and stars—have been created "in the beginning" (1:1) and also on the fourth day? And how could the author speak of a "day and night" during the first three days of creation if the sun had not yet been created? Furthermore, are we to understand that plants and vegetation were created on the third day, before the creation of the sun? (p. 129)

Gentle reader, do these strike you as real problems? Of course not. Nothing hints that all the contents of the heavens and earth were created fully formed "in the beginning." Sailhamer has asserted that they were, but he has provided no evidence to support his contention. The alternation of day and night was provided by the waxing and waning of the light source established on the first day. No problem here. Trees and grains existed for a mere 24 hours before the sun was made, and in the meantime, the light set up on day 1 sustained them. So where is the problem?

Sailhamer informs the unwary reader that many exegetes have wrestled with these problems over the centuries. They have?[16] No one did before the rise of evolutionary science. He cites the work of only two men, C. F. Keil and John Calvin, both of whom appear not to have had any problem with the text at all. They said God made the sun on the fourth day.

Now Sailhamer turns to his own position. He starts by telling us that it is clear that the sun was made "in the beginning." At the risk of boring you, let me state again that Sailhamer has provided no evidence for this assertion.

Retranslating Verse 14

Then he tells us that the proper translation of 1:14 is not "Let there be lights in the firmament to separate the day and night," but "Let the lights in the firmament be for separating the day and night." Now, if this is correct, then Sailhamer does have a case for arguing that the sun already existed. But is it correct?

First, if Sailhamer be right, then every expositor for the past several thousand years has been wrong. I find nobody who takes 1:14 the way Sailhamer does. Hirsch and Cassuto, Calvin and Keil, Wenham and Hamilton, etc.—nobody agrees with Sailhamer or even raises the issue.

Second, Sailhamer asserts that there is a clear difference in the Hebrew phrasing of verses 6 and 14. Verse 6 says, "Let there be a firmament between the waters, *and let it be* for separating," while verse 14 says, "Let there be lights in the firmament-heavens *to separate* between the day and between the night." Sailhamer's own discussion is not very clear, but he is arguing that if the traditional view were

[16] The wrestling that early and medieval exegetes did with the firmament was not over whether the sun had already been made on the first day but mainly with how it held up the waters above it. See Stanley L. Jaki, *Genesis 1 Through the Ages* (London: Thomas More Press, 1992).

correct, verse 14 should read, "Let there be lights . . . *and let them be* for separating. . . ."

Let me try and make this clearer. Verse 6 says God made the firmament, and then it says He gave it the purpose of separating the waters. Verse 14 "ought to say" that God made the luminaries and then add that He gave them the purpose of separating day and night. This would make it clear that God made the luminaries as He made the firmament, and then He assigned them their purpose. Because the verb is not repeated, Sailhamer argues, verse 14 should be read that on the fourth day God made (appointed) the luminaries to separate day and night. This implies that they already existed.

Now, as I mentioned above, no other exegetical expositor seems to think that this distinction in phrasing amounts to anything other than a simple variation in the way the text is expressing matters. I am not sufficiently skilled in advanced Hebrew syntax to express more than a very meagre opinion (see following). But I can point out that if Sailhamer's reading were correct, it would create a significant problem, to wit: The light set up on the first day *already* separated day and night. If that light is the same as the sun, then what is God doing on the fourth day? What does it mean for God to appoint the sun to this task on the fourth day if the sun already had this task from the first day?

Now, it is to Sailhamer's credit that he recognizes this problem and attempts to deal with it on pages 134–35. He affirms that the sun (in his view) was already marking day and night. What is new on the fourth day, he states, is that God *announced* the purpose of the luminaries. That works as far as the luminaries being for signs and festivals, etc., but it does not work so clearly as far as the luminaries being there to separate day and night. In Sailhamer's view, the text has already told us this in verse 4. Why repeat it here?

I submit that for Sailhamer's view to be tenable, verse

14 should simply read, "Let the lights in the firmament-heaven be for signs and for festivals and for days and for years," without repeating the business of separating day and night, since it is clear that they already had that purpose.

Now, Sailhamer asks, "Why did God wait until the fourth day to announce the purpose of the sun, moon, and stars?" (p. 135). His answer is that days 4–6 parallel days 1–3: "On the fourth day, God commanded the sun, moon, and stars to distinguish day and night and all the signs and seasons (1:14–15). On the fifth day, God commanded the seas to swarm with fish and sea creatures, and on the sixth day, He commanded the land to bring forth animal life" (p. 135). This parallelism looks good until we notice that on the fifth day God also made birds to dwell upon the land (v. 22)—and the land was made on the third day, not the second. Moreover, the second day is not focally concerned with the seas, which are not named until the third day, but with the firmament.

Additionally, Sailhamer says that the first three days are days of preparation, while the next three announce the purposes of the things made on the first three. But that's not true either. The firmament made on the second day is given a purpose immediately (v. 6). If Sailhamer's parallelism were correct, the fifth day should announce the purpose of the firmament, something it does not do.

My conclusion is that Sailhamer has not at all solved the problems his translation of verse 14 creates. On his reading, verse 14a is simply a redundant repetition of what has already been said in verses 3–4.

A Correct Understanding

The traditional understanding is that on the fourth day the sun, moon, and stars simply replaced the primordial light of day 1, which was the light of the Spirit and glory of God. Eventually, the sun, moon, and stars will be gone, because the firmament-boundary between heaven and earth will be gone and the light of the Spirit of Christ will return as the light of the cosmos (Rev. 21:23). In the meantime, the firmament stands between us and God while we live out the course of history by faith and not by sight, "under the sun," as the book of Ecclesiastes tells us.

With the traditional understanding in view, we may be able to account for the slight difference in grammar between verses 6 and 14:

> *Verse 6*—"Let there be a firmament in the midst of the water, and let it separate the waters from the waters." Were the waters already separated? No.
>
> *Verse 14*—"Let there be lights in the firmament-heavens to separate the day and the night, and let them be for signs and for festival assemblies and for days and for years." Were day and night already separated? Yes, by the light of the first day.

Now, if the text read, "Let there be lights in the firmament-heavens, and let them separate the day and the night," someone would say, "Aha! This contradicts verse 4, which says there was already a light separating day and night." But no one can make this mistake because of the way the grammar stands. Originally there was (divine) light above the earth separating day and night. Now God makes luminaries in the firmament for that purpose.

Notice how verse 14 continues, "and let them be for signs and for assemblies and for days and for years." Did the light of the first day do these things? No. They are added here, and so a finite verb rather than an infinitive is used to introduce them.

In short:

> "Let there be a firmament, and let it divide the waters," because dividing the waters is new.
>
> "Let there be lights, and let them be for signs, etc.," because these functions of light are new.
>
> "Let there be lights to separate day and night," because

> this function is not new but is now taken over by the newly-created lights.

This distinction fully accounts for the grammatical difference, and it does so simply and in line with the flow of the passage.

One other matter may be addressed here. I have asserted that the light that shone on the first day is the light of the glory-Spirit of God. This may stand to reason without a prooftext, but is there anything in Genesis 1 that points to this? Yes, there is. Notice:

> *Verses 6–7*—"Let there be a firmament. . . . And God made the firmament."
>
> *Verses 14–16*—"Let there be lights. . . . And God made the lights."
>
> *Now verses 3–4*—"Let there be light. And there was light."

We don't read that God made the light. The contrast indicates that God Himself was the source of the light. To be sure, there are creational aspects of God's light when it shines into the creation: Photons carry the packets of light (to use one way of speaking about it), and such photons are creatures. But the Source of the light in verses 3–4 is, by implication, God Himself, specifically the third Person of the Godhead.

The Fifth Day

Another large problem awaits Sailhamer on the fifth day. Up to now, he has been able to argue that when God is said to "make" things in Genesis 1, this really means that He "appoints them" or "sets them up" (pp. 106–08). He has been able to assert that these things already existed but were appointed to their various purposes during the creation week. The verb translated "make" can indeed have this meaning, though Sailhamer has not convinced us that it has that meaning in Genesis 1.

On the fifth day, however, God did not "make" the great sea monsters; He "created" them (v. 21). On the face of it, this is something brand new. In chapter fourteen of his book, Sailhamer wrestles with the sea monsters.

He points out the traditional understanding, which is that there are three acts of creation in Genesis 1: the heavens and earth, the living creatures, and humanity. Each is a new "wondrous work" of God, indicating a beginning of something radically new. But for Sailhamer, this is not acceptable, because he maintains that the animals had been created during the "beginning period." Because he is absolutely certain of this, he argues that "Genesis 1:21 is best explained as a comment on verse 20. It is a comment to remind the reader that God 'created' all kinds of animals 'in the beginning.'" (1:1) (p. 138)

He states, "The author does not say God created all the animals on the fifth day; he merely says it was God who created all the animals and that now He commands some to fill the waters and the skies over the promised land" (p. 139). But that is *not* what the text says. It does not read: "And it was God who had created the great sea monsters, etc." If that had been the writer's intention, the word order in Hebrew would be different. As it stands, the Hebrew reads, "And (He) created, God, the great sea monsters, etc." The verb comes first, stressing the action, as it does routinely in Genesis 1. For Sailhamer to be correct, the Hebrew should put the noun "God" first: "And God, (He) created the great sea monsters, etc." In fact, if the stress is on the fact that it was God who created, the Hebrew would likely include the pronoun explicitly: "And God, He Himself created the great sea monsters." But that is not how the text reads.

Conclusion

It is not necessary to survey the remainder of Sailhamer's book, some of which I have dealt with already. Nothing he writes after his discussion of the fifth day adds any new arguments for his thesis. His discussion of the sixth and seventh days is, in the main, unproblematic. The last section of his book is a return to general principles, and those parts that are relevant have already been discussed.

The conclusion is that while Sailhamer's thesis is interesting, it is not correct. The author's arguments, such as they are, consist mainly of statements of his thesis over and over again and an attempt to interpret Genesis 1 in the light of it. We have found his thesis to be unsupported by any credible argument and his interpretation of Genesis 1 to be replete with errors.

Chapter 8

The Sequence of Events in the Creation Week

Now that we have examined three unacceptable approaches to the events recorded in Genesis 1, it is only fair for me to set out what I think does seem to be recorded there. The reader should bear in mind that whether my suggestions in this chapter are correct or not, they do not alter the criticisms offered in the other parts of this book. Perhaps many of my points are in error or could be significantly improved upon. My actual interpretation of the details of Genesis 1 is not fully germane to the present book, which in its bare bones is just a defense of the normal six-day reading of the text. One can surely agree with me that the Day-Age, Framework, and Limited Geography interpretations are wrong without agreeing with all my suggested alternatives. Still, I feel I would be remiss not to offer somewhere in the present study a collected, coherent, and fairly full discussion of the text as I think it should be read.

To begin with the source of this narrative: Since no human being was present to observe these events, we must assume that this narrative was revealed directly by God to a human author. There are three ways this might have happened. First, we might read, "God said to Abraham (or Joseph or Moses): "In the beginning I created the heavens and the earth. . . ." This is not what we find, however. Thus, if Genesis 1 was originally dictated to a human author (as God dictated Leviticus to Moses), that author rephrased it in the third person.

Second, it might be that Genesis 1 came about indirectly through divine inspiration, as the Psalms, for instance, came about. In this case, the human author would be reflecting on God and creation and would be moved by insight into composing this narrative. This, however, seems quite unlikely. After all, what information would the human author have to reflect upon?

Third, and this seems most likely to me, God revealed these things to a human author, who then, under inspiration, wrote up the matter in this form. It may well be (and probably is the case) that God told all this to Adam, who passed it on in documents to his heirs, through Noah, to whoever wrote up the final version that we have in Genesis.[1]

Now, who was the human author of Genesis 1, and when was it written? As noted previously, it is usually assumed that Moses wrote Genesis, but the Bible never says this, and there is no particular reason to think Moses was

[1] We have to question the notion of some "oral tradition" from Adam forward. Human memory is quite selective, and that is why some form of writing has always accompanied human endeavor. Written language is for the purpose of memorializing and functions differently from oral language. God both speaks and writes, as He wrote the Ten Words, and so we can be pretty sure that Adam—His image—wrote as well as spoke. Common sense tells us that if someone lives nine hundred years, he will at some point learn the need to write things down because of his fallible memory and the conflicts he encounters with the memories of others.

Oral traditions do not last for hundreds and thousands of years. They constantly change as creative poets find themselves unable to resist altering them and as societies undergo transformations (as all do). The people using them may believe that they have remained essentially unchanged for millennia, but that is not the case.

Oral tradition is something quite different from written documentation. Most societies have both, and need both, because they function so differently.

For a good discussion of the limitations of oral tradition, see R. K. Harrison, *Introduction to the Old Testament* (Grand Rapids, MI: Eerdmans, 1969) pp. 68, 209, 762.

the author. To put it another way, all the arguments for Mosaic authorship are purely circular; to wit, some parts of Genesis lay the foundation for Exodus, something that would be true whether Moses wrote it or not. My own best guess is that Joseph wrote Genesis in its definitive form (requiring only a few additional notes from Moses and Samuel), so that Genesis was the Bible the Hebrews had with them while they were in Egypt.

It is important to reflect on this question because there are many commentators on Genesis 1 who try to explain various parts of the passage against the background of Moses' experiences and education in Egypt. Supposedly, for instance, in Genesis 1 Moses is providing a reply to the cosmological notions of the Egyptians. Such an assumption is wholly gratuitous and is a dangerous red herring drawn across the path of the interpreter, diverting him from paying close attention to what the text actually states.

With these things in the back of our minds, let us now turn briefly to what Genesis 1 does say.

Heaven and Earth

The creation narrative describes God's making the world over the course of a week. God's work is cosmic and covenantal. The language in Genesis 1 is used in covenant-making events later on in the Bible, and some have noted this and then asserted that Genesis 1 is concerned with covenantal ordering, not with cosmic ordering. But the only cosmos that exists is God's covenantal cosmos, so any attempt to pit covenant against cosmos is unwarranted. Indeed, any such attempt moves in the direction of gnosticism and "heilsgeschichte," the modern gnostic notion that God's "salvation history" operates outside the realm of spatio-temporal cosmic history.

Sometimes it is argued that either the first statement of the narrative, or else the first two verses, are an introduction and are not part of the seven days. I fail to see how one can argue one way or another grammatically with any certainty, and it makes no difference to the chronology in any event. If God created the heavens and the earth, with the earth unstructured, empty, and dark, and left it that way for a trillion years—so what? What does it matter? Indeed, what would be the point? We should note, however, that the darkness of the original condition is directly related to the light-making work of the first day, which certainly implies that all of this was the work of the first day. Not having any sound reason for separating verses 1 and 2 from the first day, we shall consider them as part of it. After all, since the first day is the *first* day, clearly it is also the introductory day.

In the beginning God created heaven and earth. He created two things, not one. These two things are, by implication, related to one another, linked in some way. Later this will be spelled out. For now, we notice two things that are linked: a covenantal structure, comparable to the covenantal relationship between God and man, Yahweh and Israel, man and wife, etc.

The earth as it was made was good, of course, but not yet developed. It lacked structure, was empty, and was dark. Nothing like this is said of heaven. Indeed, it is clear from the rest of the Bible that heaven was made structured, full, and bright from the beginning. The angelic host does not multiply, and so new angels do not appear in the process of time. Humanity was created as a race that matures into a host, while the angels were created as a host from the beginning.

The earth matures in a way that heaven does not. Heaven is thus the model or paradigm for the earth. The earth is to grow more and more heaven-like. In the rest of the Bible, when heaven opens, men see the models they are to reproduce on the earth, as when Moses was shown the model for the Tabernacle and David the model for the Temple.

Right away we notice something that has somehow escaped the notice of virtually all commentators, which is that the earth must mature in three areas, not just in two. Genesis 1 is not concerned only with structuring and filling, but also with light.[2]

The original earth had three zones: the earth below the waters, the waters, and a space of darkness over the waters. Above these, and not yet separated by any barrier, was the heaven. These four zones correspond to the four elements, the four states of matter, both as they were known by the ancients and as they are known today:

Heaven	fire	energy
Air	air	gas
Water	water	liquid
Earth	earth	solid

Day One

Assuming that God created this configuration at the beginning of day 1, in the evening that precedes the morning, we find on the second half of this day that He makes light. This would have been in the morning of that day.

Verse 2 presents two things over the earth:

> Darkness was over the face of the unstructured deep.
>
> The Spirit of God was hovering over the surface of the waters.

Thus, the Spirit had been inserted into the earthly realm from the heavenly realm, proceeding from the Father and the Son, evidently at the precise moment of the act of creation. The creation does not exist apart from the presence of the moving Spirit within her. God never needs to "enter" the creation; by His Spirit He has been present within her from the very beginning.

Then God said, "Let there be light." The only source

[2] Why has this rather obvious fact eluded so many modern commentators? I think the answer lies in the pervasiveness of the notion that Genesis 1 shows "three days of forming and three days of filling." As we have seen and will see again, this is not the case.

for that light is the Spirit Himself. When God appears later on in the Bible, He is surrounded by the glory, which is associated with the Spirit. Indeed, His glory hovers over Israel in the pillar of cloud and fire. Thus, the initial light came from the Spirit. Light is energy, fire; and so now fire is brought into the earth from heaven. Fire transforms things, and so begins the transfiguration of the earth, from glory to glory.

Confirmation of the idea that the Spirit is the light-bearer at this point comes from Psalm 104—if confirmation is even needed. Psalm 104 is a reflective commentary on Genesis 1, and it proceeds through the seven days in order.[3] The first day is discussed in the first four lines (vv. 1–2a). There God is said to cover Himself with light as with a cloak. Thus, the Psalmist understood the light of the first day as a light from God.

If we think of this configuration in terms of a flat earth—which we may certainly do since that is how we experience the earth—we see it as a four-deck universe. Nothing in the passage, however, excludes also seeing an earthly sphere, covered with water, covered again with airy space, and surrounded by heaven. The passage can be read equally well either way.

We conclude by noting that the insertion of the Spirit of God into earthly life is the way God always renews and reinitiates His covenant. Compare the glory's moving into the Tabernacle in Exodus 40, into the Temple in 2 Chronicles 7, and into believers in a new, more glorious way in the New Covenant.

Day Two

On the second day God created the "firmament" and separated waters above and below it, and He called it "heaven." As the first day took care of the darkness problem, so the

[3] See appendix E for a translation and analysis of Psalm 104.

second day begins to take care of the unstructuredness problem. God does not call the work good, however, until the mid-point of the third day, when the separation of land and sea completes the structuring work. We may ask why God did not do both structuring works on the second day. At least part of the answer is so that the third day is chiastically related to the fifth, so that land and sea are answered by the creatures of land and sea.

Structure seems to be related to water here. The word we have translated "unstructured" is in Hebrew *tohu*, and the word for the "deep" (which we rendered "unstructured deep") in Genesis 1:2 is *t-hom*—apparently the same root word.[4] Thus, the unstructured nature of the primeval creation is primarily associated with the waters over the earth, and when those waters have been structured, then the problem is solved. (Compare also in Genesis 2, where the four rivers that flow from the Edenic plateau structure the lands of the rest of the world.)

This enables us to correlate the three zones of the earthly creation with the three problems and solutions:

Air	Dark/Light
Water	Unstructured/Structured
Earth	Empty/Filled

We now have a heaven within the original earth. The fact

[4] The relationship between *tohu* and *t-hom* is obvious to the ear and to the eye, yet recent scholars have ascribed them to two different semitic roots. Even if this dubious attempt to separate these two terms is correct, they are clearly related by "pun" here in Genesis 1. After all, the Bible was written to be heard, to be read aloud, and thus sound-associations such as these are very important. Not only so, but in Genesis 1 it is precisely the *t-hom* that is *tohu* and that needs to be separated and structured. (Widespread literacy only came into human civilization after the invention of the printing press, and then only after paper became cheap in the eighteenth century. Silent reading, as opposed to reading out loud, is also a very recent development; only a handful of people practiced it before the last couple of centuries.)

that this firmament is called "heaven" means that it is an image of the original heaven. Being above the waters, it is in the same place as the light. As we observe the flow of events here, it seems pretty clear that the created substance of the original glory-light of the first day is now expanded to form the firmament, a realm of light over the waters below.[5] Later, the light of the firmament will be congealed into sun, moon, and stars, which give great light during the day and less light during the night.

The word "firmament" (*raqia'*) is used for a beaten-out, flat surface, like a shell or a curtain over the earth. There is nothing mythological about this, for that is how the sky actually looks. A full examination of this place called the firmament, however, will show that it is also a chamber between heaven and earth. In Genesis 2, as we saw in chapter seven, the Garden of Eden, located between the higher ground of the Land of Eden and the lower ground of the world, is a replica of the firmament. Moreover, the chiastic structure of the seven days of creation establishes that man, made on the sixth day, is positioned in the firmament. Man is located between heaven and earth, under God but over the world. In that place, man worships God, and from that place he goes out to exercise dominion. The firmament chamber corresponds to the glory-cloud of God when it appears within the earthly cosmos and to the Holy Place of the Tabernacle and Temple. Thus, the Holy Place contained a seven-lighted lampstand, positioned with the luminaries leading from the earth (courtyard) to the highest heavens (Holy of Holies), displaying the seven moving (and therefore ruling) luminaries of the sky.[6]

The firmament, considered as a shell, separates heaven and earth for the first time. There is now a barrier between

[5] Recall that though the light comes from the Spirit, light within the creation is a creaturely phenomenon consisting of physical "waves" and/or "photons."

[6] In order as they appear from the earth: Moon, Venus, Mercury, Sun (central), Mars, Jupiter, and Saturn.

them, and this points to eschatology, for it is implied that when the earth has fully matured the barrier will be removed. This barrier is replicated in the two veils of the Tabernacle and Temple, which put a barrier between the symbolic heavens and earth. These are removed at the crucifixion of Jesus—pointing to the complete removal of this barrier at the end of history.

Covenantally, we see God separating one thing (the sea) into two things and then putting them into a new relation with one another. This act of separation happens whenever a covenant is made. In Genesis 2, God separates Eve from Adam and marries them. In Genesis 15, God separates animals, representing Abram and the land as two estranged parties, which He then links by moving His Spirit between them. In the sacrifices, the animal is always cut into pieces, and the blood is separated from the flesh.[7]

Cosmically, the picture becomes a bit more complicated. From a phenomenological flat-earth perspective, we just have a sky above the earth, with heaven above it. We act in terms of this picture whenever we look up to God, lifting our faces toward the heavens.

In terms of the physical cosmos there are two aspects to discuss. First, the Bible is clear that heaven is now in another "dimension" from the earth. When heaven is opened or God appears, it always turns out to be very near, as in the vision of Isaiah 6. Thus, we cannot reach the highest heaven by means of a spaceship, as we might have on the first day before the firmament was established. The idea that the biblical revelation is "unsophisticated" in this regard is unwarranted, as we have just seen. While many ancient people doubtless thought of heaven as being located on the other side of the stars, they were also aware that in another sense their gods' heaven was "near" as well as "far away." Thus, for us to refine their thinking is not to

[7] The only exception is the annual passover lamb, which is not cut up but which does experience the separation of flesh and blood.

depart from their fundamental understanding.

Additionally, the firmament is shortly to become a chamber, perhaps another "dimension" between heaven and earth. From later passages in the Bible, it seems that the departed saints resided here while they waited for heaven to be opened, when the Seed of the woman, the man Jesus Christ, would ascend to the throne of God and they would be allowed to accompany Him fully inside. The evacuation of that firmament chamber, as described in Revelation 6:9–11; 15:2 and 8; and 20:4, raises the possibility that this aspect of it no longer exists today. God's people no longer worship Him in a place between heaven and earth; in Christ they are now in heaven itself when they draw near to God. Recall that man, made on the sixth day, is symbolically positioned in the firmament at the beginning. Similarly, he is positioned in the Garden of Eden between Eden and the world. That firmament-place is glorified in the New Jerusalem, which is between heaven and earth as a star (Rev. 21:11), and from that place men may now ascend in Christ into the highest heavens for worship and yet go down to the world for work. In the New Creation, the top of the firmament is no longer an impassible barrier between heaven and the earthly cosmos.

At the same time, stars are "in" the firmament, while birds fly "in front of" it (vv. 14 and 20). In this sense, the firmament is outer space, the matrix in which luminaries are positioned. Cosmologically, the firmament is the place where the stars will be put in two days. We shall defer further comments on the cosmological aspect of the matter until we get to the fourth day.

The waters above the firmament are in heaven itself, on the far side of the firmament. They are not clouds, nor are they a water-vapor canopy over the earth. If such a canopy ever existed, the Bible does not speak about it; such theories must be grounded in other lines of evidence and argument. The waters below the firmament include the clouds, which recycle the waters below, continually baptizing and cleansing the earth through rain. All the water in the cloudy sky starts out as water in the sea, which through evaporation is drawn up into the air. Thus, the cloudy waters are part of the earthly sea. As the one world ocean surrounds the various lands, so that same ocean also surrounds them in the air above them.

God reached down into the earth and took some of the water up into heaven. This is an eschatological picture. It differentiates not only between lower and upper waters but also between first and last waters. The first waters covering the earth were an initial baptism, while being sprinkled with waters from above is the sign of our final baptism. We begin on earth, with earthly waters; we enter the final kingdom of God by passing through heavenly waters. Agreeable to this, the laver of cleansing in the Tabernacle and the great sea and laver-chariots of the Temple were all mounted on pedestals and thus represented the waters above: Water was lifted up and put into them and then taken back out and down to wash the sacrifices and the priests. The sea of glass, crystal, and ice that is seen in visions of heaven in Ezekiel and Revelation is the water taken into heaven on the second day.

Psalm 104:2b–4 comments on the second day as follows. We are told that God stretched out the firmament heaven like a curtain. Then we are told that God's upper chambers (His palace) are built upon the waters above the firmament. Then the psalmist refers to clouds, the wind, and to fire. It seems that the firmament can by extension be considered as including these lower phenomena in the atmosphere, though possibly "fire" here refers to the luminaries in the sky (in outer space).

Day Three

The third day completes the initial structuring work and the initial filling work. First, God separates land and sea, putting the sea below the land. This reproduces the configuration that has just been set up in heaven: land over sea. The earth is being modeled after heaven. There is now an altar-platform on the earth as well as one right below heaven (the firmament). The configuration of the whole universe at this point can be diagrammed as follows:

Heaven:	Throne (fire-air-matter)
	Sea
Firmament:	Outer space
	Blue sky
Earth:	Fire (firmament-heaven light)
	Air
	Land
	Sea

If we allow the symbolic representation of this model, found in the Tabernacle, to inform our thinking, we can see that the fourfold world is found at all three levels:

Holy of Holies:	God's "consuming fire" cloud, positioned above:
	Air, above:
	Wings of the (material) cherubim, standing on:
	The Ark Cover ("Mercy Seat"), a golden firmament-sea[8]
Holy Place:	The Altar of (cloudy) Incense
	The Lampstand of stars
	The Table of (material) Facebread
	The outer blue veil of the Holy Place[9]
Courtyard:	The fire of God above the altar
	Air between the fire and what is below it
	Wood and land animals and birds on/within the altar
	The blue veil of the courtyard (the sea)

[8] Also correlating with the cherubim veil of the Holy of Holies.

[9] The blue veil of the Holy Place should be correlated with the water in the Laver of Cleansing, a representation of the baptismal firmament

Only at this point, in the middle the third day, is the structuring work "good," because now the earth has been made after the image of heaven.

Verse 9 does not say that the land was thrust up above the sea, but that the sea was gathered so that the land appeared. In other words, part of the land sank down and the water ran off from the rest of the land. The downward flow of the water is baptismal, as we have noted earlier.

The land is now ready to be productive; things can be generated out of it. Up to this point, conditions were not right; now they are. Plants appear. Plants are "machines" that convert water, air, fire (light), and earth into food and decoration. Plants are the initial form of glory over the land, replicating God's glory in blossoms, scents, and food. Let us recall that man is made of soil and so is destined also to be covered in glory.[10] Perhaps it is noteworthy that glory was to be conferred on man by eating of the Tree of Knowledge, after the temporary probation. (That it was temporary is clear from Genesis 1:29.) Plants, the glory of the land, would pass on glory to man, made of the land.[11] In

waters. Hebrews 9:3–4 associates the Altar of Incense with the Holy of Holies as the part of the Holy Place closest to it. On the degrees of "holiness" of these objects, which proves their relative positions as I have given them here, see my monograph, *From Glory to Glory: Degrees of Value in the Sanctuary.* Biblical Horizons Occasional Paper 2 (2nd ed., February, 1994; available from Biblical Horizons, Box 1096, Niceville, FL 32588).

[10] Hair, the "plants" that grow on the man made of earth, is associated with glory throughout the Bible. Plants make the earth smell good, and human beings also smell (though the odors given off by fallen man are all bad smells, which we cover with perfumes and by bathing). Plants are also eaten, and in the Bible the holy kiss symbolizes our "eating" one another as we participate in the body of Christ, which we eat in the Lord's Supper (the bread representing not just Jesus but also each other; 1 Cor. 10:15–18). Thus, the parallels between plants and men are replete.

[11] Note Adam's attempt to cover and glorify himself with leaves, which God rejected. Since Adam had chosen to follow the serpent, God covered him with skins of beasts. The priests, however, wore linen, as do the saints in Revelation.

the Church, we get the glory of Christ from plants: bread and wine.

Only two kinds of plants are specified as having been made at this point. Only grain plants and fruit-bearing trees are mentioned. According to 2:5, the "shrubs of the earth" were not made at this point. This leaves many kinds of plants unaccounted for. We simply don't know when God made other kinds of food plants or the plants of the water.[12] Grape vines, which are not trees, were not made on the third day. They are associated, as we have seen earlier in this book, with man's mature estate as king. Since Noah was the first to plant a vineyard, perhaps they did not appear until after the Flood (9:20, according to one way of translating this verse).[13] All the same, fruits and grains are the foundation of fermented juice and bread and oil, the sacramental plant-products used in the Bible throughout. Every Israelite was to have his own field, vineyard, and olive grove: his own cosmos as an image of God (Deut. 14:23; 24:19–21).

Let me suggest that the three kinds of plants mentioned in Genesis 1–2 are the root of the three special plants of the kingdom: fruit trees (olive; oil); grains (bread); shrubs (vines; wine). We shall find this same kind of triple list later in the chapter also.

Plants are the vestments of glory for the land. If we study covenant-making events later on in the Bible, we find that being vested by God as His glorious servant is part of the covenant event, one way or another. This is most obvi-

[12] Many children are unsure whether it was God or the devil who made broccoli and brussels sprouts!

[13] Note that Noah is the first man given the right to rule, to execute criminals, by God. He is the first "king" in the full biblical sense. Adam was to serve in the Garden as a priest (literally "palace servant") until he had matured enough to be given the right to rule at God's right hand. Thus, first priest, then king. Thus, first bread, then wine.

ous in the vesting of Aaron, but baptism (which clothes us with water) is another example.[14]

At the end of the third day, God has finished taking care of the three problems facing Him at the beginning. The world is no longer dark, unstructured, or empty. I shall be bold and suggest that these three problems reveal in a very general way the three Persons of God. Clearly, the Spirit gives the light, but we begin at the throne of God with the Father's speaking the Word and sending the Spirit. The filling or glorifying is to be associated with the Spirit, for He is the glorifier. The structure of the creation is to be associated with the Son, who holds all things in their place (Col. 1:17); and the Son is the Firmament, the Mediator between heaven and earth.

Theologically speaking, when God acts outside of Himself, all three Persons are involved: All of God does all that God does. Yet, at the same time, in every action of God, one Person is preeminent. Beginning at this point in my discussion, I shall be bold and suggest ways in which Genesis 1 hints at aspects of the Trinity that are more fully revealed later in the Bible. Thus, note:

grain, bread – Son
olive oil – Spirit
wine – Father (the drink of rest and enthronement)

The plants, from which we get garments of glory, filled the land. We no longer think of garments as "filling" items, but the gems on Aaron's garments of glory and beauty symbolized the twelve tribes of Israel arrayed around his person as high priest. Similarly, in most societies, and to a degree in ours as well, a person's garment identifies his place in society: the clergyman's collar, the lawyer's black

[14] Properly performed, baptism is a shower of water (not a mere drop) that immerses or drenches us with waters from above, heavenly waters. Sprinkling a pitcher of (airified) water on someone is very similar to putting a garment on his or her shoulders.

three-piece pin-striped suit, the soldier's uniform, the doctor's gown, the auto mechanic's shirt, etc. Baptism, an investiture with water sprinkled upon us, not only places Christ upon us, but also places the Church as a community around us as well. With this in mind, we can understand more fully the covenantal association between the glorification and filling of the earth with beautiful plants on the one hand, and its meaning to human beings on the other.

Finally, the completion of the initial work on the third day opens up the third-day theme that is found throughout the Bible. The third day (hour, week, month, year, event) is always the time of initial completion and judgment, which makes possible the last four days of the week.

Psalm 104:5–18 comments as follows. Initially the waters were over the mountains, but then they fled down to the seas. God set a boundary that they might not again cover the earth. This seems to include the Flood in its perspective, for only after the Flood was it true that the waters would never cover the earth again. Various kinds of watering are mentioned: springs, streams, and rain. Then the two kinds of plants created on the third day are mentioned: grass for cattle and bread for man in verse 14, and wine, oil, and bread in verse 15.

Day Four

Coming after the third day, when the initial work was completed, the fourth day is a preliminary sabbath. A study of the sabbath in the Bible will show that it is associated with enthroned rest, and the enthronement of rulers is the fourth-day theme.[15]

The fourth day is the center of the week, and the cen-

[15] On the sabbath and enthronement, see James B. Jordan, *Sabbath-Breaking and the Death Penalty: A Theological Investigation* (Tyler, TX: Geneva Ministries, 1986) chap. 3.

ter of the narrative, chiastically considered. If we read the narrative in a linear fashion, the climax is the sabbath; but if we read it chiastically, we move inward to the central thought, which as we have just noted is a preliminary sabbath. It is the beauty of chiastic writing that enables the writer to do several things at once. He can put the opening and final thoughts at the beginning and end and the central or governing thought in the center. Also, he moves in and up to the central or pivotal thought and then back out and down.

Thus, the fourth day is central. Man, made on the sixth day, is symbolically positioned in the firmament, made on the second. Now man is implicitly described in terms of luminaries placed in the firmament. Under the Old Creation, these angelically-administered luminaries governed time, festivals, and important days and years, and ruled the earth. In the New Creation, in Christ, man now does these things, which is why the Old Creation calendar is superseded in Christ. Note that man, positioned symbolically in the firmament, is under the angelic heaven, governed by it. In the New Covenant, as we have mentioned above, humanity rises with Christ Jesus to the formerly angelic highest heavens, no longer staying under angelic tutors.

The fourth day is pivotal. It provides a second completion to the first three days and introduces the latter three days. In terms of completion, the fourth day finishes the fourfold orientation of the world displayed in the Tabernacle:

West	Ark-throne	Heaven (day 1)
East	Altar-platform	Firmament before God (day 2)
North	Table of Bread	Plants on land (day 3)
South	Lampstand	Lights in firmament (day 4)

Again:

Day 1	Throne	Father
Day 2	High Altar of incense	Son
Day 3a	Low Altar of sacrifice	Son
Day 3b	Glory Plants	Spirit
Day 4	Glory Lights	Spirit[16]

The fourth day also completes a movement down and back up. We began in heaven, moved down to the light in the sky, down to the firmament, down to the land and then down to the sea (v. 10), back up through the plants that grow toward heaven, and farther up into the firmament of stars.

On the other hand, the fourth day begins the second half of the week. We have moved from light to structure to filling already. Now we begin again with light, move to filling (days 5 and 6a), then to structure (man as ruler, "subduer"), and end with the Great Day of the sabbath, a return to eschatological light.

Thus, the fourth day is chiastically related not only to the second and sixth days, but also to the first and seventh. We begin with the primordial light of the Spirit. At the center we find the luminaries within the cosmos, which, being located between them, signify both angels and men. At the end we come back to the day of God, the eschatological Light. This is essentially a movement from Spirit to Son to Father.

We find another triplex of created objects here:

Great Light	Father (the source of light)
Lesser Light	Son (reflects the Father as His Eternal Image)
Stars	Spirit (who gathers the host)

[16] For an extended discussion, see my monograph *Behind the Scenes: Orientation in the Book of Revelation*. Biblical Horizons Occasional Paper 19 (2nd ed., May, 1999; available from Biblical Horizons, Box 1096, Niceville, FL 32588).

The Expansion of the Firmament

On the fourth day, God congealed the light within the original earth into bodies inside the visible firmament. We saw that the light originally came from the shining of the Spirit, and then by implication was spread out in the firmament, which was located where the Spirit was. The alternation of evening and morning was an alternation of a bright sky with a relatively dark one. Now that light sky congeals to form the heavenly bodies.

This congealing formed the stars and galaxies that we see in the sky. In terms of how the universe works, it is perhaps no surprise that in congealing, this energetic matter acquired rotation, forming spinning stars, double stars, planets, moons, and rotating galaxies. This did not take millions of years, however, but happened quite rapidly. It is entirely conceivable, however, that some of the currently proposed mechanisms of how the universe came to have its present configuration are correct—but the timing is way off. Possibly the earth began her rotation at this point as well.

Isaiah 40:22 may shed a good deal of light on the firmament and the starry heavens. The second half of the verse reads:

> The One stretching out like a thin veil heavens,
> And spreading them out like a tent for dwelling.

Note that in the first phrase, the heavens are a thin veil, as thin as a layer of dust (as the Hebrew implies); while in the second phrase the heavens are a spacious tent.

On the basis of this, and from Genesis 1, I suggest that the following is the sequence of events:

First, on day 1 a light of glory is positioned above the earth.

Second, on day 2 the substance (the created aspect) of that light is stretched out as a thin veil over the earth.

Third, on day 4 that veil is spread upwards and outwards to form outer space. The substance of the veil is broken up and congeals to form stars, planets, asteroids, dust, etc. This rapid spreading upwards and outwards from the earth may account for some aspects of "red shift" phenomena.[17]

Housebuilding

The appointment of rulers and governors is always part of a covenantal act of God, as when Abraham was set up to minister to the nations, or when Israel was given rulers in Exodus 18. The appointment of servant-rulers by God is part of the "victory-housebuilding" pattern in the Bible. God defeats His enemies and builds His house out of the spoils. As a last action, He lights the fire on His hearth and appoints servants to tend it and care for the house.

For example: The Tabernacle was made of the spoils of the Egyptians. Once it had been built, God lit the fire on the altar-hearth (Ex. 40, Lev. 9:23–24), simultaneously appointing the priests to tend it and care for the house. Similarly, the Temple was made of the spoils of David's wars against the Philistines. Once it had been built, God lit the fire on the altar-hearth (1 Kgs. 8:54). Again, the Church was set up out of the spoils of the Old Creation, especially of Israel. Once it had definitively been built in the Person of Jesus, God lit the fire on His altar-persons on the day of Pentecost (Acts 2).

Now, the Tabernacle and Temple contain features only of the first three days of creation. In them are lights (the glory of God above the cherubim, the lampstand, and burning incense), structure (the "mercy seat" cover between the Ark and the cherubim, and the veils), and plants (the

[17] Some recent models of the universe provide possible explanations of how this upward and outward expansion might have worked. See Douglas F. Kelly, *Creation and Change: Genesis 1:1–2:4 in the Light of Changing Scientific Paradigms* (Ross–Shire, UK: Mentor–Christian Focus Publications, 1997) chap. 7.

pot of manna, the face-bread and the beer [strong drink] on the table,[18] olive oil, and the materials used to make the incense and to perfume the oil). As built, these cosmic models do not contain any animals or human beings. When these houses were built, God's glory filled them so that no human beings could enter (Ex. 40; 2 Chr. 7:2; compare Acts 5:12–13). At that point, the "fourth-day" point, God lit the fire on the altar-hearth, the fire that was used to light the lamps and incense within once the priests entered. Only after the fire was lit were priests allowed within to bring the representative blood of animals and birds within also.

From this we see that the firmament is the altar-hearth before the Throne of God in heaven, and the lighting of the fires on that altar is the establishment of the sun, moon, and stars. God's house has been built and furnished. The servants of that house will be created on the fifth and sixth days.

And from all this we can see more clearly that the fourth day is a kind of preliminary sabbath. The initial work has been completed, and God lights His fires. Historically, this corresponds to the arrival of fire on the day of Pentecost in Acts 2, after the third-day resurrection of Jesus from the grave. From that Pentecost onward, God's new house (the Church) is to be filled.[19]

[18] The Table only has grain products on it, not wine. See Numbers 28:7. Wine was poured on the sacrifices of the outer court Altar (Numbers 15), but beer was poured into the vessels on the Table of Facebread.

[19] If I may be bold, let me suggest as a possibility that the Apostolic Church period bears a general relation to the fifth day, as the birds of the land (Jew) and the fishes of the sea (Gentile) are woven together into one new body in the Church, a process completed by the time of the destruction of Jerusalem. Thereafter, men (the saints) and animals (the unbelievers) exist together in this world, in an extended sixth day that awaits the coming of the final sabbath.

Cosmology

In terms of cosmology, a few further thoughts are warranted. Physically speaking, we have seen that the firmament is outer space, above the atmosphere where the birds fly. In the Old Creation, the departed saints seem to have dwelt in the firmament. Whether this was in another dimension or in outer space, we don't know. We do know that they were near the highest heaven and were able to communicate with God (Rev. 6:9–11; the altar spoken of is the Incense Altar, located in the firmament of the Holy Place, which is the symbolic ladder that reaches from the firmament heavens to the highest heavens).

At the same time, it does not appear that we can see through the firmament with telescopes and discern the throne of God. The firmament continues to be a barrier between heaven and earth until the full end of history. Heaven is located somewhere else, it is not contiguous with the physical cosmos we can travel in.

There are a couple of possibilities. One is that somehow the firmament (outer space) is closed in upon itself, circular in some way, so that to travel far enough in one direction is to return to one's starting point. This is one modern theory. Another is that the universe is truly infinite. This is not unacceptable to Christian belief. God is infinite in Himself, independently infinite, while an infinite universe is dependently infinite. Consider that human beings will live forever and are thus infinite in that sense. Possibly the universe goes on forever; the removal of the firmament at the end of history will mean that heaven is near to every part of it.

Turning to another question: At the present time, it is widely assumed that the speed of light is the same everywhere in the universe and has always been the same. Thus, the stars are said to be trillions of miles away from the earth, measured in terms of the span of time it takes light to travel in a year (light-years). This notion, we must insist, is simply an assumption. The modern view is that space is "nothingness" and therefore the same throughout. From the standpoint of creation, however, space is created, a "something" called the firmament. Space is a matrix in which all the bodies in space move and through which light moves.

There is no good reason to think that the speed of light is the same everywhere in the universe. Light may travel much faster between stars, and still faster between galaxies; that is, light may travel much faster away from "gravity wells" like the sun and the earth. Light from the farthest places in the universe may well reach us in only a few years.

Moreover, there is no good reason to think that the speed of light has remained the same throughout history. It may have begun at near infinity and slowed down exponentially since then. If the curve of the speed of light's diminution is hyperbolic, then it may be that by now it is slowing down at a very slow, almost imperceptible rate. Or, to put it another way: If the matrix of space expanded rapidly on the fourth day, as I have suggested, then perhaps the "thinning" of that firmament-matrix resulted in a diminution of the speed of light through it.

In short, there is no reason to reject the notion that the starry universe rapidly expanded and congealed on the fourth day, or the notion that light from faraway objects reaches us rather rapidly. Modern scientific theories and constructs are against this idea, but until we actually move into space and measure light's speed in various places, we shall not know. Human research has only begun to scratch the surface of the outer foyer of the starry universe.

The Nature of Government

The heavenly luminaries were made to govern, and government is not primarily spatial but temporal. The governing luminaries separated day and night and were established as symbols for setting up festival times (mistranslated "seasons"), days, and years. We see this throughout the Old Creation. The people of God knew when to celebrate Passover, a day, by observing the sun's vernal equinox and then the first new moon thereafter, and then counting fourteen days to the full moon. The signs of the zodiac, to which the Bible refers more than once, were also part of the symbolic display of the firmament.

We may learn from this that the real power of government is the appointment of times, the kinds of times mentioned in Ecclesiastes 3:1–8, and after the fall, the time to bring judgments against sinners.

Geocentricity

Finally, we should say a few words about geocentricity. The Bible is frankly geocentric in two important respects. First, the earth was made before the starry heavens and the sun. Everything moves out from the earth in Genesis 1. Second, the earth is the center of affairs, where humanity is placed and where Christ died and was resurrected. The Bible does not, however, teach that the earth is geographically or cosmically located at the center of the physical universe. Indeed, this is an unimportant concern, and possibly a fallacious one. If the universe be infinite, or if it be closed in upon itself, any point in it may be considered central. In fact, when Jesus says, "Wherever two or three are gathered together in My name, there I am," He is saying that wherever the Church is planted is the center.

Along these lines, consider where the center of the surface of a sphere is located. Any point on the surface of a sphere can be considered the center. Is Ararat, or Jerusalem, or Rome, the physical center of the world? Yes and no. Since humanity proceeded from Ararat after Noah, that is the center. Or it was. Is it still? To ask such a question is virtually to answer it. Whether or not the earth is physically located at the center of the physical universe, I know not. I do know that it is not a question dealt with in the Bible.[20]

[20] For more on this matter, see my essay "The Geocentricity Question," available from Biblical Horizons, Box 1096, Niceville, FL 32588.

Day Five

The fifth day sees the creation of land and sea creatures. These are said to swarm, to form clouds in the sea and air, and thus they are associated with the Spirit; for it is the Spirit who gathers the host of God around Him, forming the glory cloud.

The fifth day is often mistakenly put parallel to the second, as if birds are creatures of the firmament and fishes creatures of the original deep.[21] This is not the statement of the text. Birds fly "across the face of" the firmament—in front of it, not within it (v. 20). They are not part of the firmament, like the sun and moon, but dwell below it. While birds travel (usually) in the air (which is *not* the firmament), they are said to multiply on the earth (v. 22). Indeed, birds generally nest in trees. Also, the fishes are in the "sea," which is the name given to the *gathered* waters of day 3, not to the original "deep" waters of days 1 and 2. Thus, the fifth day is chiastically parallel to the third: land and sea :: creatures of land and sea.

Once again, three groups of creatures are made, to wit:

Tannins (aquatic dinosaurs)	the mighty Father
Fishes (sea)	the Son (the Fisher of Men)
Birds (air and land)	the hovering Spirit (1:2)

The tannins, or aquatic dinosaurs, call for comment. The word "create" is used in connection with their making, and this word always indicates a special, wondrous act of God. These great creatures show up at the end of Job as signs of God's power and rule. The fact is that stories of dragons are found all over the world, and the Bible (Job) refers to them. The notion that these great creatures had died out long before humanity arrived on the scene is contradicted by the clear testimony of history.

This is the first of three days of blessing. The blessing here is to multiply and fill. This is the blessing of the Spirit,

[21] See appendix B for a fuller discussion of this matter.

the Divine Matchmaker, who brings man and woman together, Bride and Christ together, and who creates a host for God.

The verb "be fruitful" contains the word "fruit" both in Hebrew and in English, linking the animals conceptually with the fruit trees of the third day.

The phrase "and it was established" is not found regarding the work of the fifth day. Rather, it is delayed until verse 24, after the creation of land animals. The text thereby groups the animals of the fifth and sixth days. Similarly, while the fishes and birds are blessed on the fifth day, the land animals are not given a similar blessing on the sixth day. The blessing of the fifth day surely extends to the land animals of the sixth, again linking all the animals together.

There are those who say that Genesis 1 presents three days of realms and three days of rulers. Nothing is said about the fishes ruling the sea or the birds ruling the air or land. This scheme is fallacious.

Covenantally, God's people always form a host around Him when the covenant is renewed.

Psalm 104:24–26 mentions the swarms of the sea and the great leviathan dinosaur.

At this point it might be well to take up a criticism of creationism, which is that there is a vast plethora of fossils in the world today, including coal and oil—too many (it is claimed) to have been deposited by the Great Flood. I cannot answer this objection fully here, but I can suggest some lines of an answer. I assume that the seas before the Flood were shallow throughout, and thus all teemed with life. Genesis 7:11 says that at the Flood "all the fountains of the great deep burst open." This indicates to me that the depths of the present oceans came into being at this point.

Moreover, since all the world was to be explored and occupied by men and animals, there is reason to believe that all the world was habitable at this time. There were no deserts, nor great mountain ranges, nor polar ice. Evidence for this is found in the quick-frozen mammoths in Siberia with warm-weather flora in their stomachs and mouths.

Thus, the world may well have teemed with far more life than it sustains at present, and this would account for the vast fossil deposits found on the earth today. Since the Flood Year was a "year of miracle," we are also free to assume that angels arranged these deposits in such a way that they would be useful for the coming generations of man.[22]

Day Six

The sixth day provides the creation of land animals and of humanity. As we saw above, the second day spills over to the first half of the third day, for only at that point did God say that it was good. Similarly, it seems that the fifth day spills over onto the first half of the sixth.

Day 1	Throne	Father
Day 2	High Altar	Son
Day 3a	Low Altar	Son
Day 3b	Glory Plants	Spirit
Day 4	Glory Lights	Spirit
Day 5	Swarmers	Spirit
Day 6a	Animals	Son
Day 6b	Man	Son
Day 7	Sabbath	Father

As the High Altar of the Firmament is related to the Low Altar of the land as structures, and thus is associated primarily with the Son, so also in reverse order, the land animals (lower; land) and man (upper; firmament), both structuring creatures rather than swarming creatures, are associated with the Son. (Land animals are much more territorial than fishes and birds, and thus they are more

[22] For more on this question, see James B. Jordan, "Creation With the Appearance of Age," in *Open Book* 45 (April, 1999).

associated with structure.) As regards the land animals, we once again have three groups:

Cattle	Domestic-sacrificial animals	Son
Creeping things	Swarms[23]	Spirit
Beasts	Ruling animals	Father

As we have seen, no parallel exists between the second and fifth days, eliminating the notion that the first three days are parallel to the next three. There is a parallel between the sixth day and the third. This is because humanity is related to every day of the creation week.[24] On the third day, the land was created as a throne for the plants. Similarly, the cattle (*behemah*) are a throne (*bamah*) for human life, for human beings depend, in the main, on domestic animals—or at least they did before the technological era. Notice in Revelation 17 that the Harlot is enthroned (*bamah*) on the Beast (*behemah*).[25]

No particular blessing is given to the land animals; we may assume that the Spirit's blessing upon the fishes and birds applies to them as well.

When we come to the second work of the sixth day, we come to the creation of humanity. The word "create," in-

[23] Within the world of land animals, creepers are more like swarmers than are cattle and beasts. But Genesis 1 calls them creepers rather than swarmers, I believe, because swarming is specifically associated with day 5 and the host-gathering Spirit.

[24] In terms of literary structure, this is because chiasms are cumulative. A chiasm is a way of structuring a literary flow, a "narrative" of one sort or another. Naturally, as the narrative proceeds, everything said before plays a part in what is said after. For a decent discussion of the whole phenomenon of chiasm in the Bible, see John Breck, *The Shape of Biblical Language* (Crestwood, NY: St. Vladimir's Seminary Press, 1994).

[25] The word *bamah* means "high place," or as Hirsch puts it, "an elevation which serves for raising a object." Hirsch associates *bamah* and *behemah* from the root *bvm.* See Samson Raphael Hirsch, *The Pentateuch: Genesis,* trans. Isaac Levy (Gateshead: Judaica Press, [1963] 1989) p. 29.

dicating a special wondrous work, is used for the third time here. Thus:

Create all things	Father
Create tannins[26]	Spirit
Create man	Son

Humanity is positioned between God and the lower creation in the firmament symbolically. He is to rule over the lower animals, which are listed as five:

Fishes
Birds
Cattle
Beasts (the "earth")
Creepers

This list of five is odd in this passage, which heretofore has been authored in terms of lists of two and three. I think the list is given this way to call attention to what is not listed: the tannins. The omission is striking. Humanity is not to rule over them. From the end of Job, we see that only God can rule them.

Let me suggest that the tannins no longer exist in the earth precisely because angels no longer rule humanity. We shall someday judge the angels (1 Cor. 6:3). At the present time, angels are God's servants for our good, but they no longer rule us as sergeants over raw recruits because in Christ we have graduated from officer boot camp and are now His officers in the world (Heb. 1:14). We are no longer positioned in the firmament under the angels. Tannins are (were) associated with angels, a part of creation that serves God but that we do not rule.[27]

God's blessing upon humanity starts with the blessing

[26] That is, the chief of the swarmers.

[27] In Job, the fire-breathing Leviathan ruled by God at the end of the book relates to the fire-sending Satan at the beginning of the book. Tannins also signify great gentile powers in the Scriptures, those nations that God's people did not rule over.

of the Spirit, to be fruitful, multiply, and fill the earth: As the land bears trees that bear fruit, so man, made of soil, is to bear fruit. It continues with the blessing of the Son: to subdue and rule over the earth.

God also lists the initial food given to man and to the animals. To man is particularly given the grains and fruit trees. We note that *all* the fruit trees "shall be" food for man, so we realize that the prohibition on the fruit of the Tree of Knowledge of Good and Evil, given in Genesis 2, is temporary.

The list of animals to whom food is given is:

Beasts
Birds
Creepers

Fish are omitted since God is speaking of the plants on the surface of the earth. Cattle are omitted, I believe, because man supervises their food; thus, they do not receive it directly from God.

In Psalm 104:27–30, the stress is on the food God gives to the animals, and by implication, to humanity.

Covenantally, a communion meal is always part of the covenant-making ceremony.

Day Seven

The seventh day is blessed with the blessing of the Father. That blessing comes when the work is finished and thus is eschatological. Because God has finished His work, He enters into His rest, which is unending. The Spirit, who has worked with the world during creation week, now enters into man (Gen. 2:7), and through man will complete the work He has begun. Humanity, empowered by the life of the Spirit, has a work to do, so man's weekly sabbath ends and ushers in another week, and then another, age after age until the end.

There is another triad here: the heavens and the earth were completed and all their hosts:

Heavens	Father
Earth	Son, "growing up" to be like Father
Hosts	Spirit

Covenantally, the sabbath day is the preeminent day of the Lord, coming after the first six days of the Lord. It is the normal time of covenant renewal in the Scriptures, for it is the time when God comes to visit His people (as He did on the first sabbath in Genesis 3).

Psalm 104:31–35 speaks of God's coming down on the mountains to be with His people, to judge the wicked, and to receive His people's praises.

Appendix A

Evening and Morning

Do the days of Genesis 1 begin in the evening or in the morning? Does the day run from twilight to twilight or from dawn to dawn? This question has divided exegetes for decades, and no consensus is in sight.

Let the well respected Old Testament scholar Gerhard Hasel present a summary of the evidence for an evening-to-evening day:

> The astronomical day was reckoned by the Hebrews from evening to evening (Gen. 1; Ex. 12:18; Lev. 23:27, 32); i.e., the day began at sunset and ended at sunset (cf. Lev. 22:6f.; Deut. 16:6; Neh. 13:19; Ps. 55:17; Esther 4:16; Is. 34:10; Jer. 27:3 [?]; Matt. 28:1; Luke 23:54; Mark 16:1f.; Acts 20:7; 2 Cor. 11:25) or evening. . . . In the creation account of Genesis 1 appears the repeated phrase "and there was evening and there was morning . . . day" (vv. 5, 8, 13, 19, 23, 31). The formula indicates (1) that "evening and morning" should be understood alike in all six days, (2) that the day begins with evening, (3) that each day is a real twenty-four-hour day, and (4) that thus the daily rhythm of time has its beginning. The creation day is understood as a normal twenty-four-day in Ex. 20:8–11; 31:15, 17. . . . The Hebrew compound "evening-morning" *('ereb boqer)* in Daniel 8:14 is a circumlocution for "day." It is the equivalent of the expression "there was evening and there was morning"—and emphasizes again that evening or sunset is the beginning of the

> twenty-four-hour calendar day in the OT and NT (cf. Mark 4:27; Luke 2:37; Acts 20:31; 26:7). In antiquity the Babylonians began the day likewise with sunset, but the Egyptians with sunrise. The custom of beginning the day at midnight derives from the Romans.[1]

The equally redoubtable Umberto Cassuto, however, argues just the opposite:

> An examination of the narrative passages of the Bible makes it evident that whenever clear reference is made to the relationship between a given day and the next, it is precisely sunrise that is accounted the beginning of the second day. For example: *They made their father drink wine that night . . . and* ON THE NEXT DAY, etc. (Gen. 19:33–34). Similarly: *When he arose early* NEXT MORNING (Judg. 6:38); *and* ON THE MORROW *the people rose early* (Judg. 21:4); *If you do not save your life tonight,* TOMORROW *you will be killed.* (1 Sam. 19:11); *and* TOMORROW *you and our sons shall be with me* (1 Sam. 28:19). Consonant with this tradition is the use of the expressions: *hayyom* ['the day' = *today*], *hallayla* ['the night' = *tonight*], *'emes* ['yesterday' = *last night*].
>
> Nor is this all. If we consider the Scriptural sections dealing with the ritual laws, particularly those that prescribe that the observance of Israel's holy days must begin in the evening, we see clearly that these passages corroborate, in their method of reckoning the dates, the evidence of the narrative portions. In Exodus 12:18, it is stated: *In the first month, on the* FOURTEENTH *day of the month at evening, you shall eat unleavened bread.* It is on the evening preceding the fifteenth day that the obligation of eating unleavened bread comes into force, yet that evening is refered to as the *fourteenth.* So, too, in Leviticus 23:32, with regard to the Day of Atonement, it is enjoined: *and you shall afflict yourselves on the* NINTH *day of the month beginning at evening, from evening to evening shall you keep your Sabbath;* thus the evening before the tenth is called *the ninth of the month.*

[1] G. F. Hasel, "Day," in *The International Standard Bible Encyclopedia*, 1979 edition (Grand Rapids, MI: Eerdmans, 1979) 1:877.

> It will thus be seen that throughout the Bible there obtains only one system of *computing time:* the day is considered to begin in the morning; but in regard to the festivals and appointed times, the Torah ordains that they shall be observed also on the night of the *preceding day.*[2]

I have to admit that I have no settled opinion on the matter. The following comments explain some of the difficulties.

First, it seems to me that both an evening-to-evening day and a morning-to-morning day are found in the Bible. Compare the following, both of which describe the same event:

> Now late on the sabbath, as it began to dawn toward the first of the week, Mary Magdalene and the other Mary came to look at the grave. (Matt. 28:1)

> And when the sabbath was over, Mary Magdalene, and Mary of James, and Salome, brought spices, that they might come and anoint Him. (Mark 16:1)

Matthew says the women came late on the sabbath, before the new day dawned. Mark says they came after the sabbath was over. It looks as if Matthew considers the new day as beginning at dawn, while Mark regards the old day as having ended the preceding evening, and thus the new day to have begun.

Second, while "day" is used for the whole 24-hour period of time, Genesis 1:5 defines it more closely as the time of light. Thus, the many passages of the Bible that speak of something's being done on such-and-such a day usually refer to the daytime part of the day.

Third, while Cassuto's evidence is impressive, the Bible distinguishes two evenings in Exodus 12:6: "[The Passover flockmember] is to be guarded by you until the fourteenth day of this month, and all the people of the congregation

[2] Umberto Cassuto, *A Commentary on the Book of Genesis, Part I: From Adam to Noah, Genesis I-VI 8,* trans. Israel Abrahams (Jerusalem: Magnes Press, [1944] 1961) p. 28f.

of Israel must slaughter it *between the evenings*" (cf. Ex. 29:39, 41; Lev. 23:5; Num. 28:4, 8). There is no difficulty understanding what the two evenings are; they are sunset and full dark, with twilight in between. With this in mind, we might answer Cassuto by saying that yes, the *first* evening and subsequent twilight are considered the last part of the preceding day, while the new day begins with the coming of the *second* evening, when it is fully dark.

The third problem for this reading is that the word for morning *(boqer)* does not mean daybreak. The Hebrew word for the edge of the end of night is *shahar,* "dawn." Morning is a period of time after the sun has risen. Night does not end in the morning in English or in Hebrew; it ends at dawn. For the morning-to-morning view to be correct, the text might better read, "and there was evening and there was dawn, a second day."

A similar way to read the text is that "there was evening and there was morning" refers not to the whole day but to the period of night only, which ends in the morning. Thus:

1. God makes the firmament.
2. Evening comes.
3. Morning comes.
4. A second day (the day ends).

There is a certain attractiveness to this view, because it provides a different explanation for why there is no such summary statement after the seventh day. That day goes on forever, in a sense, so there is no evening after it, and that is why we don't read that after God rested "there was evening and there was morning, a seventh day."

Attractive as this approach is, the arguments we have already provided can stand against it as well. As we have seen, "morning" is an extended period of time, which would take us into the next day. Nor does Leviticus 24:3, which says that the Lampstand was to be ordered "from evening to morning," stand against the fact that morning is not dawn.

Since there was no sunlight coming into the Tabernacle, the Lampstand had to burn all day as well as all night. At least it had to burn well into the morning, long enough for the priest to accomplish his daily morning tasks. Second Chronicles 29:7 indicates that it was sinful to put out the lamps on the Lampstand, implying that they burned perpetually.

Genesis 1 initially defines "day" as the period of light, which in context comes after a period of darkness (1:5). If we assume that this is the only meaning of "day" in Genesis 1, then the meaning of the phrase in question would be:

1. God makes the firmament.
2. Evening comes.
3. The period of morning comes.
4. The second day *begins.*

In that case, God made the firmament on the first day and rested on the sixth. But since we are told that He rested on the seventh, this interpretation is impossible.

Let me suggest that the sabbath is the key here. Leviticus 23:32 says "from evening to evening you shall keep your sabbath." This statement applies directly to the Day of Covering, but since it is called "sabbath" and nothing otherwise is said about how the other sabbaths were kept, I submit that evening-to-evening applied to all sabbaths. Exodus 20:11 tells us that the seventh day of creation was the first sabbath, the Divine prototype. Thus, it follows that this first sabbath ran from evening to evening. Whether the Bible consistently refers to other days as beginning in the evening, or sometimes speaks of them as beginning in the morning, is immaterial. The sabbaths began in the evening.[3]

[3] Though one can argue that since "sabbath" is singular and not plural in Leviticus 23:32, the evening-to-evening sabbath only applied to that one occasion. My argument, thus, is not water-tight.

The statement immediately preceding the seventh day is: "And there was evening and there was morning, the sixth day" (Gen. 1:31). If this sentence speaks of the close of the sixth day and the beginning of the seventh, then the sabbath did not begin in the evening. Thus, the evening and morning in 1:31 must refer back to the sixth day, in which case the previous occurences of this phrase must also refer back to the day they are associated with. Each day begins with evening, consists of evening and morning, and runs to the next evening.

Does this solve all problems? Not quite. First, does day 1 really begin with an evening? It seems to begin in absolute darkness and then move to the light of day. We think of the evening as a time of diminishing light, not of absolute night-darkness, and that seems to be the way the biblical term is used also. We can salvage the traditional view, however, by noting that Genesis 1:1 says that God made heaven and earth. The heaven is full of light. The earth is full of darkness. Thus, the sequence heaven-earth is a sequence from light to dark, and in that sense the earth is created in evening, as light dies away.

Second, "morning" is only the first part of the day. Summarizing the entire day, the text of 1:8 might have said, "and there was night and there was day, a second day." But that is not what is said. We can paraphrase the actual text this way: "The light waned (evening), and the light waxed full again (morning), a second day." In other words, the text is not contrasting night and day but is speaking of the rhythm, the movement, from light's diminishing as the whole day begins to light's return as the full day arrives. The rhythmic flow of time is emphasized.

Thus, a full day is characterized as beginning with the waning of light and then the return of light. That is what makes a full day a day, a time of light (1:5, "God called the light day"). There is a wee bit of light at the beginning of the full day (at evening), followed by a time of relative darkness (but with the moon and stars showing some light still), which then advances to full light in the morning. This is a very temporal way of speaking, a way of speaking that actually anticipates the course of history as one vast day of the Lord: beginning with the light of His covenant making, proceeding through times of struggle, and then coming to the morning of the kingdom and the fullness of day.

Thus, I believe that the traditional view is most likely correct. The word "day" is defined as the time of light, and that meaning is expanded to encompass the entire 24-hour timespan. The whole period is named for the second, more glorious part of it. In their essence, all these periods of time are days, though they start with night and move to day, more narrowly conceived. Day 1 began when God created bright heaven and dark earth, moved through a period of darkness, and then into the light of day, the whole of which was one day.

Understanding that each day moves from darkness to light also shows us that the work of each day is an amplification of the first work of sending forth light. Each new work is a new light, a new work of the Spirit, and thus a new manifestation of God's glory. I submit that this is an important aspect of the theology of Genesis 1, which would be far less in evidence if the evenings followed the mornings.

Appendix B

Chiasm and Structure in Genesis One

I have pointed to the chiastic structure of the days of Genesis 1 several times in the course of the present study (pp. 43, 195). My purpose here is to summarize and briefly illustrate the chiastic literary form, particularly for readers not familiar with it.

The word "chiasm" (KY-azm) comes from the Greek letter *chi*, pronounced "kh," and written X. This X shape, when we look at it from bottom to top, represents a literary structure that presents certain ideas (the bottom of the X), moves to a central pivot point (the center), and then upwards to the representation of those same ideas in a transformed way (the top of the X). An extended chiasm is also called a palistrophe.

A chiasm is not merely a structure of ideas; in narrative passages it is also a flow of events that move in time. We use the term "inverse parallelism" for a passage that says the same basic thing twice, in reverse order. Psalm 19:1, in Hebrew, is an example of "inverse parallelism" that is not a full or pure chiasm, because it does not have a flow to a central pivot and then a flow out from that pivot:

The heavens
declare
God's glory;
His handiwork
displays [is displayed by]
The firmament.[1]

An example of inverse parallelism in Genesis 1 is found in verses 14–16:

Let them be for signs
And for festival times
And for days and years . . .
The greater light to govern the day,
And the lesser light to govern the night;
The stars also.

Stars are for signs primarily. Festival times in the Old Creation were governed by the moon (first month, fourteenth day, etc.). The sun determines days and years.

In inverse parallelism, the second set of phrases adds something to the first set and usually intensifies it in some fashion. A true chiasm, however, is not just a series of balancing ideas that when compared bring out further associations (as the balances in Genesis 1:14–16 do). Breck argues that for an inverse parallelism to be considered a chiasm, there must be a central idea or pivot that is the most important, so that the phrase or passage rises to a central point and then descends again.[2] For instance, arguably Genesis 1:14–16 should be seen as a chiasm, since the sun is the most important of the heavenly luminaries and it is central.

Another example, one of hundreds in the Bible, where the central idea is most important is Genesis 9:6:

[1] The verb "displays" is active voice in Hebrew, but the subject of the second phrase is "the firmament." There is no way to translate this into English without either putting "displays" in the passive voice or changing the word order to "the firmament displays His handiwork."

[2] John Breck, *The Shape of Biblical Language: Chiasmus in the Scriptures and Beyond* (Crestwood, NY: St. Vladimir's Seminary Press, 1994) chap. 3.

Whoever sheds
the blood
of *man,*
by *man*
shall his blood
be shed.

There is one additional element in a full chiasm, and that is that as the sequence of ideas moves upward to the pivot, and on up to the top of the X, the second half carries with it all the ideas of the first half, and thus the entire sequence is cumulative. The second half intensifies the first half and brings the entire chiasm to a second climax at the end. Thus, a full chiasm has two places of climax.[3] For instance, the narrative of the Tower of Babel in Genesis 11 is a full chiasm:

A. One lip, one vocabulary (culture), v. 1
B. Shinar, v. 2a
C. Dwell together, v. 2b
D. Said to one another, v. 3a
E. "Lend your strength," v. 3b
F. Bricks and tar, v. 3c
G. Build city and tower, v. 4a
H. Name of their own, v. 4b
I. Lest we be scattered, v. 4c
H' Yahweh as Name, v. 5a
G' Examine city and tower, v. 5b
F' One people and one lip, v. 6
E' "Lend your strength," v. 7a
D' Confuse one another, v. 7b
C' Scattered, v. 8
B' Babel, v. 9a
A' Confused lip, many cultures, v. 9b

Notice that the pivot of the narrative, where the people reject God's command to take dominion over the entire

[3] Ibid., chap. 4.

earth, is answered by the second climax at the end, where God forces them to do so.[4]

Another example is Psalm 98, which celebrates the arrival of the king; this is signified by taking up musical instruments and singing (compare Rev. 4–5):

A Psalm.

1:A Sing to Yahweh a new song,
For He has done wonderful things,
His Salvation-worker is His right hand and His holy arm.
Yahweh has made known His Salvation;

B Before the eyes of the nations He has revealed His righteousness.

C He has remembered His lovingkindness and His faithfulness to the house of Israel;

D All the ends of the land have seen the Salvation of our God.

2:E Shout joyfully to Yahweh, all the land;
F Break forth
G and sing for joy
H and make music *[play musical instruments]*.
I Make music *[play musical instruments]*
J TO YAHWEH
I' with the lyre;
H' With the lyre
G' and the voice of song.
F' With trumpets and the sound of the ram's horn
E' Shout joyfully before the King, Yahweh.

3:D' Let the sea roar and its fullness,
The world and those who dwell in her.

C' The rivers: let them clap their hands;

B' The mountains all together: let them sing for joy before Yahweh.

A' For He is coming to judge the land.
He will judge the world with righteousness and the peoples with equity.

[4] Comparing F and F', we see that the bricks joined with tar symbolize the people bound by one lip, or religious confession. For a full

Analysis. The center of this psalm is a clear and unmistakable chiasm, which indicates to us that we should read the whole psalm as a chiasm. Reading it this way we see a very clear progression. Section I focuses on God's new Savior coming to the nations and to Israel (land). Section II is a call for praise. Section III shows us the response of praise in the nations (sea, world), in Israel ([Edenic] rivers), and in all the world (all mountains together). More specifically:

B Nations
  C Israel (as house)
    D Israel (land) (third day imagery)
    D' Nations (sea) (third day imagery)
  C' Israel (as garden of rivers)
B' Both

Each group is chiastically matched with its complement, but the overall progression is from Israel to the nations, or as the last two lines put it, from the land to the world. It is worth noting that Psalm 98 is the central psalm in the chiasm of Book 4, and it is itself wholly chiastic.[5]

We have seen that Genesis 1 is just such a full chiasm. The passage is focused on the idea of day/light, with each day moving from evening to morning, so that the work of each day is an expansion of God's original work of light-bringing. This rises to a climax at the center on the fourth day, and then it moves upward to an even greater climax on the seventh, the day which has no ending: the light is now permanent and there is no longer any darkness at all.

Genesis 1, in fact, can be seen as having three climactic points. The central pivot is the enthronement of the luminaries to govern the world on the fourth day. The final

analysis of this passage, see James B. Jordan, "Babylon and the Babel Project," in *Studies in the Revelation* 11–15 (November, 1996 March, 1997), especially Nos. 11–12.

[5] On the chiastic structure of Book 4 of the Psalter, see James B. Jordan, "The Fourth Book of the Psalter," in *Christendom Essays, Biblical Horizons* No. 100 (Niceville, FL: Biblical Horizons, December, 1997) pp. 136–173.

climax is the picture of God enthroned in heavenly rest. A preliminary final climax comes on the sixth day, which is by far the longest section of the narrative, which concerns the creation of the images of God, His earthly light-bearers.

Now, a chiasm may just present a set of ideas, but when a chiasm is used to describe historical events, it is also an historical flow.[6] The fact that Genesis 1 is also an historical flow is clear from the enumeration of the days—not just one day after another, but a first, second, third, etc. day. It is also clearly an historical flow from the use of the repeated refrain "there was evening and there was morning." Thus, when the Frameworkers strip Genesis 1 of its historical time flow, they not only deny a huge part of its revelatory meaning, they also grossly corrupt its literary structure.

The heptamerous (seven-fold) chiasm of Genesis 1 is picked up as a model for a number of creation/decreation passages in the Bible. One such is the Night Visions of Zechariah 1–6, to wit:

[6] For instance, the Abraham, Jacob, and Joseph narratives in Genesis are large chiasms. So are the whole books of Judges, Kings, Esther (two parallel chiasms in the two stories), Jeremiah, and Matthew. For outlines, see *Biblical Horizons* 110 (October, 1998; Abraham); 111 (November, 1998; Jacob); 113 (January, 1999; Joseph); 79 (November, 1995; Judges and Kings); 94–95 (April–May, 1997; Matthew); James B. Jordan, *Esther in the Midst of Covenant History* (Niceville, FL: Biblical Horizons, 1995); Jordan, *Countdown to Exile: The End of the Kingdom of Judah.* Biblical Horizons Occasional Paper 29 (July, 1997; Jeremiah; available from Biblical Horizons, Box 1096, Niceville, FL 32588).

Day 1: **"I saw at night, and behold" (Zech. 1:8).**
Yahweh and His host, by (not "in") the deep.
Spirit of God over the face of the deep.
Preparation for action.

Day 2: **"And I lifted up my eyes, and looked, and behold" (Zech. 1:18).**
Old altar torn down; new altar being erected.
Firmament platform over the world.

Day 3a: **"And I lifted up my eyes, and looked, and behold" (Zech. 2:1).**
Separation of God's people from the world system.
Separation of land from the sea.
God's glory in and around His people.

Day 3b: **"And he showed me" (Zech. 3:1).**
Day of Covering restores priesthood: vine and fig tree (Feast of Booths) ensue.
Grain and fruit plants on the land.
Change of (linen, vegetable) garments.

Day 4: **"The angel returned, roused me as from sleep, and said, 'What do you see?' . . . I see, and behold" (Zech. 4:1–2).**
Lampstand.
Sun, moon, and stars.

Day 5: **"And I lifted up my eyes again, and looked, and behold" (Zech. 5:1).**
"Leprosy" (anti-glory) uncleanness on the houses of secret sinners.
Swarms of birds and fish: glory clouds.
Contrast houses of Israelites gathered around God.
Contrast Feast of Booths (vine and fig tree; 3:10).

Day 6: **"Lift up now your eyes, and see" (Zech. 5:5).**
Ephah of Wickedness given temple in Shinar.
Humanity set in Garden of Eden.

Day 7: **"And I lifted up my eyes again, and looked, and behold" (Zech. 6:1).**
Horses and chariots ride forth and cause God's Spirit to rest in the North.
Sabbath rest.

Numerous other biblical passages also track the chiasm of Genesis 1.[7]

The Three Panel Structure in Genesis One

That there is also a three panel literary structure in Genesis 1 cannot be denied, but at the same time, this structure is not the primary one. What I am calling the "three panel" structure is this: There is at least one general correlation between the first three days of creation week and the second three:

1. Light	4. Luminaries
(2. Firmament between waters)	(5. Fishes and birds)
3a. Land	6a. Land animals
3b. Plants	6b. Humanity

The fact that both the third and the sixth day have two parts, and that humanity is parallel to plants in Genesis 2, indicates a literary correlation that we should not miss. (On plants and men, see appendix D.)

At the same time, the Framework Interpretation (in particular) has made too much of these parallels. Some have tried to make these two sets of days into Days of Forming followed by Days of Filling. The problem with this approach is threefold. First, Genesis 1 is concerned with three matters, not two (i.e., darkness, shapelessness, and emptiness). Second, the world is filled with plants on the second half of the third day, which is in the first part of the week. Third, the birds do not fill the firmament, or even travel in it; they only travel across the face of it. They are said to

[7] For instance, the tabernacle-building in Exodus 25–40; see James B. Jordan, *The Tabernacle: A New Creation,* Biblical Horizons Occasional Paper 5 (2nd ed., June, 1993: available from Biblical Horizons, Box 1096, Niceville, FL 32588). On the seven feasts of Leviticus 23, see James B. Jordan, *Covenant Sequence in Leviticus and Deuteronomy* (Tyler, TX: Institute for Christian Economics, 1989) p. 38. The seven trumpets and the seven bowls of Revelation both have judgments against the sun in the fourth position. Etc.

multiply on the land, which goes with the third day, not the second, so that there is no real parallel between the second and fifth days. Thus, this approach to the passage fails to account for all the significant details.

Others have suggested three days of Realms and three days of Rulers. The problem here is that the creatures of the fifth day are not said to rule anything, nor are the land animals of day 6a. Accordingly, this approach to the passage also fails.

We must not toss out the baby with the bathwater, however. There is a relationship between the light of day 1 and the luminaries of day 4—though this relationship is fully established by the chiastic structure of the passage, which lines up days 1, 4, and 7 (but also lines up days 2, 4, and 6). More importantly, there is a parallel, as noted, between days 3 and 6. And we can add that while the birds do not dwell in or travel in the firmament, the words "waters" and "firmament" do occur in day 5, creating a slight parallel with day 2. Indeed, taking later passages of the Bible into account, the great tannins of day 5 are once associated with the "deep" sea of day 2 (Psalm 148:7), and the birds (symbolizing angels and the Spirit) with the firmament of day 2.

Thus, a three panel literary arrangement of Genesis 1 is indeed present, but it is more subtle than the traditional "forming and filling" and "realms and rulers" approaches allow. Moreover, the three panel structure only takes in a few of the details of Genesis 1, as compared with the chiastic structure of the passage, and thus it is of only secondary importance.

My larger point is this: The Framework Interpretation claims to take the literary structure of Genesis 1 with the utmost seriousness and even pits that literary structure against the historical claims of the narrative. In fact, however, the Framework Interpretation has utterly failed to discern the true literary structure of the narrative.

Some Additional Literary Structures in Genesis One

Not only are the seven days to be understood as a chiasm, but there are other chiastic flows in the passage as well, providing a beautiful "polyphonic" symphony of melodies that harmonize with one another perfectly.

A. The refrain "And God saw that it was good" occurs seven times in the passage, and the arrangement is chiastic:

A. Day 1 Light good
  B. Day 3a Both separations good
    C. Day 3b Plants good
      A' Day 4 Luminaries good
    C' Day 5 Fishes and birds good
  B' Day 6a Animals good
A" Day 6b Man good

Just as the chiasm of the seven days associates light with the luminaries and with the sabbath, so this chiasm associates humanity with the light and the lightbearers. The B sections link the emergence of the land with the land animals. The C sections link the glorifying of the earth by two hosts of plants with the glorifying of the seas and air by the two hosts of fishes and birds. The central section links most closely with the A sections, of course, but in that it glorifies the fourth realm, it also links with the C sections in terms of glorification.

B. The refrain "and it was established" occurs six times in the passage, and it too is chiastically arranged; to wit:

A. Day 2 Firmament established
  B. Day 3a Sea and land established
    C. Day 3b Plants established
    C' Day 4 Luminaries established
  B' Day 6a Fishes, birds, and land animals established
A' Day 6b Man established

As the chiasm of the seven days links man with the firmament, so it does here. The B sections link the sea-land distinction with the creatures of sea and land. The C sections link the glorifying of the lower altar (the earth) with the glorifying of the higher altar (the firmament).

The Shekinah Light of day 1 was not "established" because it was destined to give way to the luminaries of day 4.

C. The refrain "and God said" occurs nine times in the passage, and once again it is chiastically arranged:

A. Day 1 Light
  B. Day 2 Firmament
    C. Day 3a Dry land appears
      D. Day 3b Plants
        E. Day 4 Luminaries
      D' Day 5 Fishes and birds
    C' Day 6a Land animals
  B' Day 6b Man as image and ruler
A' Day 6c Plants for man and animals

As always, the luminaries of the fourth day are central. The D sections link the glorifying plants with the glorifying fishes and birds, as above. The C sections link the land with the land animals. The B sections once again link the firmament with man. The A sections don't seem to correspond, but perhaps we are intended to see a link between the light produced by the Spirit and the life given by the Spirit through the consumption of plants.

Indeed, we can add on the outside of this structure that the narrative begins with God in eternal rest, creating the world, and ends with Him in sabbath rest, having finished His work of creating and making.

D. In terms of the Trinity, we move chiastically:

A. Day 1 Throne of Father
B. Day 2 High Altar of Son
C. Day 3a Low Altar of Son
D. Day 3b Glory Plants of Spirit
E. Day 4 Glory Lights of Spirit
D' Day 5 Glory Swarms of Spirit
C' Day 6a Low Images of Son
B' Day 6b High Images of Son
A' Day 7 Sabbath Enthronement of Father

We have pointed out that the firmament is the high altar, parallel to the Altar of Incense in the Tabernacle, and that the land is the low altar, parallel to the Bronze Altar in the Tabernacle courtyard. That animals are "low images" of the Son is seen in that they are offered in sacrifice as representatives of men, the "high images" of the Son. At the center is the glorification, associated with the Spirit, of the four aspects of the creation:

Fire – glorified firmament (day 4)
Air – glorified by birds (day 5)
Land – glorified by plants (day 3b)
Sea – glorified by fishes (day 5)

E. In the first half of Genesis 1, we descend from God's heavenly throne to the land and sea, rising back up with the plants and then moving back up to the firmament; we then descend to the sea creatures and then ascend back up to the highest heaven. Thus:

At the heavenly throne
Down to the firmament
Down to the land (God called the land earth)
And to seas below it (God called the waters seas)
Plants grow back up toward the firmament
Back up to the firmament
Down to the sea below the land (Let the waters teem)
Back up to the beasts on the land (birds, and then beasts)
Back up to man "in the firmament"
Back to the heavenly throne

F. There may be a hint of chiasm in the things God specifically named on Days 1–3, with the Heaven at the center. The Earth, lighted from above by the Day, would contrast with the Seas, which in their depths are full of Night:

God called the light Day and the darkness Night (day 1)
    God called the firmament Heaven (day 2)
God called the land Earth and the waters Seas (day 3)

G. We have noted the inverse parallel structure of the fourth day in the discussion above. Note the following also:

Waters gathered (v. 9a)
    Dry land appears (v. 9b)
        And it was established (v. 9c)
    Dry land: earth (v. 10a)
Gathered waters: seas (v. 10b)

Be fruitful, multiply, and fill (v. 28a)
    Subdue (v. 28b)
    Rule over animals (v. 28c)
Plants, which already fill the earth (vv. 29-30)

Heavens and earth (2:1a)
    Completed (2:1b)
        All their (gathered) hosts (2:1c)
        Seventh (sabbath) day (2:2a)
    Completed (2:2b)
His work that He had done (2:2c)

God rested from His work (2:2d)
    God blessed the seventh day (2:3a)
God rested from His work (2:3b)

H. Note the *inclusio* of the entire passage, which brackets the chiasm of the seven days:

God created the heavens and the earth (1:1)
  The work of the days: creating and making
Created and made (2:3b)

This is, again, a true chiasm. We start only with creating. During the days we add the idea of making things out of created things. The conclusion collects both actions.

I. The triadic lists in the passage can be summarized thus, in the order they are presented in the statements "and God made":

Father:	Sun	Tannins	Beasts
Son:	Moon	Fishes	Cattle
Spirit:	Stars	Birds	Creepers

J. The following dyads also appear, though not always in the same configuration. It would be pointless to try and find a chiastic structure here. Rather, we should note the relationship of inferiors to superiors. The dyads marked A proceed from superior to inferior and from first to second. The dyads marked B move from inferior to superior. In every case, the movement is eschatological, as the inferior is to grow up to be equal to the superior in some sense. Thus:

A. Heavens – Earth (v. 1)
  The earth is to mature to become like heaven.

A. Light – Darkness (v. 4)

A. Day – Night (v. 5)

B. Evening – Morning (vv. 5, 8, 13, 19, 23, 31)
  Darkness and night are to become like day, as evening precedes morning.

B. Waters below – Waters above (v. 7)

The waters below are lifted up to become waters above, a type of humanity, the soil that emerges from and is baptized by these waters.

A. Waters – Dry Land (v. 9)

A. Earth – Seas (v. 10)
Initially the waters were over the dry land, so they are mentioned first at the beginning; once they are below the land, we find the order Earth – Seas.

B. Grains – Fruit trees (vv. 11 and 12)
Grains precede fruit trees, as bread precedes wine in daily life and in the Lord's Supper. (You start the day with bread; you end it with a glass of wine.)[8]

A. Day – Night (v. 14)

A. Symbols – Festivals (v. 14)
The luminaries as symbols precede the luminaries as festival markers, because the Word precedes the Sacrament.

A. Days – Years (v. 14)
Days precede Years because the Day of the Lord is the primary symbol, while the Acceptable Year of the Lord is secondary. The Day of God is foundational and endless, while solar years will end at the final Day of the Lord.

A. Heavens – Earth (v. 17)

A. Day – Night (v. 18)

A. Light – Darkness (v. 18)

B. Fishes – Birds (v. 20)
Fishes precede Birds because the waters below preceded the emergence of land.

B. Fruitful – Multiply (v. 22)
Fruitfulness is the precondition for multiplication and is a more general term, for we bear many kinds of fruits (such as the fruits of the Spirit).

[8] The wine of the not-yet-created "shrub" is the final form of the fruit of the trees made on the third day.

B. Fill the seas – Multiply on the land (v. 22)

Filling the seas precedes multiplying on the land because the sea preceded the land.

B. Image – Likeness (v. 26)

Man *is* the image of God, even in hell, but he is to grow in the likeness of God, maturing to fullness.

A. Male – Female (v. 27)

Male precedes Female. In history, man rules woman, but the initial Adam also grows to become the Bride of Christ. Masculinity is protological in humanity, while feminity is eschatological. Men initiate; women glorify.

B. Fruitful – Multiply (v. 28)

B. Fill – Subdue (v. 28)

Filling the earth must precede subduing it.

B. Grains – Fruit trees (v. 29)

A. Heavens – Earth (2:1)

B. Completed – Rested (2:2)

Completing His work precedes God's resting from it.

B. Blessed – Sanctified (2:3)

Blessing is the precondition for sanctification.

A. Created – Made (2:3)

Creating is the initial work, making the secondary.

Appendix C

Paul H. Seely on the Waters in Genesis One

Paul H. Seely, "The Firmament and the Water Above," *The Westminster Theological Journal* 53(1991):227–240; 54 (1992):31–46.

Paul H. Seely, "The Geographical Meaning of 'Earth' and 'Seas' in Genesis 1:10," *The Westminster Theological Journal* 59 (1997):231–55.

In these two essays, Mr. Seely provides a very careful exegesis and explanation of the meaning of the firmament, the waters above the firmament, the land, and the ocean, according to Genesis 1. There is much of value in these essays, and I have drawn upon them in these studies, but I believe they also contain significant errors that are in need of correction.

Seely holds that the Bible is inerrant, but he agrees with B.B. Warfield that the Bible was also written in terms of the scientific understanding of its times. Thus, the biblical picture of the cosmos should not bind us as we consider the actual arrangement of the universe.

In each of his essays, Seely begins by surveying the views of a wide range of the primitive peoples of the world and of ancient cultures. He concludes that before the arrival of modern understandings, men pretty universally believed that there was a hard shell or dome over a flat, circular earth that floated on water and was surrounded by water. (A few cultures did not believe that the earth floated on water.)

Seely turns to the Bible and attempts to show that the same understanding of the physical cosmos is found there. He is quite clear that neither the early cultures nor the biblical people took this world picture as a mere metaphor, but that they believed this is how the world really is.

Turning to Seely's first article, we find that throughout the history of the Church until the modern era, it was universally held by expositors that the firmament was a hard shell supporting a heavenly ocean. Only after the development of modern views of the universe did expositors suggest that the firmament might just be the atmosphere with clouds in it, or that the waters above the firmament might refer to a water vapor canopy over the earth before the Flood.

Seely does a good job of demolishing these modern notions. The firmament, or *raqia'*, was "made" according to Genesis 1. Thus, it cannot be merely the absence of something, for it is something actually made. Genesis 1 might have said that God put "room" or "space" between the waters, but it does not. Further, the firmament is the place where the sun, moon, and stars were later put. Thus it cannot be the atmosphere, and the waters above the firmament cannot be a water vapor canopy over the earth.

In this first article Seely is quite firm on the point that the firmament is something hard, and that it in fact holds back the heavenly waters. In his second article, however, Seely admits that the verb *raqa'*, and thus the noun *raqia'*, can refer not to something hard that is stamped out but simply to something spread out, as in Psalm 136:6.

Now, as Seely shows in his first article, the ancients used to argue over what this hard firmament is made of. The Bible does not say what it is made of. In light of this, Seely might have suggested that perhaps the firmament is not made of any kind of metal or stone at all, or anything hard. All we know is that God made it of some created substance. It might, in fact, have been made of "spread out" empty space, if we consider "empty space" as actually having a matrix of some sort.

Seely comes at Genesis 1 from the perspective of the ancient world, assuming that it was written in terms of the science of that time. It would be better to assume that God inspired Genesis 1 in such a way that it is not written in terms of the science of any time, though it does not conflict with the true arrangement of the cosmos, rightly understood.

Hidden in his procedure is the notion that the Bible arose in and out of a Hebrew culture, something the Bible emphatically denies. The Bible came down as the Word of God to stand over and against and to criticize the Hebrew culture. The prophets stood outside their culture and spoke down to it from a standpoint on high. To the extent that the Hebrews learned about the heavens from the Babylonians and the Egyptians, that learning is brought into question on every page of the Bible, for the Babylonian and Egyptian skies were full of gods. Many Hebrews may well have thought like the Babylonians and Egyptians, but the prophets sent by God to write the Bible did not.

Just as some modern conservatives err by stuffing modern science into Genesis 1, so Seely stuffs ancient science into it. He imports into the text notions of a hard shell and a hard-domed sky that are in fact not present there at all. However common such notions may have been among the idolatrous nations roundabout, and however common they may have been in the minds of ancient Israelites, they are not found in Genesis 1. All that is present in the text is a "stretched out something."

Here is where Seely overlooks something important. Genesis 1 clearly states that God put the sun, moon, and stars in the firmament. If the firmament were a rotating hard shell over the earth, the sun, moon, and stars would all have to move together. In fact, they do not, and everyone in the ancient world knew it. (It is, after all, impossible not to know it!) They also knew that the moving stars (planets) were not fixed to any hard firmament. For them, the hard firmament was the area of the fixed stars, not of the sun, moon, and planets. But this is *not* what Genesis 1 states. Genesis 1 puts all these various moving bodies in the area called "firmament," and that means that the firmament cannot be a hard shell.

I have argued that the proper interpretation of Genesis 1 is this: On the second day, God made a spread-out of something and set it to divide the waters above and below, creating an earthly and a heavenly sea. Given the meaning of *raqia'*, this "spread out something" was essentially flat. Then, on the fourth day, God expanded this firmament outward, breaking up the primordial light into the sun, moon, and stars (Is. 40:22). Later passages of the Bible speak of the firmament both as a surface (as it continues to appear) and as a three-dimensional environment (as the fourth day of Genesis 1 clearly implies).

As to the waters above the firmament, Seely is absolutely correct. Those waters were literally taken up into the angelic heaven, where they form the sea of glass/ice/crystal.

The finished firmament of Genesis 1 is what we now call outer space. The "substance" of that firmament is the matrix of space itself. The hard shell (if it was hard) of the second day has been broken up and expanded to form stars, planets, and cosmic dust, as well as the spatial matrix in which these subsist.

To be sure, Genesis 1 was doubtless read in the ancient world in terms of their view of the universe, but it can also be read without compromise or difficulty in terms of a modern understanding of outer space.

The waters beyond the firmament are on the other side of outer space, in heaven. I am not at all sure that heaven is a place that can be reached by travel in a spaceship; rather it seems to exist in "another dimension," so that when heaven is opened, it is very near to the people who see into it. The starry universe is, however, finite. The notion of an infinite universe gives rise to what is called Olbers's Paradox: If the universe goes on forever in every direction, our eye will see a star in every direction—in which case the sky would be white at night, every nook and cranny filled in with a light-streaming star. The fact that the sky is not white with light indicates that in some sense the universe is finite and in some sense boundaried.[1] Thus, while modern science shows us a vastly larger and deeper firmament than the ancients believed in, that firmament is still bounded, and in some sense heaven is on the other side of it.

We now turn to Seely's second article, which is on the land and sea in Genesis 1. As noted, Seely shows that premodern people believed (and still believe) that the earth is a circular island surrounded by water and (usually) floating on a vast sea. He then tries to argue that the Bible presents such a flat earth, and not simply as a metaphor in passages comparing the earth to an altar or a house but as a reality.

His case for this is not convincing. He argues first, from Daniel 4, that since the great tree reaching to heaven was "visible to the ends of the earth," this presupposes a flat earth. Seely errs in assuming that "earth" here means exactly what it means in Genesis 1. First of all, the Bible often speaks of empires as ruling the entire earth, when in fact they only ruled part of it. The ancients spoke the same way, even though they knew full well that there were nations and peoples outside the boundaries of their lands. Thus, "all the earth" and "to the ends of the earth" does not mean, in such contexts, the entire physical earth but

[1] For a full discussion, see Stanley L. Jaki, *The Paradox of Olbers' Paradox* (New York: Herder & Herder, 1969).

rather a "political earth."[2] Second, of course, Daniel 4 is a vision, and in a vision the pictures are to be taken symbolically, not literally. The other (few) passages that Seely discusses are also speaking metaphorically and must not be pressed to imply a literal notion. Job 38:13, for instance, does not say that the earth is hard and flat but that it is like a carpet that can be shaken (as in an earthquake). The passage is metaphorical, not scientific.

Genesis 1 says that the waters are under the earth. This is quite literally true, but it does not imply that the earth is one circular continent, or that it is flat. There is only one world ocean, and all the land in the world rises above it.[3]

Seely then attempts to show that the Bible teaches that the earth floats on a vast underground ocean, from which arise springs and rivers. Not all of his arguments for this are sound, as when he refers to the great bronze ocean in Solomon's Temple. That laver portrayed the heavenly ocean raised up above the earth on the backs of bronze bulls and resting in the firmament of the laver itself.

Clearer are Psalm 136:6 and 24:2, which speak of the earth as spread out upon waters and as founded upon water. Similarly, Genesis 49:25 speaks of the blessings that come from the sea below, which cannot refer to any body of water but to water below the ground.

All of this is quite true, but it does not mean or imply that there is a body of water under all the ground of the

[2] In fact *'erets* always refers to a political earth. In Genesis 1, God is the ruler of all the world, so that all the world is His *'erets*, His political empire.

[3] It may be that the notion of a one-continent world has a root in historical fact. When I was in college, the notion of continental drift was disparaged as a discredited theory. Nowadays it seems back in vogue. If all the continents were joined before the Flood, this could partially account for the perpetuation of a one-land world in cultures unaware of the real configuration of the post-deluvial world. On continental drift and the Flood, see Douglas F. Kelly, *Creation and Change: Genesis 1:1–2:4 in the Light of Changing Scientific Paradigms* (Ross–Shire, UK: Mentor–Christian Focus Publications, 1997) p. 184.

earth. These passages might well be symbolic or metaphorical. At the same time, if you dig down far enough, you will find water. Some degree of wetness is under the ground everywhere in the world. From that underground wetness come springs and rivers. We call this underground water the "water table."

Genesis 1, however, does not say anything at all about water under the earth. It contrasts the sea with "dry" land. The moist soil under the dry surface of the land is all that "water under the earth," mentioned elsewhere, need imply.

We conclude that Genesis 1 could readily have been read by ancient people in terms of their cosmology (though with some difficulty given their view of a solid firmament), but it can also be read by us in terms of our more developed and sophisticated cosmology. God has written it in such a way that it is valid for all times and seasons of human experience and understanding; it is for those with ears to hear and eyes to see.

Appendix D

Mark Futato on Genesis 1 and 2

Mark D. Futato, "Because It Had Rained: A Study of Genesis 2:5–7 with Implications for Genesis 2:4–25 and Genesis 1:1–2:3," *The Westminster Theological Journal* 60 (1998):1–21.

Professor Futato's essay is built on a series of assumptions that we have found questionable in the course of this book. For one thing, he assumes that Moses wrote Genesis and that Genesis 1 is addressed first to the people Moses shepherded out of Egypt. We have seen that there is no evidence for either of these notions.

Assuming Moses wrote it, Futato then argues that we need to read Genesis 1–2 in terms of what the Israelites were familiar with. Thus, since they were familiar with idols, we need to read these chapters as polemics against idolatry. Such a procedure reads into the text of Genesis 1–2 matters that are simply not there at all. Nothing in these texts so much as hints that they were written as polemics against anything.

Turning to the details of Futato's essay, we find him arguing that the plants of Genesis 2:5 are not all plants but only shrubs and grains that spring up after rain falls. This is how things happen in the land of Palestine, he points out, and he asserts that this is what Genesis 2:5 describes (p. 3). I do not believe that such an understanding of shrubs and grains can be demonstrated from the terms involved, but even if it could be, how familiar would this situation be to the people Moses brought out of Egypt? The crops of Egypt were watered by the flooding of the Nile, not by rain. Had any of these people ever experienced rain and its results? If we were to assume a wilderness context for the authorship of Genesis, it would be far more likely that the *'ed* water in Genesis 2:6 was water emerging from the ground or from a river, not from rain.

Futato argues that since the Garden was planted "in Eden, in the east," we must assume that the passage "is narrated from the perspective of one living in the Syro-Palestinian Levant" (p. 3, n. 8). But Moses was *never* in this area, nor were the people at the time he supposedly wrote the book of Genesis. Futato assumes that Eden was Mesopotamia, but as we have seen in chapter seven, it is far more likely that Eden was in the area of Ararat. Thus, the Garden "in the east" means "in the eastern part of the land of Eden."

Perhaps more to the point: Assuming that the early chapters of Genesis need to be taken in terms of the world of Moses' day begs the question: How much alike were these two worlds? Did the people of Moses' day live to be nearly a thousand years old? Even if we think Moses wrote Genesis, why should we think that his presentation is fitted to the people of his own time? Rather, we should look at what the text says in its own context.

Now, Futato, rightly I believe, analyzes Genesis 2:5–7 as a triple parallelism:

> No wild plants
> No sprouted grains
>
> Because no rain water for the wild plants
> Because no man for the cultivated plants
>
> God provides *'ed* water for the wild plants
> God provides man for the cultivated plants

This is fine as far as it goes, but Futato then insists that the wild plants *must* be watered by rain, because that is how things are in Palestine, and thus *'ed* must mean "rain," not "ground water." He admits that the scholarly consensus is in favor of ground water, but he submits that the arguments behind this consensus are trumped by the Palestinian context of the passage.[1]

Futato also argues that the parallel between "no rain" and the provision of *'ed* shows that *'ed* is rain. But if that is so, why not use the word "rain"? Yes, the two are parallel, both being water for the wild plants, but there is also a contrast because a different word is used, one that is associated with ground water. The usual understanding of the passage is that there was no rain, and God did not provide rain at this point but instead provided ground water.[2]

On page 7 Futato argues that Job 36:27–28 should be translated:

> [27]When He draws up drops from the sea,
> they distill as rain from his rain cloud (*'ed*).
> [28]The clouds pour down their moisture
> and abundant showers fall on mankind.

But the parallelism as well as the flow of the passage is better preserved if we translate it thus:

> [27]For He draws up drops from the sea,
> they distill as rain from his stream (*'ed*).
> [28]The clouds pour down their moisture
> and abundant showers fall on mankind.

[1] For a full discussion of *'ed* (a word that only occurs twice in the Bible) and its meaning as ground water, see David Toshio Tsumura, *The Earth and the Waters in Genesis 1 and 2: A Linguistic Investigation.* Journal for the Study of the Old Testament Supplement Series 83 (Sheffield: Sheffield Academic Press, 1989). Futato's attempts to answer this book are, I submit, very unconvincing.

[2] If Moses wrote this passage, then an Egyptian context makes more sense than a Palestinian one. However, the wild plants of Egypt were not watered by rain but by ground water, by the annual flooding of the Nile!

In this latter translation, both phrases of verse 27 refer to evaporation, which leads to a pair of phrases that refer to rain. Thus, the *'ed* of the second half of verse 27 is not parallel to the clouds in verse 28, but to the seas in the first half of verse 27. Far from confirming Futato's rain-interpretation, Job 36:27 (which is the only other time in the Bible that the word *'ed* appears) argues against it.

Futato now moves to the fact that men and plants are discussed together in Genesis 2, and with this I completely agree. The *'ed* mingles with the ground to make the plants grow, and the Spirit of God mingles with the ground to make the man (2:6–7).[3] Moreover, Genesis 2:8, which states that God planted a garden and then that he put the man into it, is expanded in 2:9–14 and 2:15. Additionally, the discussion of the Garden in 2:9–14 concerns both plants and water (though as rivers—ground water—a problem Futato tries to resolve). Thus, Genesis 2:5–15 is organized as a whole series of conceptual parallels:

Wild plants (v. 5a)
    Man-cultivated plants (v. 5b)
No rain (v. 5c)
    No man (v. 5d)
'ed water for plants (v. 6)
    Spirit for man (v. 7)
Garden (v. 8a)
    Man in garden (v. 8b)
Garden and water (vv. 9–14)
    Man in garden to cultivate it (v. 15)

Having noted that man and plant are discussed together in Genesis 2, Futato calls attention to the parallels between days 3b and 6b to argue that men and plants are related together in Genesis 1 by this parallelism. From this fact he draws the totally unnecessary and incorrect conclusion that Genesis 2 is going over days 3 and 6 together, so that they must have happened at the same time. We have seen that

[3] Futato does not make this point.

the plants of day 3 and the plants of Genesis 2 are completely different plants, so this conclusion on Futato's part is clearly wrong. It is curious that Futato recognizes that the plants of 2:5 are not all plants but fails to realize that neither are the plants of day 3.

Futato is right that days 3 and 6 are parallel to one another, in addition to being chiastically linked with days 5 and 2 respectively; to wit:

Land as throne
  Plants on throne
Land animals *(behemah)* as throne *(bamah)*
  Man's life built on animals[4]

As I showed in appendix B, in a true chiasm the later part of the chiasm takes up everything in the earlier part. Everything in Genesis 1 up to the creation of man is included in the meaning of man.

Futato tries to support his contention that days 3 and 6 happen at the same time by arguing that days 1 and 4 must be the same. I have gone over this at length already in this book. It is true that the light of day 1 separates day and night, as do the luminaries of day 4, but (a) the situation of day 1 is not said to be "established," and this is because the light is going to be taken over by the luminaries, and (b) there is simply no conceptual problem with the idea that the light's function is passed to the luminaries; there is no contradiction here, only progression.

In the last section of his essay, Futato builds on his misreading to assert that the text of Genesis 1–2 was pointed as a polemic against the Canaanite religion. How this could be so and Moses could still be the author (which is his position), he does not explain. Neither Moses nor the wilderness Israelites had had any experience with Baalism at the time he says the text was written. Futato does not address this problem or provide any reason to think that a

[4] Genesis 2:18–20 does not mean that animals are not helpers for the man, only that they are not the *fitted* helper for the man.

group of people who had just left the ground-watered land of Egypt and had not yet encountered Baalism would understand the rather subtle and unobvious polemic supposedly contained in Genesis 1–2. Thus, all that he writes here about an anti-Baal polemic, showing that Yahweh and not Baal was cloud-master, is irrelevant.

Well, then, what *is* going on in Genesis 2:5–7? The following discussion is extracted from a larger work of mine in progress.[5]

Genesis 2:5 says that no shrub yet existed in the earth and no field plant had sprouted for two reasons. The first is that "Yahweh God had not caused rain upon the earth," and the second is that "there was no man to serve the soil." Then verse 6 explains that "a spring used to rise from the earth and water the whole face of the soil," answering the first problem. Verse 7 answers the second problem by the creation of man, .the gardener.

This is the first reference to rain in the Bible, and rain is not mentioned again until the story of the Flood, where the phrasing is very similar: "For after seven more days, *I am causing rain on the earth*" (Genesis 7:4). The Bible implies, but does not state, that God never sent rain until the Flood, which has been taken by same creation scientists as a clue to the nature of the ante-deluvian world. Whatever the value and/or limitations of such a use of Genesis 2:5–6 and 7:4, we want to ask *why* God set up the world this way. Why are we told that God did not send rain but instead caused water to spring up from the ground?

The land and Garden of Eden were watered by a spring. Why call attention to the fact that God did not send rain? Why not just mention the spring and leave off the statement about rain? The reason, I believe, is to call our minds back to Genesis 1:2–9. We find in Genesis 1:2 that there

[5] James B. Jordan, *Trees and Thorns.* This is an ongoing commentary on Genesis 2–4 presented as a series of monthly essayletters available from Biblical Horizons, Box 1096, Niceville, FL 32588.

was an ocean over the original earth. Then God created the firmament, and separated the waters above from the waters below. On the third day God gathered the waters below into areas below the surface of the land.

Now we have a clear distinction between waters above the firmament, which being above are parallel to rain, and waters below, which would have to come up from under the earth. Both Genesis 1:2–9 and 2:5–6 set up the distinction eschatologically; ground water comes first, and then heavenly water.

With this distinction in mind, we can begin to see associations between ground water and the first creation, which is earthy and Adamic, and heavenly water with the second creation, which is heavenly and Last Adamic: "The Spiritual [world order] is not first, but the natural [world order]; then the Spiritual [world order]. The first man is from the earth, earthy; the second Man is from heaven. As is the earthy, so also are those who are earthy; and as is the heavenly, so also are those who are heavenly" (1 Cor. 15:46–48).

Ground water is associated with the first world, the world defiled by sin. Originally the land of promise centered on the "circle of the Jordan," which "was well watered everywhere—before Yahweh destroyed Sodom and Gomorrah—like the Garden of Yahweh, like the land of Egypt as you go to Zoar" (Gen. 13:10). This Edenic spot was chosen by Lot, who went for the obvious blessing of ground water—so much more reliable than rain, which must be prayed for. Notice that Genesis 13:10 interjects the statement that God would soon destroy this area. Why is this inserted here? I submit that it is to point to the fact that ground water is not going to be the place of salvation. The waters below, the original Garden of Eden, cannot be recovered. We shall have to move forward to the eschatological waters above and the heavenly Jerusalem.

Just so, Moses contrasts the old land of Egypt, watered from the ground, with the promised land, which is watered by rain: "For the land, into which you are entering to possess it, is not like the land of Egypt from which you came, where you used to sow your seed and water it with your foot like a vegetable garden. But the land . . . drinks water from heaven's rain" (Deut. 11:10–11). Moses quotes God's promise, "I will give the rain for your land in its season, the early and late rain" (Deut. 11:14).

The laver of the Tabernacle and the bronze ocean and water-chariots of the Temple stood off the ground on pedestals and thus represented heavenly water. This was the water for cleansing and baptism. The rivers that flow from the Temple in Ezekiel 47, Zechariah 14, and Revelation 22 are flowing from these heavenly containers.

The first time it is said to rain is at the Flood. Perhaps it rained before this, but theologically speaking the first "rain from heaven" was at the Flood. Let us probe the significance of this. Rain comes from heaven. Too much rain is dangerous to mankind and constitutes a judgment, as does frozen rain (the plague of hail; Ex. 9:22–35). Water from above is, thus, judgmental. It is judicial. In the Levitical law, it sprinkles the righteous, judging and cleansing him of ceremonial death (uncleanness). It hails upon the wicked and drowns him.

The ground waters are in subjection to the heavenly waters. Gentle rains produce streams in the desert and water the land of God. The heavy rains of the Flood were accompanied by vast amounts of ground water: "On the same day all the fountains of the great deep burst open and the windows of the heavens were opened and the rain came upon the earth for forty days and forty nights" (Gen. 7:11–12). When the Flood was announced, however, it was announced in terms of rain only (Gen. 7:4). Similarly, the hail on Egypt was followed by Pharaoh's drowning in the Red Sea, while God sprinkled baptismal rain from heaven upon the Israelites as they passed through the sea dry-shod (Ps. 77:17–19).

The reason that the grains had not sprouted in Genesis

2:5 is because it remained to be seen whether man would sin or not (Gen. 3:17–19). Similarly, part of the reason it had not rained is because it remained to be seen whether man would sin or not. Grains could have sprouted in such a way as to be relatively labor-free; instead, harvesting grain is labor-intensive (by the sweat of the nose). Similarly, the rain could have been gentle and baptismic, or it could have been stormy and full of hail. Because of sin, the latter is often the case, and the first instance we see of it is at the Flood.

We now come to verse 7: "Then Yahweh God formed man of dust from the ground, and breathed into his nostrils the breath of life; and man became a living soul."

The word for man is *'adam* and the word for ground is *'adamah*. Commentators routinely point out the similarity between these two words, noting that the first is masculine and the second feminine. We can see the motherhood of the earth expressed here. Humanity is the offspring, so to speak, of heaven and earth, of God and the soil.

Another word in this passage that is surely related to these two is the word *'ed* in 2:6, which refers to the water that flowed out of the earth (*'erets*) and watered the *'adamah*.[6] The *'ed*, we notice, does not flow from the *'adamah*. Rather, the *'ed* waters the *'adamah*. The *'ed* carries out the same function as the *'adam*, the man. There is no *'adam* yet made to cultivate the *'adamah*, but for the time being *'ed* does so.[7] Once the *'adam* is created, he will work with water and become the cultivator of the *'adamah*.

[6] Vowels in Hebrew are secondary; what count are consonants. (Notice for instance how Old Testament Edom becomes New Testament Idumea; "ay-dom" becomes "ee-dum.") Thus, *'d*, *'dm*, and *'dmh* can be seen to be quite similar, particularly when we take note of the context and theology of this passage. Also, taking these word similarities into account helps explain the choice of the rare word *'ed* in this passage instead of one of the more common words for springs of water.

[7] *'ed* is masculine, *'adamah* is feminine.

The *'adamah* is the mother, but she has no water in herself. She must get water from a father. *'ed* from the earth (*'erets*)[8] acts as the father-fluid, and later *'adam*, ruler of the earth, acts as father, to make mother *'adamah* fruitful. More precisely, man takes over God's function as High Father to bring *'erets* and *'adamah* together in fruitful marriage.

But where does man himself come from? Is he the offspring of mother *'adamah* and *'ed* from father *'erets*? By no means. Man is made from dust, which is dry and without water. Genesis 2:7 sets us up for the question: "Then Yahweh God formed man of dust from the *'adamah*." A man-shape has been made of dust (*not* clay). Now, where will father-water come from to quicken this dust? The answer is that the "water" is the (moist) breath of the Spirit of God.

Genesis 2:5–6 pictures plants being generated by water and soil, by *'ed* coming from the *'erets* combined with soil (*'adamah*). Only man, the ruler of the *'erets* (earth) is made of God's breath and the dust of the soil. Only man is the "offspring (generations) of the heavens and the earth" (2:1).

The Spirit of God, His divine breath, is heavenly. The firmament of Genesis 1:7 separated the waters, and the firmament is called heaven. Thus, the waters above the firmament are heavenly waters. The Spirit's breath should be seen to impart the moisture of the heavenly waters to the dust. This creates an association between wind, water, and the Spirit of God, an association that continues throughout the Bible. When God sends a dry, desiccating wind that dries up our moisture, we die (Ps. 32:4). Similarly,

[8] *'erets* has common gender, that is, it can be either masculine or feminine in its grammatical gender. For instance, in Genesis 1:11–12, where the *'erets* brings forth vegetation, the verb used with it is feminine. There the *'erets* is considered as mothering the plants. *'erets* is by implication masculine in Genesis 2:4, which speaks of the offspring of heaven and earth, and also in 2:6, the verse we are considering here.

God's Spirit is not found in a flood of water devoid of air (Ps. 32:6). But when God sends sprinklings of water from above, mixed in air, we are baptismally revived.

Earlier we reflected on the fact that the first Adam was of earth while the last Adam is of heaven (1 Cor. 15:46–49). We associated this with the original ground waters and the later heavenly waters. Now we need to refine these reflections. Even the first Adam was made of heavenly water mixed with earthly soil. Thus, the contrast is not really between waters but between "soils."

The first world-order is characterized by earthly soil and earthly waters, but ruled over by a man made of heavenly water and earthly soil. The last world-order, inaugurated by the resurrected and heavenly Adam (Christ) is ruled over by a Man made of heavenly water and heavenly soil. What Paul argues in 1 Corinthians 15:35–50 is that all along, the implication of Genesis 2 was that humanity would move toward an eschatological transfiguration from earthly soil to heavenly "soil."[9]

Thus, in conclusion, the parallels between human beings and plants are very important to the theology of Genesis 1–3, but not in the way Futato supposes. They have nothing to do with Baalism and everything to do with biblical theology.

[9] See the full discussion of verse 44b in R. B. Gaffin, *Resurrection and Redemption: A Study in Paul's Soteriology* (Phillipsburg, NJ: Presbyterian & Reformed Pub. Co., 1987) pp. 78ff. The first edition of this study was published as *The Centrality of the Resurrection*.

Appendix E

Psalm 104[1]

Day 1:

Bless Yahweh, my soul.
O Yahweh, my God, You are very great.
With splendor and majesty You are clothed,
Covering Yourself with light as with a cloak.

Day 2:

Stretching out heaven like a curtain,
Laying beams in the waters of His upper chambers,
The one appointing clouds His chariot,
The one walking on wings of wind,
Making His angels winds,
His ministers flaming fire.

Day 3:

a He established the earth upon its foundations,
So that it cannot move, everlastingly and forever.

[1] On the position of Psalm 104 (creation psalm) as it matches Psalm 92 (sabbath psalm) in the chiastic structure of Book 4 of the Psalter, see James B. Jordan, "The Fourth Book of the Psalter," in *Christendom Essays. Biblical Horizons* No. 100 (Niceville, FL: Biblical Horizons, December, 1997) pp. 136–173.

b With the deep as a garment He covered it;
Above the mountains stood waters.
  At Your rebuke they fled;
  At Your loud thunder they hurried away.
  They ascended mountains;
  They descended valleys to the place You established for them.
A boundary You set that they may not cross;
Never may they return to cover the earth.

c The one sending forth springs in the ravines.
Between the mountains they flow.
  They give drink to every beast of the field.
  Wild donkeys quench their thirst.
  Above them the birds of the heavens dwell.
  Among the branches they give forth voice.
Watering the mountains from His upper chambers,
With the fruit of His works is the earth satisfied.

d Causing the grass to grow for the cattle;

e And grain for the service of man;
  To bring forth bread from the earth,
    And wine, which makes a man's heart glad.
  To make his face glisten with oil;
And bread that sustains a man's heart.

f Satisfied are Yahweh's trees,
Cedars of Lebanon, which He planted,
Where birds build their nests;
The stork, in the cypresses, her home.

g High mountains are for the wild goats.
Cliffs are a refuge for the rock badgers.

Day 4:
    He made the moon for seasons.
    The sun knows its setting.
        You appoint darkness and it becomes night,
        In which prowls every forest beast.
            The young lions roar after their prey,
            Yea, to seek their food from the Mighty One.
        The sun rises;
        They withdraw and in their dens lie down.
    Man goes forth to his work,
    And to his service until evening.

Day 5:
    How many are Your works, Yahweh!
    All of them with wisdom You made.
    The earth is full of Your possessions.
        Behold the sea, vast and broad-handed,
        In which are swarms without number,
        Animals small and great.
        There ships move along;
        Leviathan, which You formed to frolic in it.

Day 6:
    All of them look to You to give them their food at its time.
        You give to them;
        They gather up.
            You open Your hand;
            They are satisfied with good.
                You hide Your face;
                They are dismayed.
            You take away their breath;
            They expire and to their dust return.
        You send Your Spirit;
        They are created.
    And You renew the face of the ground.

Day 7:
a Let the glory of Yahweh endure forever;
b Let Yahweh be glad in His works,
c The one looking at the earth and it trembles.
He touches the mountains and they smoke.
a I will sing to Yahweh all my life.
I will sing praise to my God while I exist.
Let my meditation be pleasing to Him.
b As for me, I shall be glad in Yahweh.
c Let sinners be consumed from the earth,
And let the wicked be no more.

Bless Yahweh, my soul.
Praise Yah!

Analysis. Psalm 104 praises God for His provisions for man and beast using the seven days of creation as a foundation:

Day 1: The Shekinah Glory-Light of the first day.
Day 2: The firmament.
Day 3: Land and sea, grains and trees (see below).
Day 4: Sun and moon, times for food; chiasm.
Day 5: Land and sea and their creatures.
Day 6: Creation from dust and food for all; chiasm.
Day 7: Sabbath worship and praise (see below).

The day 3 section has seven subsections. The first two recapitulate the first two days of creation, with a description of the Flood in the second subsection, the Flood-event being parallel to the events of the third day. The remaining subsections celebrate the food plants made on the third day (grains and fruit trees) as they feed (c) wild animals, (d) cattle, (e) humanity (with sacramental allusions); and as they provide homes for (f) birds. Finally, we return to the land as providing a home for (g) animals.

Notice in the chiastic day 4 section that humanity is parallel to the luminaries of the firmament, something we have noted from Genesis 1 and 2.

The day 7 section has a threefold parallelistic structure. The (a) sections deal with foreverness; the (b) sections deal with rejoicing; and the (c) sections deal with fire and judgment. The psalm ends with an exhortation to praise God.

Appendix F

Archetype and Prototype

The angelic heavens relate to the earth spatially as archetype; as the heavenly patterns are impressed on the earth, so the earth gradually moves from darkness, formlessness, and emptiness to become like heaven. The first week relates to later weeks temporally as a prototype. The sequence of events in God's week of work are played out again and again by His image, humanity, as mankind progressively lightens, structures, and fills the earth, bringing her from glory to glory. These two radically different aspects of reality are not to be confused, whatever Einsteinian physics may claim. There is no earthly model-archetype, nor is there a heavenly week-prototype.

The heavens of Genesis 1:1 are brought down into the earth as archetype or model by the hovering Spirit on day 1. This is the Glory Cloud, the primary revelation of heaven within the earth.[1] Light from this cloud shines down on the earth, communicating the pattern. On day 2, the firmament heavens are set up as yet a third revelation of

[1] Moses enters the cloud to get the model, brings it back, and builds it on the earth as the Tabernacle. Kline rightly writes, "The Glory-cloud was indeed the invisible realm of heaven appearing in a veiled visibility in the midst of earthly creatures." Meredith G. Kline, *Kingdom Prologue*, 2d ed. (by the author, 1981) p. 20. See James B. Jordan, *Through New Eyes: Developing a Biblical View of the World* (Eugene, OR: Wipf & Stock Pub., [1988] 1999) pp. 42ff.

heaven, over the earth. The pattern continues to shine down upon the earth from these three heavens.

Diagram 1
The Heavens as Archetype of the Earth

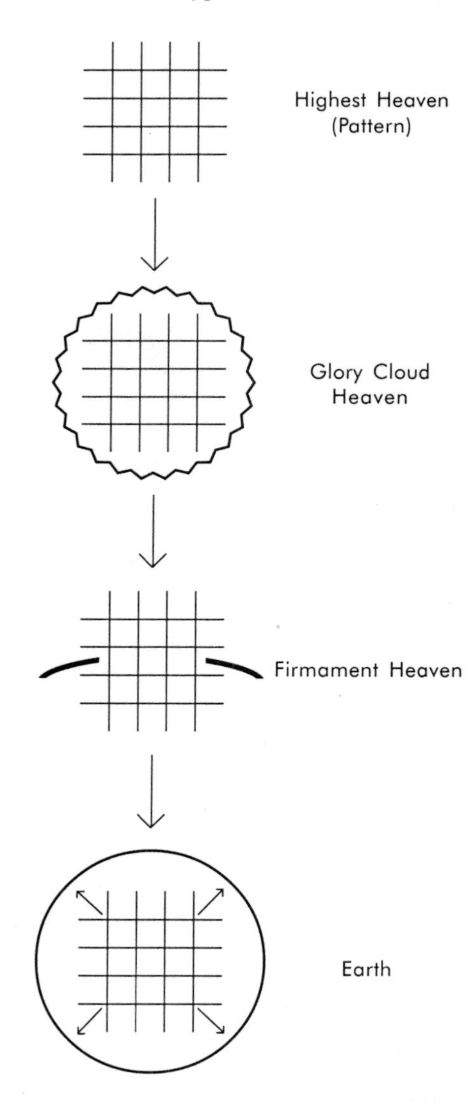

The first three heaven-like places in the earth are the world at large in Genesis 1, the land of Eden as a land in Genesis 2, and within that land, the Garden as sanctuary where God meets with man. Later on, the Garden becomes the Tabernacle and Temple complexes within the Edenic land of Israel, which is itself within the world. Each of these is symbolically related to the others, as each is, in its own way, a reflection of the heavenly archetype.[2]

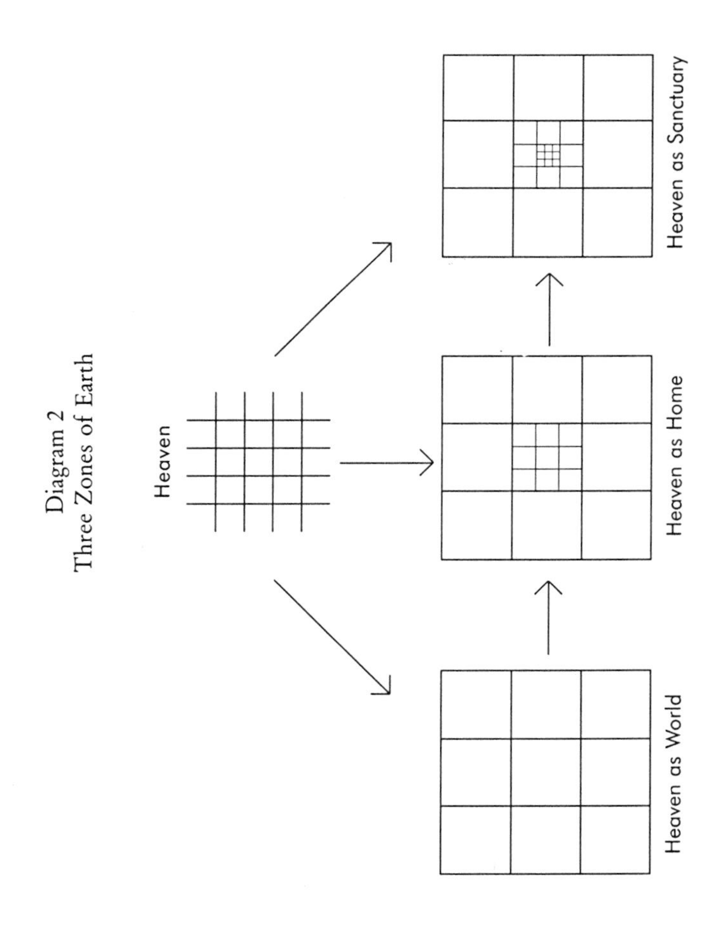

Diagram 2
Three Zones of Earth

[2] On the environments of Garden, Home, and World, see Jordan, ibid., pp. 152ff.

The first week was a real week of time, just as the original heaven was (and is) a real place in space. It is the prototype of later weeks of seven days. There are also larger "weeks" of history that expand from this original week, such as the large week of Old Creation history from Adam to the sabbath enthronement of Jesus, and the large week of New Creation history from the formation of the new Church on Pentecost to the sabbath rest of the Bride at the Final Judgment. After this there are no more weeks after the model of the first week, no more evenings and mornings, only everlasting sabbath.

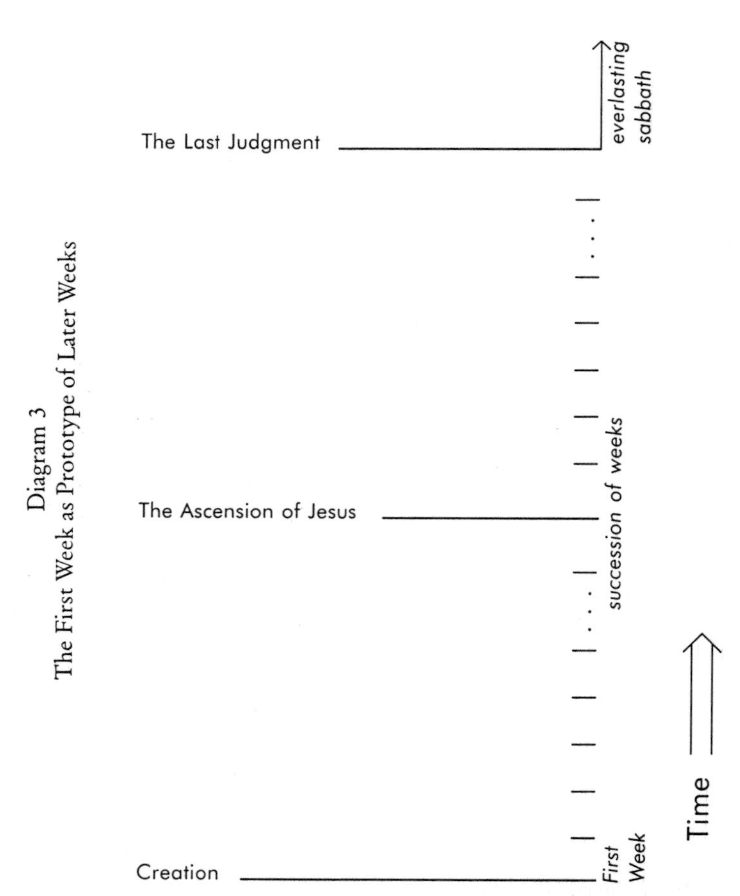

Diagram 3
The First Week as Prototype of Later Weeks

The heavenly model is applied to the world progressively, from glory to glory, by Spirit-empowered humanity. Thus, there is a succession of "week-worlds," age after age, until the coming of the final sabbath, when earth will be fully like heaven in the final manifestation of the new heavens and earth. The Old Creation "Week" consists of seven covenantal "weeks," seven "worlds" in succession.[3]

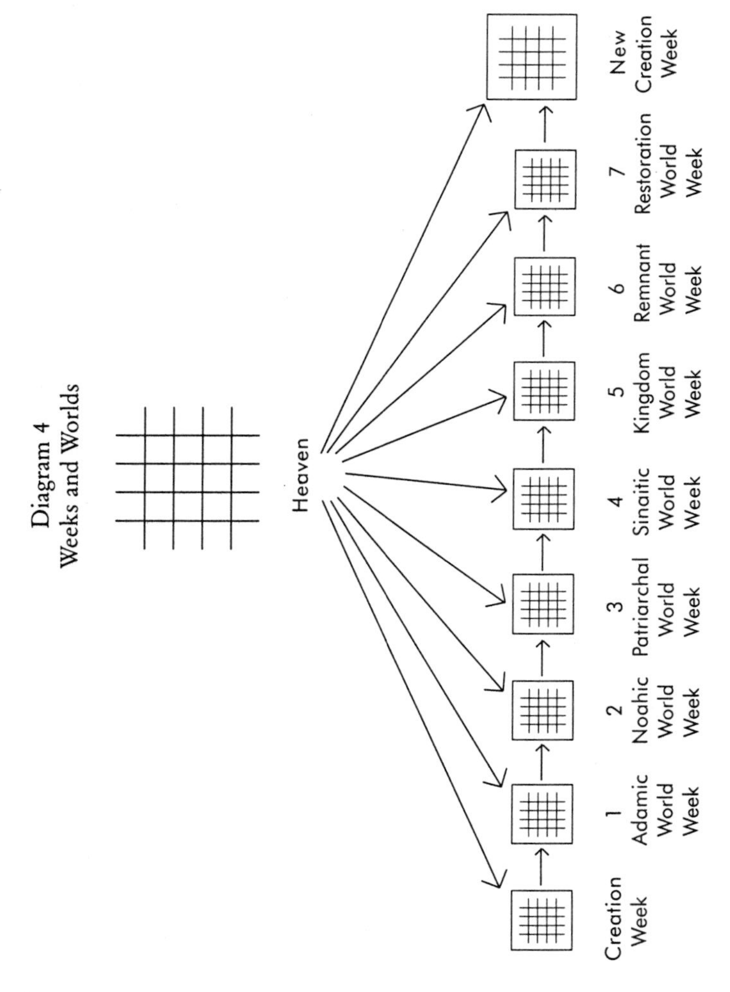

[3] On the succession of covenantal "worlds," see ibid., especially chaps. 13–19.

Scripture Index

Subject/Author Index